Palgrave Studies in Financial Services Technology

The Palgrave Studies in Financial Services Technology series features original research from leading and emerging scholars on contemporary issues and developments in financial services technology. Falling into 4 broad categories: channels, payments, credit, and governance; topics covered include payments, mobile payments, trading and foreign transactions, big data, risk, compliance, and business intelligence to support consumer and commercial financial services. Covering all topics within the life cycle of financial services, from channels to risk management, from security to advanced applications, from information systems to automation, the series also covers the full range of sectors: retail banking, private banking, corporate banking, custody and brokerage, wholesale banking, and insurance companies. Titles within the series will be of value to both academics and those working in the management of financial services.

More information about this series at
http://www.palgrave.com/gp/series/14627

Roberto Moro-Visconti

MicroFinTech

Expanding Financial Inclusion with Cost-Cutting Innovation

palgrave
macmillan

Roberto Moro-Visconti
Catholic University of the Sacred Heart
Milan, Italy

ISSN 2662-5083 ISSN 2662-5091 (electronic)
Palgrave Studies in Financial Services Technology
ISBN 978-3-030-80393-3 ISBN 978-3-030-80394-0 (eBook)
https://doi.org/10.1007/978-3-030-80394-0

This Palgrave Macmillan imprint is published by the registered company Springer Nature Switzerland AG
The registered company address is: Gewerbestrasse 11, 6330 Cham, Switzerland

Contents

List of Figures

List of Tables

CHAPTER 1

Introduction

Microfinance is a renowned albeit controversial solution for giving financial access to the unbanked, even if micro-transactions increase costs, limiting outreach potential. The economic and financial sustainability of microfinance institutions (MFIs) is a prerequisite for widening a potentially unlimited client base. Automation decreases costs, expanding the outreach potential, and improving transparency and efficiency. Technological solutions range from branchless mobile banking to geo-localization of customers, digital/social networking for group lending, blockchain validation, big data, and artificial intelligence, up to "MicroFinTech"—FinTech applications adapted to microfinance. This study examines these trendy solutions comprehensively, going beyond the existing literature and showing potential applications to the traditional sustainability versus outreach trade-off.

Microfinance is by now a consolidated and successful mean to provide credit to the neediest. Going beyond traditional banking, it helps the poor to sort out bank exclusion, which is one of the main misery traps (Collier, 2007) that prevents billions of underserved, especially women, from escaping atavistic poverty.

While the success of microfinance, since the pioneering intuition of Yunus, has gone beyond any expectation, its implementation is still typically subsidized and raises growing concerns. Self-sufficiency and economic sustainability represent, in most cases, a mighty goal, whose

R. Moro-Visconti, *MicroFinTech*, Palgrave Studies in Financial Services Technology, https://doi.org/10.1007/978-3-030-80394-0_1

attainment would allow microfinance institutions (MFIs) to broaden their clientele (potentially unlimited, being represented by billions of unbanked poor).

Microfinance is a renowned solution for giving financial access to the unbanked, even if micro-transactions increase costs, limiting its outreach potential.

The economic and financial sustainability of microfinance institutions is a prerequisite for the capacity to widen their potentially unlimited client base.

Microfinance, however, suffers from a business model that is typically expensive and inefficient, with high operational fees that, unless subsidized by forward-looking donors, translate to interest rates, up to the boomerang point of promoting poverty, instead of eradicating it. Recent evidence suggests only modest social and economic impacts of microfinance. Favorable cost–benefit ratios then depend on low costs (Morduch et al., 2018).

Consistently with this view, microfinance cannot be a silver bullet for development and profit-oriented MFIs are problematic ("better unbanked that unable to repay loans"). The business industry remains opaque, and mission drift[1] is a constant temptation, especially in India (Saxena & Deb, 2014). Microfinance must be regulated and subsidized, and other strategies for viable financial inclusion of the poor and small producers must be more actively pursued. Financial inclusion[2] is generally considered as a pro-growth strategy and improved access to (micro)finance reduces income inequality and poverty (Agyemang-Badu, 2018). Mader (2017) however claims that high expectations of financial inclusion serving as a core pro-poor, private-sector-led development intervention lack justification. Bateman and Chang (2012) are even more skeptical, arguing that microfinance constitutes a powerful institutional and political barrier to sustainable economic and social development, and so also to poverty reduction.

Technology, starting from electronic payments, may foster financial inclusion and availability/affordability of financial services in developing economies, softening the perverse effects of microcredit (Dos Santos & Kvangraven, 2017).

[1] See Armendariz De Aghion and Szafarz (2009).

[2] See World Bank (2018).

While there is an impressive literature on microfinance (for a comprehensive introduction, Armendariz De Aghion & Morduch, 2010; for recent surveys, Garcia-Perez et al., 2017), and m-banking (Shaikh & Karjaluoto, 2015), little attention has been dedicated to other more innovative strands, as FinTech (Gai et al., 2018) or social networking applied to microfinance group-lending (Ali et al., 2016) and peer-to-peer (P2P) lending (Bruton et al., 2015; Dorfleitner et al., 2019). Whereas some studies examine the impact of technology on microfinance (Ashta, 2011; Moro Visconti, 2015; Moro Visconti & Quirici, 2014), little attention has been dedicated to "MicroFinTech," a neologism that combines financial technology with microfinance, reshaping the delivery of financial services to make them more accessible and affordable. In emerging markets where financial inclusion is a challenge, FinTechs are helping bridge the exclusion gap and may be financed for instance by social impact funds (described in Chiappini, 2017). Rapid urbanization, mobile and Internet penetration, and ease of use are driving individual demand for FinTech services. Leapfrog innovation can provide cutting-edge solutions for the unbanked (Ernst & Young, 2019).

This study represents an advance in the debate about the trendy opportunities of microfinance.

Consistently with this framework, the research question is the following: ***given the economic and organizational bottlenecks that prevent an optimal outreach of traditional microfinance, which is the impact on microfinance sustainability of technology-driven innovation?***

Traditional banking systems are unfit for illiterate poor with no guarantees, while ad hoc products, tailored to suit the needs of potentially billions of peculiar and unconventional borrowers, might prove successful in widening financial access, with a positive side effect of reducing inequalities and fostering economic development. Financial innovation and flexibility are key solutions for forms of lending that are collateral, or cash flow-based only to a small extent.

Precursors of MFIs include rural moneylenders, often like usurers, or credit and group lending cooperatives, while more formal MFIs are increasingly like standard banks, albeit with peculiar characteristics. Microfinance is proving a useful device for pooling risk and cross-subsidizing borrowers; its greatest success is the demonstration that even the poorest can become reliable borrowers.

Group-lending with self-monitoring, short repayment installments, and small loans can help to soften otherwise unbearable governance problems, such as ***adverse selection*** (the problematic distinction between those who deserve credit and those who do not), ***moral hazard*** (temptation to "take the money and run away"), and ***strategic default*** (false bankruptcy to avoid repayment). Social networks mastered by digital platforms reshape group lending patterns,[3] linking them to P2P crowdfunding.

The supply of synergic products such as microdeposits, microinsurance, or micro-consultancy allows passing from microcredit to microfinance and represents a good parachute against endemic adversities.

High interest rates to repay substantial operational costs, due to the small size of loans, make borrowing expensive for the poorest, even if subsidized credit might worsen the situation.

The classic trade-off between maximum outreach to the destitute and financial sustainability[4] is related to an evolutionary growth pattern from subsidized NGOs to commercial banks, together with proposals for improving impact, using also lending sources from socially oriented international funders, who might even look for a reasonable risk-return profile.

Microfinance allows institutional investors and individuals to embrace socially responsible opportunities and might offer a reasonable risk-return profile, diversified from other investments.

The most exciting promise of microfinance is that—even without being a panacea—it can reduce poverty with a self-fulfilling mechanism, once adequately ignited, without requiring continuous donations that often spoil and humiliate the poor, emptying the donors' pockets.

Unsubsidized sustainability and profitability combined with deep outreach to the underserved stands as the most ambitious and challenging goal.

A key strategic issue to improve the micro-loan and make it a competitive financial product should include minimization of intrinsic problems as substantial costs with HR and offices, high default risks due to poverty, geographical barriers, and low educational levels of borrowers.

Operational costs of MFIs that operate in rural communities (where clients are scattered, and technology is less diffused) tend to be higher,

[3] See Sangwan and Nayak (2020).

[4] Tutino (2013).

and the banking model is performed through agent selling. Physical branches are often far and last-mile proximity with the final client is often hindered by organizational or physical bottlenecks.

Digitalized transactions that pass through the web allow for timely recording of financial data with positive consequences on the business model. They can fuel big data that nurture artificial intelligence patterns for applications like credit scoring, insolvency forecasting, and client segmentation.

FinTech solutions, using blockchains that secure payment recording or other innovations, reshape the business model of traditional banks and increasingly impact on MFIs, disrupting and reengineering old-fashioned managerial patterns.

Technology and smartphones can revolutionize this system, replacing sales agents with mobile banking and social media channels. User-friendly Mobile Apps can re-engineer to the operativity of group lending, whose members can use technology to build up digital networks. Internet platforms, consistent with peer-to-peer lending or borrowing and crowd-funding, bypass digital divide concerns and link customers to MFIs in real-time and ubiquitously.

Technology can so play an important role in decreasing unitary costs per transaction, widening the outreach potential, and improving transparency and efficiency. Technological answers are represented by complementary solutions ranging from branchless mobile banking to geo-localization of customers, digital/social networking for group lending and crowdfunding or peer-to-peer lending, FinTech (with blockchains), and other applications. The latest frontier is represented by big data and artificial intelligence, where information is stored and processed, fuelling machine learning patterns. Technology is a multiple-sided strategy that enables MFIs to cut operating costs increasing flexibility, with a scalable effect that improves marginality. Corporate governance interactions among the main stakeholders through the supply and value chain are reshaped by technology.

This study examines these trendy solutions comprehensively, going beyond the extant literature and showing potential applications to the traditional sustainability vs. outreach trade-off.

The business model of MFIs can be synthetically represented in Fig. 1.1.

Technology has an impact on all three supply chain blocks.

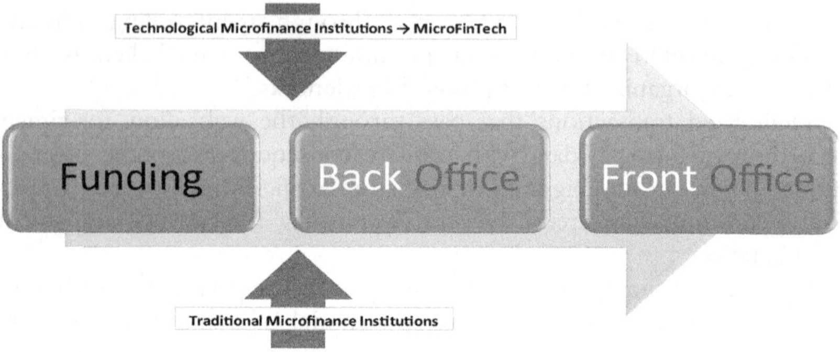

Fig. 1.1 MFI simplified business model

Consistently with this simplified framework, the book is structured as follows: Chapter 2 is dedicated to the microfinance background, analyzing its main characteristics. Chapter 3 considers the main microfinance issues, again within a traditional context. Chapter 4 describes the technological devices and processes that may have an impact on microfinance. Chapter 5 illustrates FinTechs, considered as an innovative template that may inspire upgrading MFIs. Chapter 6 is eventually dedicated to trendy MicroFinTech applications, where FinTech solutions are made compliant to microfinance peculiarities.

The canvas of Fig. 1.1 will be adapted to each consequential step, representing the backbone of the whole book.

This book is dedicated to my wife Alessandra and to our beloved son and daughter, Luca and Elisa.

Università Cattolica del Sacro Cuore, Milan, Italy, August 2021
roberto.morovisconti@morovisconti.it www.morovisconti.com

References

Agyemang-Badu, A. (2018). Financial inclusion, poverty and income inequality: Evidence from Africa. *Spiritan International Journal of Poverty Studies*, *2*(2).

Ali, A., Jamaludin, N., & Othman, Z. H. (2016). Modeling microfinance acceptance among social network women entrepreneurs. *International Journal of Economics and Financial Issues, 6*(S4), 72–77.

Armendariz De Aghion, B. A., & Morduch, J. (2010). *The economics of microfinance*. MIT press.

Armendariz De Aghion, B. A., & Szafarz, A. (2009). *On mission drift in microfinance institutions* (Working Paper CEB 09.015.RS). Université libre de Bruxelles. Available at http://ideas.repec.org/p/sol/wpaper/09-015.html.

Ashta, A. (Eds.). (2011). *Advanced technologies for microfinance*. IGI Global.

Bateman, M., & Chang, H. (2012). Microfinance and the illusion of development: From hubris to nemesis in thirty years. *World Economic Review, 2012*(1), 1–13.

Bruton, G., Khavul, S., Siegel, D., & Wright, M. (2015). New financial alternatives in seeding entrepreneurship: Microfinance, crowdfunding, and peer-to-peer innovations. *Entrepreneurship: Theory and Practice, 29*(1), 9–26.

Chiappini, H. (2017). *Social impact funds. Definition, assessment and performance*. Palgrave Macmillan.

Collier, P. (2007). *The bottom billion: Why the poorest countries are failing and what can be done about it*. Oxford University Press.

Dorfleitner, G., Oswald, E.-M., & Zhang, R. (2019). From credit risk to social impact: On the funding determinants in interest-free peer-to-peer lending. *Journal of Business Ethics, 170*, 375–400.

Dos Santos, P. L., & Kvangraven, I. H. (2017). Better than cash, but beware the costs: Electronic payments systems and financial inclusion. *Developing Economies, 48*(2), 205–227.

Ernst & Young. (2019). *FinTech ecosystem playbook*. Available at https://www.ey.com/Publication/vwLUAssets/EY-fintech-ecosystem-playbook/$FILE/EY-fintech-ecosystem-playbook.pdf.

Gai, K., Qiu, M., & Sun, X. (2018). A survey on FinTech. *Journal of Network and Computer Applications, 103*(1), 262–273.

Garcia-Perez, I., Munoz-Torres, M. J., & Fernandez-Izquierdo, M. Á. (2017). Microfinance literature: A sustainability level perspective survey. *Journal of Cleaner Production, 142*, 3382–3395.

Mader, P. (2017). Contesting financial inclusion. *Development and Change, 49*(2), 461–483.

Morduch, J., Cull, R., & Demirgüç-Kunt, A. (2018). The microfinance business model: Enduring subsidy and modest profit. *The World Bank Economic Review, 32*(2), 221–244.

Moro Visconti, R. (2015). Leveraging development with technology and microfinance. *ACRN Oxford Journal of Finance and Risk Perspectives, 4*(3), 19–33.

Moro Visconti, R., & Quirici, M. C. (2014). The impact of innovation and technology on microfinance sustainable governance. *Corporate Ownership & Control, 11*(3–2), 420–428.

Sangwan, S., & Nayak, N. C. (2020, July). Factors influencing the borrower loan size in microfinance group lending: A survey from Indian microfinance institutions. *Journal of Financial Economic Policy, 13*(2), 223–238.

Saxena, A., & Deb, A. T. (2014). Paradigm paranoia or mission drift? Lessons from microfinance crisis in India. *Journal of Business Thought, 4*, 38–49.
Shaikh, A. A., & Karjaluoto, H. (2015). Mobile banking adoption: A literature review. *Telematics and Informatics, 32*(1), 129–142.
Tutino, M. (2013). Matching outreach and financial sustainability. An assessed accounting framework in evaluating performance of microfinance project. *GSTF Journal on Business Review, 2*(3), 46–50.
World Bank. (2018). *Financial inclusion—Financial inclusion is a key enabler to reducing poverty and boosting prosperity*. Available at http://www.worldbank.org/en/topic/financialinclusion/overview.

CHAPTER 2

The Microfinance Background

The supply chain/business model canvas anticipated in the introduction is recalled in Fig. 2.1.

2.1 Why Traditional Banking Is Unfit for the Poor

The first and the main problem that a banker anywhere in the world faces is how to get back the lent money, minimizing the delinquency risk. Only reliable and well-known borrowers—with a positive and sound credit history—can receive money (up to a certain amount) without guarantees.

This traditional policy has always proved inapplicable to the unbanked poor who lack any positive track record and do not have any creditworthy collateral or regular income or even a register of birth. For example, in many sub-Saharan African countries, national identity cards are not issued even if voting cards might be used for identification. The credit history of destitute borrowers is also hindered by a lack of written evidence—hence the importance of digitalization for data collection that fuels credit scoring databases.

According to basic microeconomic principles, if capital was perfectly mobile, it should be flowing to wherever its marginal productivity is higher. The law of diminishing marginal returns to capital tells us that enterprises with little capital (represented by the poor) should earn higher

R. Moro-Visconti, *MicroFinTech*, Palgrave Studies in Financial Services Technology, https://doi.org/10.1007/978-3-030-80394-0_2

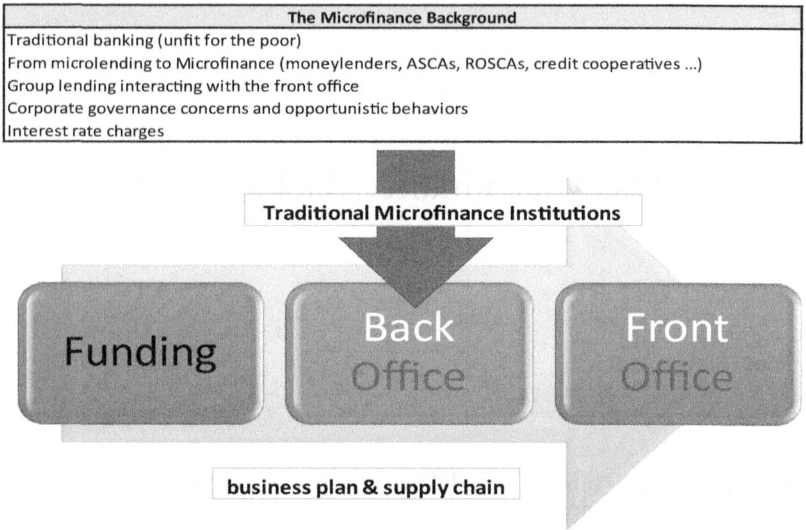

Fig. 2.1 Supply chain/business model canvas

returns compared to more capitalized enterprises, and money should consequently be driven from rich depositors to poor entrepreneurs (i.e., the microfinance target clients).[1] However, risk must be considered, and strong adverse selection problems arise when banks cannot easily discriminate between risky and safe customers, so preventing an efficient allocation of funds. See Sect. 2.4 for a description of adverse selection problems.

Market failures play a significant role in this capital rationing process that damages the deserving poor (small entrepreneurs, shopkeepers, farmers, artisans ...), stuck in an informal economic environment that does not encourage emancipation and development; together with adverse selection, often there are other problems such as information asymmetries, high transaction costs, no collateral available, no savings, no insurance, difficulties in enforcing contracts, country, and political risk. Too much for traditional banks, with a strong focus toward

[1] See Armendariz De Aghion and Morduch (2010).

Western-style markets, unable to mastermind the challenges—but also the opportunities—of other markets with completely different scenarios.

Lack of access to traditional sources of mainstream finance is often the critical element underlying persistent income inequality and slower growth.[2] Financial inclusion, driven by the removal of barriers that obstacle access to financial markets, considerably helps the talented poor with promising opportunities. Financial development also reduces income inequality.[3]

Among the main barriers and constraints that prevent poor households and small enterprises from using banking services, there are micro- and macro-connected factors, such as:

- Geographical access, if bank branches are too far or dispersed, this being the case particularly in underdeveloped (i.e., economically unattractive) and/or underpopulated regions[4]; physical access is important where the absence of technology does not allow virtual banking (that also has a positive impact in cost-cutting that represents, if absent, a competitive disadvantage);
- Lack of proper documentation (cadastral certificates of property; other legal, census, health documents …), typical of poor countries;
- Lack of sizeable and worthy collateral;
- The absence of steady jobs for which a standard payroll can be envisaged and foreseen;
- Lack of education, from illiteracy to poor schooling, and weak economic—managerial culture; cultural deficiencies bring to marketing problems since poor may not have anybody in their social network who understands the various services/products that are potentially available to them;
- Health and hunger problems, which prevent people from a regular attitude to work and create family disruptions and orphanage;

[2] See Thi-Hong et al. (2021).

[3] See Özcan (2020).

[4] The link between poverty and underpopulation is well-known since dispersion and distance from schools, hospitals, and other main services, together with lack of infrastructures, are major obstacles to social and economic development.

- Country and political risk and instability (from a general lack of civic sense to corruption, bribery, and mismanagement of public resources or so frequent changes in government and dictatorship);
- Prejudice toward the poorest, leading to refusal of admittance to banking offices and tribal/ethnical or religious discriminations (curiously typical also of Western countries, where immigrants tend to have more challenging access to credit than natives);
- Weak legal, ICT, power[5] and physical infrastructures: no justice, weak TLC, and bad roads are—unsurprisingly—a key obstacle to development, particularly in a global world.

Most of the problems that the poor face every day are, however, challenging to detect—particularly for Westerners—since they are almost neglected by the superficiality of mass media—unless a tragic humanitarian catastrophe happens—because the poor usually keep silent. Moreover, misery does not cry, has no voice. Misery suffers but in silence and does not rebel. Poor, often ashamed of their condition, tend to hide and rise only when they hope to change something but an essential aspect of most people who live in misery is the absence of hope.[6]

Limited access to finance also creates segmentation and competitive barriers, bearing ineffectiveness and weak competition, with the standard side effect of bad and highly-priced products. The negative impact on the poor is unfortunately enhanced by their limited choices and opportunities that frequently throw them in a misery trap, with few emergency exits.

Globalization with its increasingly advanced standards and the digital divide is another segmentation factor from richer countries. Little if no access to ICT products and networks is a growing problem, even if wireless devices are somewhat easier to establish even in poorer countries, where the impact of mobile phones, for instance, is having an astonishing positive impact, somewhat even bigger than that observed in developed countries since it allows for a "jump leap," circumventing other more infrastructure-intensive technologies, particularly missing in poor underpopulated areas.

[5] Lack of energy and frequent power shortages requiring emergency generators represent a common and serious problem.

[6] See Kapuscinski (2003).

Rethinking and reshaping banking for the poor is so an imperative goal, also considering the failure of so many state-owned development banks, politically driven (and consequently short-sighted and intrinsically unstable) and frequently run by non-professional and corrupt managers.

2.1.1 The Economic Lives of the Poor

An understanding of the economic lives of the poor proves useful to find proper financial solutions for an improvement of their conditions. Products and services need to be tailor-made, and technological product and process innovation must match the needs of the unbanked at the basis of the social pyramid. This background analysis will be complemented, in Sect. 6.2.1, by financial innovation practices and tools.

According to Banerjee and Duflo (2007):

- The typical extremely poor family unsurprisingly tends to be large: when every penny counts, it helps to spread the fixed costs over a greater number of people; a patriarchal family might be a potential target for MFIs, finding a social guarantee in family ties;
- The poor tend to be very young, due to high mortality as well as fertility rates; they might consequently lack skill and experience—but not enthusiasm and motivation—for entrepreneurship, so slowing or preventing financial access;
- Poor allocate slightly half of their budget to food while spending the rest on ceremonies, tobacco, alcohol, etc.;
- Ownership of assets might consist of land property—even if cadastral records are generally missing—and few assets such as radios, bicycles, or televisions (if electricity is available);
- From a psychological point of view, while the poor certainly *feel* poor, their reported levels of self-happiness are not particularly low, even if they appear anxious about health problems, lack of food, and death coming next; microdeposits and microinsurance might prove useful solutions to soften these issues; realistic acquaintance of the living condition proves good for survival but might bear to passive acceptance of poor standards, so preventing any effort or desire for improvement;
- The extremely poor spend very little on education, even if attendance to primary school is often guaranteed by free-of-charge public schools; higher levels of education are often jeopardized by

school fees, the necessity of labor force, lack of family motivation, distance from schools (particularly in underpopulated regions), lack of teachers (particularly in sub-Saharan Africa, where AIDS and other illnesses decimate young generations) so preventing socio-economic development and—consequently—making harder any access to financial institutions and products;

- Many poor households, particularly in backward rural regions, tend to have multiple occupations: they cultivate the land they own (even if without legal title to land—a typical problem in poor regions—the stimulus to invest in it collapses), and operate in other non-agricultural businesses; lack of specialization due to risk-spreading strategies and infrequent migration for job reasons—reflecting the value of remaining close to one's social network—prevent, however, many poor to grasp the economic opportunities they seek and long for; business scalability is generally very small, so preventing economic margins from growing; should the poor be enabled to raise the needed capital to run a business that would occupy them fully, they might—with the help of microcredit—increase job specialization and productivity;
- The market environment constrains choices: some save little because they lack a safe place to put their money; availability of basic infrastructures (roads, power and TLC connections, schools, health facilities, water, and basic sanitation …) varies considerably across countries and is higher in urban areas;
- Many poor are "penniless" entrepreneurs, not according to a free choice but since they are forced to do so: with few skills and little capital, it is easier, particularly for women, to be a self-entrepreneur than to find an employer with a job to offer.

In developing economies and particularly in the rural areas, many activities that would be classified in the developed world as financial are not monetized: that is, money is not used to carry them out. Almost by definition, poor people have very little money. However, circumstances often arise in their lives in which they need money, or the things money can buy.

Rutherford (2000) cites several types of needs:

- *Lifecycle Needs*: such as weddings, funerals, childbirth, education, home-building, widowhood, old age.
- *Personal Emergencies*: such as sickness, injury, unemployment, theft, harassment, or death.
- *Disasters*: such as fires, floods, cyclones, and man-made events like war or bulldozing of dwellings.
- *Investment Opportunities*: expanding a business, buying land or equipment, improving housing, securing a job (that often requires paying a large bribe), etc.

Poor people find original and often collaborative ways to meet these needs, primarily through creating and exchanging different forms of non-cash value. Common substitutes for cash vary from country to country but generally include livestock, grains, jewels, and precious metals.

A key problem in developing countries is that many poor people can provide only their work and since complementary assets require outside financing (being savings not existent or not properly "stored"), the lack of finance (together with lack of education, state aid, infrastructures ...) is an obstacle to the birth of entrepreneurship, with negative side effects on employment.

Yunus and Jolis (1999) show that if the poor are provided access to finance, they might start up microenterprises, building up a virtuous cycle and transforming underemployed laborers into small entrepreneurs.

From Adam Smith's path-breaking treaty on the Wealth of Nations (1776), we wonder why poor people usually remain indigent and how they can climb the social ladder, an easier task if mobility is culturally accepted and economic growth is powerful enough to disrupt old caste divisions and ancient dominant logic.

2.1.2 Climbing the Social Ladder from the Bottom of the Pyramid

"The Market at the Bottom of the Pyramid" is a celebrated book of Prahalad (2006),[7] which is not primarily focused on microfinance, even if many insights can be usefully applied to our topic and allow for a better understanding of the social and economic possibilities of the poorest.

[7] See also Sing et al. (2021).

Converting poverty from a burden to an opportunity is challenging and requires a mix of solutions, ranging from self-esteem to entrepreneurial drive. Money can help—albeit it might hurt too—but the true target lies in reshaping a passive mentality, transforming ancestral issues into unthinkable opportunities. Human potential has unlimited upside and development opportunities are impressive, particularly for those who start from the lowest levels. Partnering and sharing with the poor might bring to a win–win scenario—the dream target of any sustainable microfinance project.

The poverty penalty is a result of mixed causes such as local monopolies (prospering out of entry barriers), inadequate access, weak distribution, strong traditional intermediaries (such as moneylenders), lack of democracy and justice, etc., which limit competition, choice, innovation, freedom, and hope of a better future.

These segmentation barriers can be lifted or at least softened with advanced technology devices, such as mobile phones, ATM points, and PC kiosks or Internet cafés, which are readily accepted by the poor, contrary to popular belief; reduction of information asymmetries fosters price comparison and brings to competitive auctions, allowing peasants to sell their products at higher prices, bypassing trade intermediaries that traditionally keep for them most of the margins. And price comparisons can be conveniently applied even to financial products, easing the competition between expensive moneylenders and usually cheaper MFIs.

Creating the capacity to consume among the poorest is a primary task of charity or philanthropy, which, however, rarely solve the problem in a scalable and sustainable fashion; to overcome this problem—that has many similarities with microfinance, that can simply be seen as a financial product—products have to be affordable (small packages, like small loans, can considerably help), accessible (with a capillary distribution to the poorest, possibly even in not so populated rural areas) and available (the decision of the poorest to buy is based on the cash they have at that very moment and purchasing decisions are rarely deferred).

New goods and services are strongly needed and might be as successful as microfinance products; the private sector, representing greater firms (often multinationals) that traditionally serve much wealthier clients, and—on the other side—the poorest at the very bottom of the social pyramid, do not traditionally trust each other and live in distant worlds; however, when the poor are converted into consumers, they acquire the dignity of attention from the private sector and they are entitled—often for the very first time in their lives—to choose.

The opportunity for the poorest but also private firms (fighting in an increasingly competitive and global environment and always looking for new clients) is huge and consistently unexploited. Since both are struggling for survival, they should understand how much they need each other.

And this can be a lesson even for Western commercial banks that are now fronting a huge international crisis, ignited by the mistake of having lent the wrong products to the wrong people. Subprime mortgages are showing much more dangerous than microloans to the poorest! And from the financial crisis that deeply concerns the credibility of the international banking system, we can draw immediate lessons about the importance of banks in our Western life, understanding how painful it is when they are missing or not properly working.

Deskilling work is critical in Bottom of the Pyramid markets, which lack technical and learning abilities, suffering from a shortage of talent, because of an unsophisticated and not meritocratic education. Education of clients to new markets and products focused on survival objectives such as health or nutrition is strongly needed and illiteracy or media darkness, so frequent in rural areas, does not help.

The scale of operations is potentially huge, concerning 4–5 billion people; being unitary margins low, adequate returns require significant volumes. Smart and innovative solutions to create a market for the poorest must be sustainable and ecologically friendly. The design of products and services suitable for the destitute must acknowledge that infrastructures, wherever existent, are generally hostile and first-time customers need simple products with basic characteristics. The distribution system might also prove a bottleneck and trade innovations are as critical as those concerning goods or processes.

Corruption—a market mechanism for privileged access—is another, often undervalued, main obstacle to poverty alleviation and transaction (contractual) governance—the capacity to guarantee transparent and enforceable economic deals—is strongly needed to set free huge and otherwise stuck economic resources.

As De Soto (2003) points out, poor countries are often asset-rich but capital-poor since assets cannot become capital—the most wanted collateral for microloans—unless the country guarantees an efficient set of laws whereby the ownership of property is clear and unquestioned, making them fit for being bought, sold, mortgaged, or converted into other assets.

Local enforcement of contract law is another hot issue, often left in the hands of corrupted and ruthless local "strongmen"; property rights violations and unjustified expropriations, often following a *coup d'état*, are a significant source of political and country risk, while democracy provides a safety net from idiosyncratic changes. If the rules of the game are changing and unfair, smart players remain far, with no suitable background for microfinance or other market projects.

2.1.3 The Key Principles in Microfinance

Table 2.1 reports the eleven key microfinance principles.

The key principles will be reinterpreted in Sect. 6.10, examining the impact of technology on microfinance. The principles are consistent with the Sustainable Development Goals (https://sdgs.un.org/goals) (Table 2.2).

2.2 From Microlending to Microfinance: Moneylenders, ROSCAs, Credit Cooperatives, and Group Lending

The absence of microfinance—whose presence in poor regions, albeit growing, is still more an exception than a rule—does not mean a complete lack of access to simpler and informal sources of financial intermediation: poor households generally have multiple credit sources in rural economies, as well as unregulated and flexible ways to save—the starting point for self-financing a business—and get insured.[8]

Many microlending activities are the natural roots of more sophisticated tools such as microfinance and they need to be synthetically described, to understand where microfinance comes from and if its characteristics are really "revolutionary"—as some enthusiastic supporters might induce to believe—or merely represent a natural evolution and improvement of an existing model.

Selecting the right evolutionary—"Darwinian"—theory is not simply an academic game since it might help to detect if and to which extent the

[8] See Armendariz De Aghion and Morduch (2010).

Table 2.1 The key principles in microfinance

1. Poor people need a variety of financial services, not just loans In addition to credit, they want savings, insurance, and money transfer services
2. Microfinance is a powerful tool to fight poverty Poor households use financial services to raise income, build their assets, and cushion themselves against external shocks
3. Microfinance means building financial systems that serve the poor Microfinance will reach its full potential only if it is integrated into a country's mainstream financial system
4. Microfinance can pay for itself and must do so if it is to reach very large numbers of poor people Unless microfinance providers charge enough to cover their costs, they will always be limited by the scarce and uncertain supply of subsidies from donors and governments
5. Microfinance is about building permanent local financial institutions that can attract domestic deposits, recycle them into loans, and provide other financial services
6. Microcredit is not always the answer Other kinds of support may work better for people who are so destitute that they are without income or means of repayment
7. Interest rate ceilings hurt poor people by making it harder for them to get credit Making many small loans costs more than making a few large ones. Interest rate ceilings prevent microfinance institutions from covering their costs, and thereby choke off the supply of credit for poor people
8. The job of the government is to enable financial services, not to provide them directly Governments can rarely do a good job of lending, but they can set a supporting policy environment
9. Donor funds should complement private capital, not compete with it Donors should use the appropriate grant, loan, and equity instruments temporarily to build the institutional capacity of financial providers, develop support infrastructure, and support experimental services and products
10. The key bottleneckis the shortage of strong institutions and managers Donors should focus their support on building capacity
11. Microfinance works best when it measures—and discloses—its performance Reporting not only helps stakeholders judge costs and benefits but also improves performance. MFIs need to produce accurate and comparable reporting on financial performance (e.g., loan repayment and cost recovery) as well as social performance (e.g., number and poverty level of clients being served)

Source CGAP (2006), *Good Practice Guidelines for Funders of Microfinance*, www.cgap.org

microfinance model can be culturally understood by its natural targets, easing financial allocation of resources in a complex scenario with very limited room for traditional "western-style" banks, with a selection and adaptation of species to a different and changing environment.

Table 2.2 The Sustainable Development Goals and microfinance

Goal	*Link with microfinance*
GOAL 1: No Poverty	Microfinance, lending to the bottom of the pyramid unbanked, can contribute to reducing poverty
GOAL 2: Zero Hunger	Microloans can soften hunger
GOAL 3: Good Health and Well-being	Microfinance can be linked to healthcare improvements, even if these investments do not generate an immediate payoff
GOAL 4: Quality Education	Education is another pillar of development, representing a long-term investment that can be partially funded with microloans
GOAL 5: Gender Equality	Microfinance, lending mostly to women, promotes gender equality
GOAL 6: Clean Water and Sanitation	Small projects funded by MFIs can improve access to clean water
GOAL 7: Affordable and Clean Energy	Small projects funded by microloans can improve access to solar panels. Bigger infrastructural projects are out of scope for MFIs
GOAL 8: Decent Work and Economic Growth	Small jobs can be upstarted by microloans, igniting economic growth
GOAL 9: Industry, Innovation, and Infrastructure	Small size innovation is a target of microloans that are, however, out of scope if we consider infrastructural investments
GOAL 10: Reduced Inequality	Microloans to unbanked poor reduce inequality
GOAL 11: Sustainable Cities and Communities	The socio-economic impact of microloans positively affects sustainability
GOAL 12: Responsible Consumption and Production	This is not an immediate target of microfinance, even if ESG-compliant lending may be linked to responsible consumption and production
GOAL 13: Climate Action	Climate is a macro-issue, beyond the scope of most MFIs, even if micro-intervention can strengthen bottom-up contribution to the cause

(continued)

Table 2.2 (continued)

Goal	*Link with microfinance*
GOAL 14: Life Below Water GOAL 15: Life on Land	Environmental issues are not a prioritarian target of microfinance, but they can be linked to ESG-compliant schemes
GOAL 16: Peace and Justice Strong Institutions	Reduction of financial exclusion has a positive impact on peacekeeping
GOAL 17: Partnerships to achieve the Goal	MFIs improve their efficacy by working together with other players, from group lenders to crowdfunders or other financial intermediaries

[a]See Aggarwal et al. (2015)

Informal traditional microcredit is primarily involved with lending by individuals on a non-profit and often reciprocal basis, directed by intermittent lending by individuals with a temporary surplus, lending by specialized individuals (with proper or intermediated funds), individuals informally collecting deposits, group finance or moneylenders.[9]

Rural local moneylenders easily approach the poor, lending small amounts of money, with positive but also negative side effects that have gained them the reputation of "loan sharks," behaving like exploitative monopolists:

- Moneylenders reduce or eliminate the distance and the information asymmetries with borrowers that they usually known well, being so able to assess their creditworthiness and easing the monitoring during the life of the loan; since information is expensive to gather, the informal credit market is highly segmented and local moneylenders might take profit of competitive barriers, with a consequent monopolistic power (when demand is elastic and supply is rigid, prices—here represented by interest rates—can grow substantially);
- Flexibility, informal approach, and quickness are highly valuable characteristics, particularly in rural areas where borrowing alternatives are nonexistent or socially and culturally not unaffordable (this

[9] See Newman et al. (2017).

being significant and preliminary barriers, often more important than economic ones);

- Moneylenders are frequently multi-purpose stakeholders since in many cases they are not only providers of finance but might also have other economic relationships with their customers, renting land, homes or tools and equipment, buying from borrowers products, or hiring them as labor force; in such a context, the bargaining power of moneylenders generally grows and they have a "blackmail option" to exercise, should the loan not be repaid on time; this sounds dangerous for the borrower, which can easily become a sort of "slave";
- Guarantees are often nonexistent but when they are, they can be hazardous for the borrower and induce the moneylender to make repayment challenging, should the guarantee be strategic for him (e.g., a bordering piece of land to expropriate); other guarantees have a notional and affective value for the borrower much higher than its intrinsic market value: this proves a strong "psychological" incentive for repayment, even if the residual value in case of delinquency is low;
- For the moneylender to maintain his strategic power, it is essential to keep clients always in need, avoiding emancipating them; a typical strategy is that of financing consumer credit or working capital, instead of an entrepreneurial project, naturally focused on longer-term value-creating investments. According to Aesop's tale, moneylenders might prefer life-enjoying and short-sighted grasshoppers to hard-working ants!

Abusive lending practices such as lending without prudent regard for repayment capacity, deceptive terms, and unacceptable collection techniques probably cause more damage to poor borrowers than do high interest rates. It is better to be just poor than … poor and indebted.

According to the same source, "in many countries, informal lenders are more likely to engage in predatory lending, defined as a pattern of behavior in which an unscrupulous lender exploits borrower into assuming debt obligations that they may not be able to meet and uses abusive techniques to collect repayments. The cost of predatory lending can include loss of valuable collateral, transfer of wealth to lenders (particularly over time), and / or social and psychological penalties."

In the middle of the primitive model of local moneylenders and the more advanced archetype of MFI are positioned financial intermediaries such as ROSCAs[10] (*Rotating Savings and Credit Associations*[11]), ASCAs (*Accumulating Savings and Credit Associations*), or credit cooperatives.

Group lending is another embryonic form of microfinance (being the model for Grameen bank I, now surpassed by "Grameen bank II model"), again with its advantages and pitfalls, always worth knowing about for a conscious and careful choice of the fittest model in the best place.

- ROSCAs are based on pooling resources with a broad group of neighbors and friends, which particularly in rural areas belong to the same ethnic clan. Groups of individuals agree to contribute regularly to a common "pot" allocated to one member of the group each period. Each contributor has the chance to win the pot in turn and use the proceeds to buy goods. ROSCAs' apparent simplicity is, however, biased by potential conflicts of interests (e.g., participants who win the pot earlier might have limited incentives to make subsequent contributions) and are not very flexible, even if they can help credit constraint households make simple sharing agreements to purchase indivisible goods that anyone might afford only after much time, without knowing where to put his savings in the meantime;
- ASCAs are more complex—but also more flexible—institutions since they allow some participants to save mainly and others to mainly borrow;
- These primitive forms of financial intermediations rely on simplicity, direct monitoring, and lack of viable alternatives but undergo severe conflicts of interests and limits of scope;
- Credit cooperatives or unions represent a more advanced instrument, closer to MFIs and well-known in Europe since the nineteenth century (see, for instance, the German Raiffeisen model[12] since 1864); credit cooperatives represent group-based ways to provide financial services to the poor, encouraging peer monitoring and

[10] See Patrick and Squires (2021).

[11] Local names for ROSCAs range from hui in Taiwan to tontines in rural Cameroon to polla in Chile, tanda in Mexico, chit funds in India, kye in Korea, arisans in Indonesia, susu in Ghana, esusu in Nigeria...

[12] Friedrich Wilhelm Raiffeisen is a remarkable example of social entrepreneur. See Achleiter (2008).

guaranteeing loans to other neighbors. In cooperatives, savers and borrowers are also shareholders of the institution, thus at least partially aligning their interests, with a typical "one head one vote" mechanism, according to which each shareholder has one vote, irrespective of the number of shares he owns, with a consequent peculiar majority rule;

- Even credit cooperatives have their problems: a much higher complexity, if compared to ROSCAs or ASCAs since they are real—albeit simplified—banks; a usually thin capital basis, with a subsequent capital inadequacy in bad circumstances, worsened also by the limited capacity to access to funds to meet liquidity shortfalls,[13] difficulties diversifying risks (inflation shocks; country or local community hazards ...);
- Group lending overcomes the lack of collateral, which represents one of the biggest obstacles to credit access for the poor.[14] MFIs generally lend a small individual loan to a household belonging to a group of usually 5–20 people, which guarantees for him and intervenes in the case of delinquency. Should the individual borrower prove reliable, the MFI might extend credit to other members of the group. The essence of group lending is to transfer responsibilities from bank staff to borrowers, who contribute to the selection and monitoring of debtors, helping in the enforcement of contracts. In exchange, customers get otherwise inaccessible loans.

Monitoring takes place with weekly meetings between the MFI and group members and the repayment status of the borrowers is publicly checked, minimizing screening costs by meeting debtors in groups, multiplying savings and loan transactions, with some economies of scale which reduce transaction costs for the MF bank and consequent interest charges for the borrowers.[15]

Even group lending has shortcomings since it mainly works in rural areas where social control is tighter and smart individuals belonging to an unreliable group might be severely damaged by lack of flexibility (a typical

[13] See Armendariz De Aghion and Morduch (2010).

[14] Empirical evidence about group lending is surveyed in https://www.indianjournals.com/ijor.aspx?target=ijor:sjdm&volume=19&issue=2&article=003.

[15] Song et al. (2014).

group-loan might be unfit for one of its components, often the smartest). Adverse selection issues—examined in Sect. 2.4—occur when the lender finds it challenging to discriminate between risky and safer borrowers, so applying to anybody the same interest rates, with an unwanted and undeserved implicit subsidy to the worst borrowers, which in many cases disincentives honest ones from asking for loans. Reduction of information asymmetries,[16] with real customers being able to send a believable signal to the MFI about the reliability of potential joiners, might contribute to a reduction of unfair surcharges.

Honest individuals also have a powerful incentive in directly selecting fair partners within the group: actually, groups are encouraged to form on their own, even if strong clan or family ties in many rural areas are an obstacle to discrimination according to merit. In case of delinquency, bank officers might be reluctant to sanction good borrowers who have the bad luck to be part of unreliable groups.

Stiglitz (1990) argues that the group-lending contract circumvents *ex-ante* moral hazard (irresponsible behavior) by inducing borrowers to monitor each other's choice of investments and to inflict penalties on borrowers who have chosen excessively risky projects.

A strong internal incentive for monitoring within the group arises in collective lending, even if this cannot prevent any problem; social sanctions hardly prove efficient outside small rural areas where everybody knows others and this problem grows along with the urbanization process that is taking place almost everywhere. However, even in small villages, the threat of social sanctions between close friends and relatives is hardly credible.[17] Attending and monitoring group meetings can prove expensive in dispersed areas; frequency of meetings is another implicit cost. Borrowers' behavior might also prove collusive against the bank, undermining its ability to exploit social links as proper collateral.

Benefits of group lending are counterbalanced by costs; costs emerge when borrowers are risk-averse and borrowing is expensive; costs also grow together with the scale of lending since default amounts rise, and growing businesses—with a smart borrower going far beyond his peers—suffer from credit rationing issues.

[16] The standard methods of overcoming adverse selection are to have increased information to improve risk evaluation, as Akerlof (1970) has pointed out in his seminal paper.

[17] See Armendariz De Aghion and Morduch (2010).

Loan group mechanisms are efficient if not correlated—since they allow for risk diversification and reduction—but do not work well when a generalized systematic crisis occurs (such as the periodical floods which devastate Bangladesh and have masterminded the first Grameen bank model).

For many, particularly the smartest and wealthiest, individual lending is more flexible, even if it lacks group guarantees and collective monitoring; this approach is, however, hardly ever available to the poorest and does not fit rural areas where individualism is not as culturally strong as it is elsewhere, for instance in Western countries. Looking with our Western eyes at the financial issues of less developed areas might prove even in this case wrong and dangerous.

Dynamic incentives, such as the threat of not being refinanced if the group defaults (*refinancing threat*), can bring to a better group selection, particularly for risky borrowers that are of course more stimulated to have a safe borrower as a peer[18]; this might, however, not be the case in the absence of any refinancing threat, where risky borrowers have a greater probability of going bankrupt and thus a lower probability of having to repay the debts incurred by his peer, should he default.

A comprehensive representation of the evolutionary migration from the informal to the formal credit system is contained in Fig. 2.2. The evolution from Tier 4 to Tier 1 increases sustainability (Ashta, 2012).

Section 5.6 contains a restatement of Fig. 2.2 that incorporates the impact of technology on the microfinance ecosystem.

The evolution of the microfinance ecosystem should consider the actual players, synthetically described above, and new intermediaries, as shown in Fig. 2.3.

[18] Borrowers, if allowed to form their groups, will sort themselves into relatively homogenous groups of "safe" and "risky" debtors. Without dynamic incentives, a safe borrower will value having another safe borrower as a fellow group member more than a risky borrower will value having a safe borrower as a peer since a risky borrower has a greater probability of defaulting and thus a lower probability of having to pay back the debts incurred by his peer, should he default.

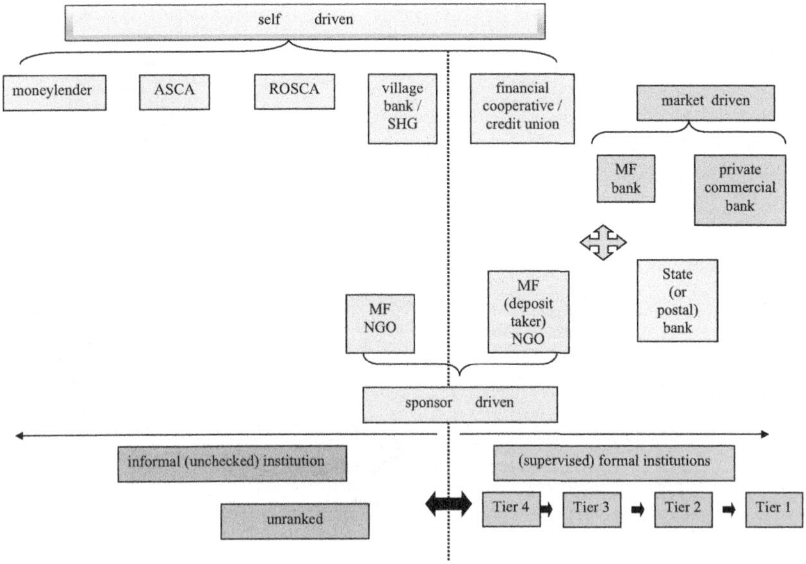

Fig. 2.2 From the (informal) micro to the (formal) macro-financial system

2.3 What Is Microfinance? Characteristics and Differences with Traditional Banking

According to the United Nations' definition: "Microfinance can be broadly defined as the provision of small-scale financial services such as savings, credit and other basic financial services to poor and low-income people. The term 'microfinance institution - MFI' now refers to a broad range of organizations dedicated to providing these services and includes non-governmental organizations, credit unions, cooperatives, private commercial banks, non-bank financial institutions and parts of State-owned banks."

In the mind of many, microfinance (Beck, 2015) and microcredit are synonymous; however, while microcredit simply deals with the provision of credit for small business development, microfinance[19]—sometimes

[19] For a survey of the literature, see Milana and Ashta (2012) and Garcia-Perez et al. (2017).

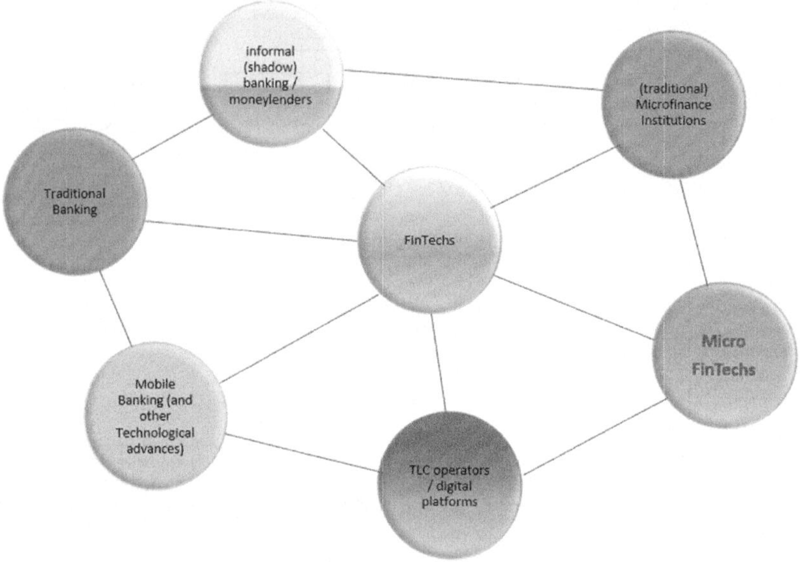

Fig. 2.3 Evolution of the microfinance ecosystem

called "banking for the poor"—refers to a broader synergic set of financial products, including credit, savings, insurance, and sometimes money transfer.

MFIs can be classified according to their organizational structure (cooperatives, solidarity groups, rural or village banks, individual contracts, and linkage models ...) or to their legal status (NGOs, cooperatives, registered banking institutions, government organizations, and projects ...) or even according to their capital adequacy standards (from Tier 1 mostly regulated MFIs to Tier 4 startup MFIs).[20]

Microfinance moves one step further, if compared to money lending, ROSCAs, ASCAs, credit cooperatives, or informal group lending, even if each new step bears some marginal (additional) complexity, this being the price to pay to solve some of the abovementioned issues: no innovation comes for free and increased complexity tends to restrict access to

[20] See Deutsche Bank (2007, p. 6).

this intermediation form, with consequent social costs due to the progressive exclusion of the destitute and often an inverse proportionality with outreach.

Microfinance firms are different from traditional banks since they have to use innovative ways of reaching the underserved and poorest clients, not suitable to mainstream institutions, mixing unorthodox techniques such as group lending and monitoring, progressive lending (if repayment records are positive[21]), short repayment installments,[22] deposits or notional collateral, as it will be seen later.

Group lending is the most celebrated microfinance innovation, making it different from conventional banking, even if microfinance goes beyond it.[23] Frequent repayments (short-term installments, starting immediately after disbursement) are another smart pragmatic device, avoiding balloon payments where the principal is all reimbursed at maturity: given the financial illiteracy of many poor (which find it hard to understand that "time is money"), postponing repayments to years to come would generally end up in a disaster, for them and the incautious lender. The dark side of frequent repayments is that they might prove unaffordable for the poorest, so preventing outreach. Regularly scheduled repayments are not generally imposed by more flexible informal moneylenders and that is probably why they appear to be thriving even in regions where MFIs are well-established.

Another frequently unnoticed but significant feature of MFIs—not typical of mainstream banks—is the marketing approach to the client: poor potential customers, particularly if living in rural and not densely populated areas, often do not know if a microfinance branch exists and where it is, cannot afford to travel long distances and suffer from cultural ignorance about financial matters. Lack of knowledge and motivation does not come out as a surprise.

[21] Moss et al. (2015).

[22] With possible negative effects since due to short repayment time, MFI risk steep deterioration of their portfolio in a matter of weeks only. Short repayment installments bring to a financial—and cultural—lack of long-term planning, which discriminates riskier projects with longer gestation.

[23] Grameen Bank II model has abandoned this model, recognizing its negative aspects, such as the free-rider problem, according to which a bad borrower has an obvious incentive to join safer ones.

Going to meet the potential client at his home—or, more realistically, barrack—is expensive and time-consuming but proves efficient not only for the possibility to reach him and his clan but also to reduce information asymmetries (getting acquainted with him and his family, life, job, and environment), speed transactions and enforce compliance.

Modern microcredit can be classified in various models or categories, in constant evolution and popular in various parts of the world, being the experience about the adaptation of a successful model to other contexts full of difficulties.

The Grameen Bank II model, popular in Bangladesh:

- has a high gender bias, being focused mainly toward women;
- does not envisage any sizable guarantee, considering fiduciary agreements and the implicit punishment of not being admitted to further installments as a significant incentive for repayment;
- still lacks financial self-sustainability—and so needs subsidies—due to its "political" decision not to charge high enough interest rates.

The Grameen generalized system allows some borrowers to remain a member of the bank, even when they are unable to pay their loan installments.[24]

Gender is a key issue in microfinance, which has a preferential social target toward women—the poorest of the poor—since they tend to spend more of their income on their households and children's education, so increasing the welfare of the family, with a positive and longer-lasting sustainable effect.

Women are generally more vulnerable since they more than men carry the burden of raising and feeding children and also have lower mobility (facing cultural barriers that often restrict them to home, for instance following the Islamic *purdah*), so ensuring a higher focus on keeping their original location, with a positive effect on the reduction of opportunistic

[24] See https://www.elgaronline.com/view/edcoll/9781788118460/9781788118460.00016.xml.

behaviors (such as the "take the money and run option") and possibilities for emancipation, due also to the participation in credit meetings[25] (which might represent an embryonic form of political gatherings).

In underdeveloped areas, social control on women is higher and easier, and blame for misbehavior is generally stronger; on the other side, empowerment chances, starting from a typically lower level, if compared with men, are higher.[26] Women are, however, often conduits for loans to men, who are the natural target for greater borrowings, to finance bigger investments (here the MFI faces a trade-off between higher profitability due to scaling and increased risk, due to gender switch but also—mainly—to increased exposure).

Another feature of recent and more sophisticated MF models—always attempting to circumvent the original sin of the lack of guarantees—is concerned with progressive loans, according to which loans are divided in regular installments that can be cashed by the borrower only if previous repayments are regular. Even in group lending systems, this sanction might be personal, so relieving the group from the misbehavior of single members.[27] Small and fractionated loans are, however, unfit for capital-intensive projects that require a high startup financing or for projects where cash flow gains are irregular and difficult to forecast. The credible threat to deny defaulters access to future loans, either with a group or with individual loans, has proven effective in minimizing delinquency.

Notional collateral—often used by moneylenders, as described in Sect. 2.2—might prove a powerful and surprising form of guarantee since it is characterized by a limited market value—bad news for the lending MFI—with a high personal or affective value for the borrower: if such a value is, in the borrower's mind, superior to that of the loan, the repayment incentive is significant. This system seems somewhat cruel but efficient against intentional misbehavior, even if it proves

[25] Attendance at meetings has also other positive side effects and is a public screening of the conditions of the women (frequency of participation has of course proven lower in abused women).

[26] See Rahman et al. (2017).

[27] There are several possible combinations, which show how the model is flexible and adaptable to different circumstances: the delinquency of one member can hit either him alone, with no access to further credit installments, or the whole group; in the latter case the monitoring incentive is stronger, but the penalty is high and somewhat unfair for the good members.

incapable to prevent involuntary default. Collateral serves to reduce the risk of strategic default when the borrower might be tempted to divert cash flows, while social sanctions (particularly within group lending and in more sensitive rural areas) and denial of further credit are efficient punishments to be imposed on defaulting borrowers.

Repayment is hard to get without adequate pressure and unsanctioned bad examples are very contagious. In the absence of guarantees, no parachutes are available for MFI: that is why repayment discipline is for them a question of life or death.

Various financial products and institutions can usefully be complementary in serving the demand for credit, flexible and segmented according to the various needs of sophisticated borrowers, duly considering also cultural aspects and various stages of development. Competition, the width of choice, specialization, and interaction are just some of the main—usually positive—aspects of the presence of various financial intermediaries, even if issues of coordination and potential new conflicts can easily arise, particularly in the presence of imbalances of regulation between "far west style" unregulated intermediaries and less flexible but more transparent ones, which can bring to "arbitrage circumventive" behaviors, should intermediaries move from one model to the other in search of milder rules and greater flexibility (within primitive intermediaries) or wider funding possibilities and more sophisticated products, present in more structured intermediaries.

This trade-off between simplicity/complexity, arbitrary freedom/overregulation, etc., has to be carefully considered. On the move toward sophistication, interest rates—representing the price of service—tend to diminish and if this might seem surprising (since complexity is intrinsically expensive and has to be paid by clients—borrowers unless somebody accepts to subsidize the intermediary), other factors might explain this phenomenon (more competition; greater effectiveness ...). This point is of crucial importance since if confirmed it states that borrowers can get better services and products at lower prices, so increasing the quality/price ratio, probably the most important parameter of choice for free consumers.

Imbalances between demand and supply remain, however huge and hundreds of millions of potential MF borrowers are not able or entitled to have access to fair (regulated) finance; this might seem strange and peculiar, in a world that usually faces the opposite marketing problem (abundant supply in desperate search of new demand, facing subsequent great competition) and where global liquidity has never been so abundant and—consequently—cheap.

The poor often face significant issues in obtaining access to credit services; microfinance tries to overcome these problems in innovative ways:

- Loan officers come from similar backgrounds and go to the poor, instead of waiting for the poor to come to them, following a bottom-up marketing approach (if Mahomet does not go to the mountain, it is the mountain that goes toward Mahomet);
- Group lending models, if applicable (we have already seen that the new Grameen Bank philosophy goes beyond, considering its negative side effects), improve repayment incentives and debt monitoring through peer pressure (particularly efficient in rural areas and with women); they also build support networks and educate borrowers with frequent meetings and discussion panels;
- Microfinance products include not just credit but also savings, insurance, and fund transfers (internal or due to remittances);
- Development activities focused on social issues, health, and education are frequently a corollary to MF activities, particularly if sponsored by NGOs.

Microloans should usually finance microenterprises, which particularly in low-income countries play a central role in economic and social development since bigger businesses are almost nonexistent, the public sector is underdeveloped and unable to absorb many job seekers but also the traditional agricultural sector has a limited upside in creating employment.

Loans are generally addressed to finance the purchase of fixed assets to start up or expand a business, while they might also finance less creditworthy consumables or working capital; little if no attention is usually paid to the possibility to provide micro-equity finance, in the form of small business startup grants. Unlike venture capital, micro-equity providers might not be supposed to become shareholders of the financed entity since social (subsidized) equity is mainly concerned with the socio-economic development of local communities, looking for a sustainability pattern that might make them sooner or later independent from international aid.

Microenterprises are firms with generally less than five employees (often, family members), usually unregistered and not paying taxes, being part of the informal sector—well-known in developing countries—that gradually tends to emerge and starts paying its toll, in exchange for public services that in the absence of taxes have obvious funding issues. Mechanized businesses are more capital intensive than commercial activity and they usually require bigger financing and additional knowledge; the wealth created by manufacturing businesses—the first step of industrialization—might be greater if compared to commercial activities, particularly in underdeveloped economies, for which production should represent a starting economic activity, followed by trade and supply of services.

MFIs are consistently smaller than traditional banks—particularly if they are startup ("greenfield") donor-driven institutions—and have small macro- and micro-economies of scale, considering their size or the size of their single loans.

MFI startups generally have a donation (or public) driven equity, while standard banks collect it within private or public entrepreneurs.

But the business of MFIs and mainstream banks does not—or at least, should not—show fundamental differences. Getting money back and proper remuneration to guarantee survival is—as shown in Sect. 2.3.1—an obvious but not-to-be-forgotten fundamental point in common. Both look for safe borrowers, try to keep positive margins containing operating costs with effectiveness, scaling, and standardization (whenever possible), and fixing interest rates at profitable levels.

The target for self-sustaining MFIs should usually be convergence to a (normal) banking model. This process has, of course, to be shared with clients, to prove feasible. Not an easy or quick target but worth anyway being considered since we go nowhere without clear aims and directions.

Lenders traditionally face:

- financial costs for collecting capital to be lent (with a mix of the cost of equity and cost of debt for the remuneration of the depositors, bondholders, interbank lenders ...); the cost of capital grows with risk and is traditionally greater in MFIs, if compared to mainstream banks;
- default costs (for delinquencies in the repayment of interests and principal);

- operational and transaction costs,[28] in MFIs that lack of economies of scale.

Small loans have great unitary costs of screening and monitoring, which substantially increase operating costs, without scale benefits that are possible only with greater loans; unitary costs per loan tend to be similar and irrespective of their size: even in this case, the issues of the ant are not smaller than those of the elephant!

Customer retention is a key marketing target for most businesses and this fundamental principle applies to both MFIs and mainstream banks, although it seems somewhat more important for the former, which do need to grow with their clients, progressively enlarging lending amounts, to reach profitability. If credit grows with positive repayment track records, MFIs usually reach their break even with a customer after the third or fourth loan.

The bridge between (not fully viable) MFIs and commercial banks can be established in both ways, either with organic growth and development of the former or with "downscaling" of mainstream banks to the microfinance market. While this bridge is greatly wanted, evolution to the profitability of subsidized MFIs is a long and challenging process, whereas penetration of commercial banks in the microfinance arena is neither easy nor common. Flexible contamination on both sides seems, however, useful for the microfinance industry and might foster financial innovation and outreach.

2.3.1 *Different Ways of Achieving the Same Result: Getting Money Back!*

Standard commercial banks and MFIs have many differences, particularly if the latter are informal and unregulated intermediaries but they tend to have at least one common aspect: they live out of repayments from borrowers.

If ways to get money back show to be different, the goal does not change, should institutions belonging to one of the abovementioned models desire to survive and, possibly, prosper.

[28] A weekly collection of money by credit officers is a high cost, particularly in underpopulated areas.

Subsidies, as it will be shown later, can soften the ways and methods to claim money back from poor borrowers but the goal is unlikely to change—and evidence shows how unwise it might prove.

When a potential borrower asks for a loan, traditional bankers demand him what he needs the money for, how he thinks to repay it, and should the answers not be enough convincing, how he can guarantee the reimbursement. No convincing answers, no money. This is the standard picture, even if opportunistic behavior such as moral hazard or strategic bankruptcy is always possible, as it will be shown in Sect. 2.4.

In microlending, fundamental rules might seem different, even if experience continuously shows that favor treatments produce disasters in the long run and if the method can and has to be different—due to the context where the collateral is typically absent—some fundamental principles, inspired to common sense, still deserve to apply.

The purpose of the borrowing is a standard question that must be linked to a feasible and credible, albeit simplified, business plan: moreover, it is the borrower's duty—if he wants to get the loan—to demonstrate how he thinks to generate adequate cash flows to service the debt. Simple questions often have challenging answers.

In countries that apply standard accounting principles, basic cash flow statements usually accompany assets & liability statements and the profit & loss account. For many illiterate poor, these basic compliance requests still look like science fiction.

Greater repayment rates also come as a natural consequence of a careful selection of the business to finance and many MFIs are not focused on risky peasants, having shifted toward "non-farm enterprises"—like making handicrafts, livestock-raising, and running small stores. A correct assessment of the volatility of the financed business—albeit challenging to detect—is a significant lending parameter even in underdeveloped countries.

2.3.2 Precautionary Savings and Risk Management: Microdeposits and Microinsurance

The poor, living on a subsistence income, might be unable to save, particularly in hard times (wars, epidemics, and illnesses to humans, livestock or plants, Biblical plagues such as famine, drought or floods, hail ...). When they succeed to save, they are often unable to find a safe harbor for their savings. Thefts, loans to relatives[29] (often unlikely to be paid back), erosion caused by shrinking purchasing power in inflated economies, are the main problems that the oxymoron represented by "poor savers" constantly face. Stashing money inside the pillow does not prove anywhere a safe strategy.

However, savings against hard times, which in underdeveloped countries are generally endemic, are in many cases the best insurance for mere survival and represent the first primordial form of insurance.

Savings help poor households to smooth consumption, keeping it above a survival break-even point, when income is volatile, without the stress of servicing debt. Saving facilities and not loans are critical for the poorest, following a "Savings first—Credit Later" motto.

Informal savings clubs, where each household contributes and makes sure that the others save, such as self-help groups in Indonesia or ROSCAs in Africa, allow making loans to the contributors on a rotating basis. Others pay unregulated deposit collectors to bring the savings to a bank or deposit savings with local money-lenders or credit unions or in the nearest post office.[30]

Microdeposits might represent, in this context, the abovementioned "safe harbour" for savings and should ignite even in poor countries—as it has happened to more advanced ones—a virtuous financial circle, with an intermediation process from micro-depositors to micro-borrowers. Microsavings should conveniently precede microlending.

Microdeposits are—perhaps surprisingly—often more requested than microlending by the poor and might well go along together, representing a partial form of guarantee for lenders, particularly if linked with insurance products (considering, for example, health insurance that might prevent ill borrowers from abandoning their job, masterminding paybacks).

Savings are also intrinsically related to borrowing since they can fuel repayments, teaching borrowers a disciplined way to save and to behave, for the sake of debt service. Being forced to repay debt might help to prevent wasting money on drinking!

Forced savings are a typical feature of group lending packages, serving as cash collateral for loans, and usually have unattractive characteristics

[29] If relatives and enlarged clan members are particularly demanding, borrowing might be a better solution than saving, to prevent "expropriation" and to justify refusals to accord them embarrassing loans.

[30] See Banerjee and Duflo (2007, p. 156).

since they pay no interest and cannot be claimed back until the member exits the group. Microloans are more diffused than micro-saving products due to:

- regulatory and compliance policies, traditionally harder for the latter;
- trustworthiness since it is harder for an MFI to persuade potential customers to deposit savings than to collect money;
- timing and entity of cash flows since debt repayments are set regularly, disciplining borrowers, whereas deposits occur randomly.

In bigger and sounder MFIs, belonging to the Tier 1 or 2 capital adequacy segment, savings collection through deposits might be replaced by cheaper funds (interbank loans; international funds; equity injections ...); MFIs should, however, try hard to attract even the penny savings—small and expensive to collect but with positive albeit underestimated effects on poverty alleviation.

Those who collect the savings need appropriate lending strategies, to make proper use of their collected funding.

The poor have little if no access to formal insurance products, even if social networks, particularly strong in rural areas, might provide some basic informal insurance, generally with loan exchanges, whose repayment schedules might, however, be severely affected by a common systematic risk, so zeroing the insurance when it is most wanted.

When the poor undergo economic issues, their "insurance" often means a drastic reduction in consumption—such as eating less—or taking children out of school: poor children tend to leave school in bad years.

Informal social insurance might conveniently be complemented by formal and professional tailor-made insurance products, provided by MFI, with a positive synergic effect since insured borrowers unsurprisingly have greater repayment records.

Interaction of microdeposits with microloans, microinsurance, and micro-consulting is depicted in Fig. 2.4.

Technology impacts on product switch and integration (e.g., deposits can be linked and compensated with loans in real-time through digital matching), as it will be shown in Chapters 4 and 6.

Farmers—most poor—find it challenging to get insured also because of typical corporate governance issues—analyzed in Sect. 2.4—such as moral hazard (insurance reduces the stimulus for avoiding losses) or adverse

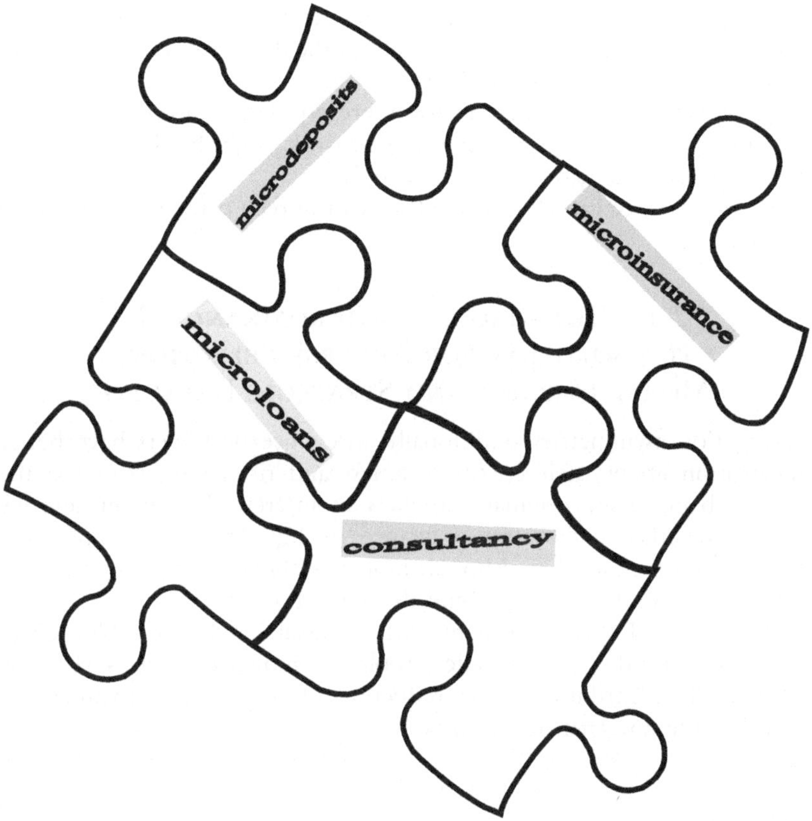

Fig. 2.4 Microdeposits interacting with microloans, microinsurance, and financial consultancy

selection (riskier farmers are the most eager to get insured but it is hard to discriminate between safe and risky ones).

Obstacles to microinsurance are generally represented by the great cost for handling each (small) risk position (unless it is part of a standard financial package, allowing for a consistent cost reduction) and by the general issues encountered in micro-lending. Lack of proper intermediaries, also considering the whole risk-handling chain, which needs reinsurance companies, is another problem.

Credit life insurance is a typical package linked to group lending, relieving other members to pay the debt of the dead borrower or to claim it from grieving widows or orphans.

Ignorance is also a primary factor in preventing the diffusion of formal insurance policies[31] whereas the social network might be the only source of (informal) insurance available to people.

Microinsurance can be upgraded with InsurTech paradigms, examined in Sect. 5.3.

2.4 The Magic in Microfinance: Is It a Solution for Adverse Selection, Moral Hazard, and Strategic Default?

Information asymmetries traditionally arise since borrowers have better information about their creditworthiness and risk-taking than has the lending bank. They originate conflicts of interest that might severely prevent the efficient allocation of finance: the liquidity allocation problem derives from the fact that although money is abundant, it is nevertheless not easy to give it to the right and deserving borrowers.

Big data and their treatment with artificial intelligence, blockchain validation, or other technological tools (as shown in Sect. 4.10) may substantially contribute to the reduction of information asymmetries, softening the governance concerns.

[31] Many people, rich or poor, are reluctant to buy insurance because they do not want to think about loss, illness, or death. Still, the low-income market may be particularly disinclined to purchase insurance for several reasons:

- The poor often lack familiarity with insurance and do not understand how it works;
- Until one receives a claim payout, insurance benefits are intangible; it is challenging to persuade someone to part with their limited resources to buy peace of mind;
- If the poor do not have to claim, they may believe that they wasted their precious income;
- Often the poor have a short-term perspective, only making financial plans a few weeks or months into the future;
- If the low-income market is familiar with insurance, they may not trust insurance providers.

Source http://microfinancegateway.org/resource_centers/insurance/focus_notes/_note_1.

Relationship lending relies on personal interaction between borrower and lender and is based on an understanding of the borrower's business, more than to standard guarantees or credit scoring mechanisms, and represents a critical factor in countries with a weak financial system counterbalanced by strong informal economic activity; multi-period and state-contingent contracts—typical of relationship lending—are an efficient device for dealing with asymmetric information.

Adverse selection is a typical problem in money lending, and it occurs even in traditional banks, when—not knowing who is who—they cannot easily discriminate between good and risky borrowers that should deserve greater interest rate charges.

The moral hazard is a classical "take the money and run problem" since borrowers might try to abscond with the bank's money or try not to engage fully in the project for which they have been financed.

Strategic bankruptcy is false information that the borrower gives about the outcome of his financed investment, stating that it has failed even if it is not true only in order not to give back the borrowed money. Poor borrowers generally have little or no collateral, so they might have little reason to avoid a strategic default.

These classical corporate governance issues are well-known in traditional banking and they naturally bring to sub-optimal allocation of financial resources and to capital rationing problems that frequently affect even potentially sound borrowers, if they are not able to differentiate themselves from those who bluff.

Standard banks in developed countries usually react by trying to reduce information asymmetries, using credit scoring analyses, monitoring, and asking for guarantees (in the form of sizeable collateral with an intrinsic market value).

Since microfinance borrowers are usually unable to give any worthy guarantee, as we have seen before, these issues are even more acute in a context that has also to take care of greater information fallacies and weak judicial systems.[32]

Therefore, any attempt or device to find a solution that can contribute to mitigating these conflicts of interest between the lending bank and the borrower is of crucial importance for the success of microfinance. As we shall see, if microfinance bears greater issues in some aspects, in

[32] See Armendariz De Aghion and Morduch (2010).

others it can intrinsically reduce risks, if compared to traditional banks. Specific microfinance loan contracts are designed with distinctive features (such as joint liability and dynamic incentives) to mitigate these pervasive problems.

The standard agency problem concerns conflict of interests between a potential lender (the principal), who has the money but is not the entrepreneur, and a potential borrower (the agent), a manager with business ideas who lacks the money to finance them. The principal can become a shareholder, so sharing risk and rewards with the agent, or a lender, entitled to receive a fixed claim. Agency theory explains the mismatch of resources and abilities that can affect both the principal and the agent: since they need each other, incentives for reaching a compromise are generally strong. In microfinance, equity stakes are typically rare and the standard model is concerned with a peculiar form of lending, which tries to overcome the abovementioned issues.

The main differences in dealing with these agency issues between traditional banks and microfinance institutions are the following:

- Limited liability businesses, where shareholders risk only the capital invested, are frequently financed by traditional banks, whereas MFIs mainly finance households or small businesses with unlimited responsibility; limited liability protects borrowers who might not be stimulated to repay their debt, particularly if it exceeds their equity stake;
- The motto "no collateral, no money" traditionally applicable in standard banking undergoes severe issues in poor areas, where the collateral is mostly nonexistent (by definition, those who have valuable collateral are not poor!) or challenging to seize, also due to unclear property rights, a primitive judicial system and ethical issues (taking resources away from poor households might severely undermine their chances of survival);
- Microfinance loans have very short maturities if compared with traditional banking loans, which can last even several years, and this gives the lender significant monitoring and enforcing power, checking weekly or monthly the repayment of interest rates, cashing early the lent capital and preventing the borrower from asking new money if he has proven delinquent with the first loan;

- Microloans generally consist of very limited amounts, which strongly reduce the magnitude of the lending risk and allow for better diversification;
- Monitoring microfinance borrowers is more expensive and challenging since credit scoring devices, computerized data, credit histories with delinquency rates, and proper bookkeeping from the borrower are usually nonexistent or present at an infantry stage; on the other side, weekly meetings between the MFI and the group members (borrowers) allow the creditor to monitor the repayment status of each debtor publicly, increasing the transparency within the group and generating a form of peer pressure that is expected to foster internal monitoring, minimizing debt screening costs[33];
- Ex post moral hazard, which emerges after the loan is made and when the investment is in the process, might lead to the abovementioned "take the money and run" temptation, even invoking a fake strategic default[34]: while this well-known phenomenon might be present in both cases, in traditional banking guarantees can represent a parachute, while in a microfinance context the absence of guarantees can be counterbalanced by a deeper in-site (on-field) control on the borrower and lower chances for him to leave his rural area (take the money without knowing where to run away might prove challenging); as a matter of fact, poor have poor chances for escaping repayments …
- Reputation also plays a significant role in preventing opportunistic behavior and poor borrowers, who at first sight do not have much to lose, in reality often are more concerned about this issue since the chances they have are very limited and new opportunities strongly depend on a good track record; they also face the abovementioned mobility issues and, in general, these "problems," which can become positive chances for enforcing reputation, are stronger in women, so introducing gender discrimination—well-known in the microfinance experience—according to which at least in some areas[35] women are better borrowers than men and might have stronger incentives to

[33] See Deutsche Bank (2007, p. 4).

[34] Dynamic incentives, such as access to additional loans, prove useful in reducing the strategic default option.

[35] This is the case in Bangla Desh, where up to 95% of the clients of Grameen Bank are women but not elsewhere, for example in sub-Saharan Africa …

pay back the borrowed money, seen as a chance for emancipation (breaking gender-based barriers, generally meaningful in underdeveloped countries), taking also profit or their better understanding of basic rural economics since they—more than men—tend to run the limited resources of the family;

- Strong information fallacies and asymmetries that affect poor borrowers are offset by good local information and enforcement mechanism that characterize rural lenders;
- Microfinance might soften information asymmetry problems if relationship lending and peer monitoring—often associated with mutual responsibility—are in place;
- Micro-saving and microinsurance can be positively linked to microloans, with a double side effect: if they are not available—as it frequently happens—then the whole microfinance circuit is weakened and more exposed to conflicts of interest.

The lender and the borrower might align their interests, paddling in the same direction—so reducing opportunistic behavior, one of the worst and most slippery hidden problems—if the borrower participates in the MFI business, also becoming a depositor and, possibly, a shareholder, this being a possible solution particularly for loyal and not-so-poor customers; multi-role stakeholders reduce many conflicts.[36]

Adverse selection and moral hazard are, as a matter of fact, mutual governance problems since they might characterize not only the behavior of the borrower toward the MFI, as it is universally known but also the strategy of the MFI that, for instance, might use its informational advantage in the money market to charge too high loan rates or to take on too much risk with depositors' money.

The high cost of capital (interest rate charges and banking fees) and short-term repayment schedules represent an incentive for proper allocation of loans to cash-flow-producing investments, able to ensure the

[36] A multi-role stakeholder simultaneously occupies different positions, and he can act as a shareholder, lender, borrower, worker, manager. This context is typical in cooperatives (even credit cooperatives). Corporate governance problems might arise if the multiple stakeholder interests are not properly known outside, due to information asymmetries, and he has an undeclared and hidden prevailing interest, potentially harmful for the other players.

service of the debt, preventing the temptation to address loans to consumables or working capital, which usually act as cash-burning devices. The property of small investment fixed assets (e.g., cars, agriculture tools ...) might sometimes represent a limited guarantee for the lender, so decreasing the overall risk of the loan.

Short-term (high-frequency) repayment installments, unrelated to the gestation timing of investments and to their ability to generate cash flows, are based on current income and assets of the borrower, marking a difference with the rigid philosophy of Basel II principles, now applying to mainstream banks in Western countries, according to which the capacity to generate adequate cash flow to service debt repayment should be the crucial parameter for lending scrutiny.

Lending is usually cash-flow based or collateral-based but with microcredit, this general banking classification seems too rigid and unable to describe its peculiar nature; poor borrowers with hardly predictable cash flows and unworthy collateral might still get credit, using typical microfinance innovative products. Improving cash-flow forecasting and/or use of worthy collateral might be of great help in reducing interest rates[37]: while this strategy seems hardly consistent with the poorest real possibilities, it might prove easier—at least to some extent—for the not-so-poor taking individual loans, with an established and growing business.

Focusing on ambitious but realistic scopes, albeit challenging to reach, is the right strategy, particularly for the illiterate poor who are not culturally used to targeting.

Progressive lending, a powerful device experimented in particular within group lending, might show some drawbacks—well-known to industrial or trading corporations that increase their sales to clients that have gained a good reputation but then start to misbehave, avoiding payments—if borrowers who lack the increased repayment capacity, go to other lenders in search for bridge loans, and pay old debts making new ones, exploiting information asymmetries and moral hazard techniques, in a well-known spiral of growing indebtedness, concealing and deferring the solution of problems that sooner or later come to a final judgment.

Adverse selection is also present since riskier borrowers have a natural incentive in looking for extreme scenarios, while safer ones are more concerned about their reputation. The social or macroeconomic scenario,

[37] Technology can also help to reduce interest rates. See Vong and Song (2015).

should external shocks occur (conflict; natural disaster; raise in interest rates ...), might worsen these governance problems. Offering a borrower a lower interest rate on his next loan is a financial innovation device that has a huge impact on repayment of the current one.

The limited size and the short time horizon of loans are, however, a significant obstacle to riskier but greater value-added projects, which become increasingly significant with the growth of the economy, and the consequent greater demand for differentiation. For these investments, other financial intermediaries are fitter, being represented by bigger MFIs (ranking as Tier 1 institutions) or ordinary commercial banks.

In synthesis, microfinance can in some cases become a "magic tool" to produce new, cheap, flexible, and simple ideas to circumvent information problems and asymmetries that are the main obstacle to an optimal allocation of capital, exploiting smart innovations in corporate governance, contract theory, and (flexible) product design. However, enchantments soon vanish and are uneasy to deal with: Microfinance soon reveals to be a challenging instrument, to manage with care, which needs fine-tuning and constant monitoring. Microfinance is a useful device, although not a miracle or a panacea that comes for free.

2.4.1 Transaction Cost Governance

Transaction cost theory (Williamson, 1979) was first discussed in the context of the decision by a firm whether to do something in-house or to outsource.

Organizations choose between two methods of obtaining control over resources in a classic "make it or buy" decision:

- the ownership of assets (hierarchy solutions—decisions over-production, supply, and the purchases of inputs are made by managers and imposed through hierarchies) and
- using the assets (the market solution—individuals and firms make independent decisions that are guided and coordinated by market prices).

The decision is based on a comparison of the "transaction costs" of the two approaches. Transaction costs are the indirect costs (i.e., non-production costs) incurred in performing an activity, for example, the expenses incurred through outsourcing.

When outsourcing, transaction costs arise from the effort that must be put into specifying what is required and subsequently coordinating delivery and monitoring quality.

Transaction costs for MFIs occur when dealing with another external party:

- Search and information costs: to find the (optimal) supplier.
- Bargaining and decision costs: to purchase the needed service.
- Policing and enforcement costs: to monitor quality with a timely audit.

Transaction costs represent a critical factor in this study since they are responsible for most of the problems that threaten economic sustainability and hinder outreach to the unbanked.

Consistently with the research question of this study, it will be shown that technology can reduce transaction costs and soften their criticalities.

2.4.2 Value Co-creating Stakeholders

Value co-creation is an innovative paradigm that examines how incremental value can be created by the cooperation of different parties that are jointly concentrated on a mutually valued target.

Co-created value arises in the form of personalized, unique experiences for the customer (value-in-use) and ongoing revenue, learning, and enhanced market performance drivers for the firm (loyalty, relationships, customer word of mouth). Value is co-created with customers when a customer can personalize his or her experience using a firm's product-service proposition—in the lifetime of its use—to a level that is best suited to get his or her job(s) or tasks done and which allows the firm to derive greater value from its product-service investment in the form of new knowledge, higher revenues/profitability, and/or superior brand value/loyalty.[38]

Co-creation allows companies and customers to create value through interaction. It is the joint, collaborative, concurrent, peer-like process of producing a new value, both materially and symbolically (Galvagno & Dalli, 2014). Collaborative innovation in new product development may also involve technological advances in microfinance, even with online and digital customer involvement.

2.5 The Interest Rate Paradox: Why Cheap Credit Might Harm the Poor

People might wonder why it is easier to buy toothpaste than to buy (borrow) money since—according to basic economic rules—prices adjust so that at market equilibrium supply meets demand. Consequently, when demand for toothpaste exceeds the supply for it, the price will rise until equilibrium is reached. If the price is too great, some might stop buying toothpaste but those willing to pay the great market price would not have any access problem.

Credit markets are somewhat similar, but they also show significant differences, as the Nobel prize winner Stiglitz explains in a seminal paper[39]: even in this case if demand for money exceeds supply, the price (represented by interest rates) grows till it reaches a market equilibrium but here an access problem might arise anyway, and information problems (such as those described in Sect. 2.4) can lead to credit rationing even in equilibrium. This happens because banks are concerned not only about the interest rates they charge on the loan but also about its risk.

High-interest rates have twofold implications and are a dangerous weapon in the hands of the lender: while providing more significant returns to banks, who cushion themselves against lacking collateral, they increase the risk of loans, which might prove too expensive and unbearable for borrowers, giving them opportunistic incentives and leading to moral hazard and in general being associated with a higher probability of failure.

[38] http://customerthink.com/my_personal_definition_of_business_with_customer_value_co_creation/.

[39] Stiglitz and Weiss (1981).

This general framework also applies in the microfinance arena, which, however, unsurprisingly shows some peculiar aspects, if compared to a standard credit market. A short historical summary might explain how interest rates have changed from primitive to modern credit markets, a pattern that is being also followed by microfinance institutions.

In the beginning, there were single, local, and informal moneylenders, providing liquidity and charging high interests, often at usury rates. In case of no repayment, ruthless actions were routinely applied to borrowers. Shylock in Shakespeare's Merchant of Venice is a bright example of how a usurer might behave, even if happy ends such as that in the drama are unfortunately exceptions more than a rule.

It is not surprising that usury, before becoming a criminal offense as it is now in most Western countries, was strongly condemned by the "Book Religions": both Jews and Christians find their source in the Deuteronomy's book of the Bible, while Muslims follow what is written in the Coran, with consequences that are still present in Islamic Finance,[40] according to which conventional interest is not allowed.

Middle Age finance, represented by Florence and the Medici family in the fifteenth century, evolved into a company scale and individual lenders were replaced by banks, with rules and costs that began to justify interest rates. Modern banks have consistently refined the model, intermediating liquidity between lenders and borrowers and providing—not for free—many other increasingly sophisticated services.

The origins of microcredit might be set back to the Italian Monti di Pietà at the end of the fifteenth century, established by religious orders to provide some sort of credit to the poor. At the end of the nineteenth century, loan cooperatives and saving banks were established in Europe to provide finance to small enterprises. Microcredit was so born long before the prominent Grameen Bank ("bank of the village") funded by Mohammed Yunus in Bangladesh in the early 1980s.

In this historical evolving context, interest rates find a rational economic and ethical explanation, even if they still undergo strong discussions and the right "price" of interest rates is among the hottest monetary questions.

In microfinance, interest rates show almost everywhere in developing countries—albeit with consistent differences—an astonishing great level,

40 See www.islamic-banking.com/. For an analysis of Islamic Microfinance, https://www.sciencedirect.com/science/article/pii/S0305750X20302576.

generating scandal among those who ideally consider that microfinance should be affordable even for the poorest. High rates particularly affect females, also because in underdeveloped countries the labor market, characterized by significant unemployment and segmentation, is for most of women essentially nonexistent. Gender discrimination unfortunately still appears challenging to eradicate.

Normal interest rates might vary from 1.5 to 4% and more and if this rate sounds cheap to westerners, it should not be equivocated that the rate is calculated per month and not per year[41]! Interests are frequently paid monthly, with a compound mechanism that substantially raises the toll. Fair levels of profit[42] have to consider interest rate burden.

The immediate explanation that these skyrocket rates are due to very high inflation does not hold since even real rates are consistently greater than in OECD countries in Bangladesh—the country where microfinance was born and is stronger—or even more in Bolivia,[43] another well-established place for microfinance. Elsewhere—not surprisingly in sub-Saharan Africa, the less developed area in the world—both nominal and real rates are even greater.

The deep presence of moneylenders who charge much greater rates shows a somewhat surprising relative insensitivity of poor households to interest rates: the main reason seems that they strongly need access to finance and, in many cases, they are forced to accept bad conditions because they lack better choices; widening the offer, easing the depth and outreach of finance, is a crucial point for economic development. Lower rates, due to increased competition, will naturally follow, as it has happened even in Western countries. Access to finance is (for the moment) more important than its price. Not taking profit from such a situation of need is a delicate ethical problem, of which not-for-profit institutions, such as NGOs, should be concerned.

How can we conciliate useful purposes—helping the poor giving them affordable access to finance—with usury interest rates?

[41] See also the reported statistics on MicroBanking Bulletin, www.mixmbb.org/.

[42] See Hudon et al. (2020).

[43] For market price conditions and setting standard comparisons within the microfinance industry around the world, see http://mftransparency.org/.

But before trying to respond to this embarrassing question, we might try to detect why interest rates empirically show to be so high in the microfinance arena. The reasons are many:

- the unitary amount of loans is very small and since each loan has to be instructed, dealt with, and monitored, fixed costs are generally very high, preventing economies of scale, due also to the fact that weekly on-field collection proves expensive; as a consequence, survival strategies require rates to be great enough to cover their running costs;
- MFIs find it challenging to collect deposits, particularly if they are not in Tier 1 or Tier 2 capital adequacy ranking; interbank deposits are also expensive; the lower the ranking of the MFI, the greater its cost of collected capital;
- MFIs also bear other fixed costs (set up and working of branches ...) that have to be repaid by borrowers...;
- Since relationship lending—typical of a microfinance context, where customer's creditworthiness is hard to detect and monitor—is costly for the lender (not being a standard product, so preventing economies of scale), it requires high spreads or large volumes to be viable and economically profitable: being large volumes for unitary loans almost nonexistent (with other barriers to cost-cutting economies of scale), high interest charges seem unavoidable.

Empirical evidence shows, however, that subsidizing microfinance to lower interest rates is hardly ever a good policy since it weakens borrowers, creating an artificial and segmented market: interest rate ceilings—like those existing in Western countries to prevent usury—have frequently shown to have severe negative side effects, failing to provide adequate consumer protection against abusive lending and weakening lender responsibility.

High interest rates charged to the poor might seem a contradictory policy, particularly from NGOs, and might result in predatory and unscrupulous lending, strongly damaging the poorest and keeping most of them outside an unaffordable credit market.

The introduction of mandatory interest rate ceilings, historically and currently used by many governments to address these problems, often hurts—rather than protecting—the most vulnerable, by shrinking their access to financial services since they generally discourage the provision of tiny loans by making it impossible to recover their great administrative costs. Among the many interacting reasons for such problems, the following are of interest:

- when faced with interest rate ceilings, MFIs often retreat from the market, grow more slowly, and/or reduce their presence in rural areas or other costlier market segments, if unable to cover their operating costs;
- not-for-profit MFIs might be discouraged from transforming into fully-licensed financial intermediaries; on the other side, subsidized MFIs are often embarrassed by "informal" fees (bribes) requested by dishonest credit officers;
- MFIs might try to circumvent the ceiling—to cover their costs—imposing new "cunning" charges, often hard to detect;
- the implementation of a transparent ceiling policy might prove challenging due to various definitions of the interest rate (nominal, real, annual percentage ...), different terms, and repayment schedules;
- interest rate ceilings are often challenging to enforce, particularly when it comes to softly regulated or unregulated intermediaries, such as many MFIs, the responsibility for enforcement is not always clear or is placed with agencies without proper technical expertise.

Cheap credit has long been a problem and lenders charging interest rates that are lower than the average market level are inefficient, misdirecting, and often face low repayment rates. "When subsidized credit is much cheaper than loans available elsewhere in the market, getting hold of those loans is a great boon. Loans meant just for the poor are thus frequently diverted to better-off, more powerful households. Even when loans go to the poor, the fact that greatly subsidized loans have generally come from state-owned banks (and the fact that loans are so cheap) make them seem more like grants than loans, and repayment rates fall sharply consequently."[44]

Interest rates are in part rationing and discriminating mechanisms, determining who chooses (or can afford) to borrow and who does not.[45]

[44] Armendariz De Aghion and Morduch (2010).

[45] Armendariz De Aghion and Morduch (2010).

Subsidized rates such as those usually provided by NGOs consequently have ambiguous results and while they might prove useful in the short run, they can be dangerous if too protracted. Even from state-run banks, we get a negative example: many of them for "political" reasons charge interest rates well below market standards, showing also weak repayment rates from intrinsically risky agricultural lending: no surprise that they are costly, inefficient, and not particularly brilliant in outreaching the poor.

The level of interest rates is, however, less dramatic than it might seem at first sight since projects of the poor usually show considerable rates of return, which are normally consistent with the service of the debt, leaving a positive economic and financial margin that can be reinvested or directed to savings, creating a virtuous circle. Interest rates depend on macroeconomic (monetary) policy (Buera et al., 2021).

Technology can help to bring down transaction costs and interest rates.

High-interest rate charges represent a limit to the ability of MFIs to serve poorer potential clients and constitute a competitive disadvantage against those who are entitled to much cheaper access to credit, even if market segmentation tends to keep a distinction between various classes of borrowers, which are generally not competing in the same markets (should this happen—and the probability is becoming increasingly concrete, due to globalization—then the problem might be worth considering and dealing with).

Consumer protection laws, including mandatory public disclosure of total loan costs (often partially hidden to unaware borrowers), might provide a desirable safeguard without the negative side effects of interest rate ceilings.

According to Zetzsche and Dewi (2018), hard interest rate caps prompt two unwanted consequences: increasing the importance of the informal credit sector and furthering the microfinance institution's mission drift.[46]

References

Achleiter, A. K. (2008). *Social entrepreneurship and venture philanthropy in Germany*. TUM Business School, Technische Universität München.

[46] See also Engels (2010).

Aggarwal, R., Goodell, J. W., & Selleck, L. J. (2015). Lending to women in microfinance: Role of social trust. *International Business Review, 24*(1), 55–65.

Akerlof, G. A. (1970, August). The market for "lemons": Quality uncertainty and the market mechanism. *Quarterly Journal of Economics, 84*, 488.

Armendariz De Aghion, B. A., & Morduch, J. (2010). *The economics of microfinance*. MIT press.

Ashta, A. (2012). Co-creation for impact investment in microfinance. *Strategic Change, 21*, 71–81.

Banerjee, A., & Duflo, E. (2007, Winter). The economic lives of the poor. *The Journal of Economic Perspectives, 21*(1), 141–168.

Beck, T. (2015). *Microfinance: A critical literature survey* (Independent Evaluation Group (IEG) Working Paper Series, no. 2015/4). World Bank Group.

Buera, F. J., Kaboski, J. P., & Shin, Y. (2021). The macroeconomics of microfinance. *The Review of Economic Studies, 88*(1), 126–161.

De Soto, H. (2003). The *mystery of capital. Why capitalism triumphs in the west and fails everywhere else*. Basic Books.

Deutsche Bank. (2007). *Microfinance. An emerging investment opportunity*. Available at https://www.db.com/usa/docs/Emerging_Investment_Opportunities.pdf.

Engels, P. (2010). *Mission drift in microfinance*. Ibidem Verlag.

Galvagno, M., & Dalli, D. (2014). Theory of value co-creation: A systematic literature review. *Managing Service Quality, 24*(6), 643–683.

Garcia-Perez, I., Munoz-Torres, M. J., & Fernandez-Izquierdo, M. Á. (2017). Microfinance literature: A sustainability level perspective survey. *Journal of Cleaner Production, 142*, 3382–3395.

Hudon, M., Labie, M., & Reichert, P. (2020). What is a fair level of profit for social enterprise? Insights from microfinance. *Journal of Business Ethics, 162*(3), 627–644.

Kapuscinski, R. (2003). *A reporter's self portrait*. SIW "Znak".

Milana, C., & Ashta, A. (2012). Developing microfinance. A survey of the literature. *Strategic Change, 21*(7–8), 299–330.

Moss, T. W., Neubaum, D. O., & Meyskens, M. (2015). The effect of virtuous and entrepreneurial orientations on microfinance lending and repayment: A signaling theory perspective. *Entrepreneurship Theory and Practice, 39*(1), 27–52.

Newman A., Schwarz S., Borgia D. J., & Wei, W. (2017). The influence of formal and informal institutions on microcredit: Financial inclusion for micro-entrepreneurs by lender type. In D. Cumming, Y. Dong, W. Hou, & B. Sen (Eds.), *Microfinance for entrepreneurial development*. Palgrave Macmillan.

Özcan, G. (2020). Financial development and income inequality: An empirical analysis on the emerging market economies. *Theoretical and Applied Economics, 3*(624), 85–96.

Patrick, F., & Squires, M. (2021). Linking mobile money networks to "e-ROSCAs": An experimental study. *Science Advances, 7*(1).

Prahalad, C. K. (2006). *The fortune at the bottom of the pyramid*. Wharton School Publishing.

Rahman, M. M., Khanam, R., & Nghiem, S. (2017). The effects of microfinance on women's empowerment: New evidence from Bangladesh. *International Journal of Social Economics, 44*(12), 1745–1757.

Rutherford, S. (2000). *The poor and their money*. Oxford University Press.

Sing, J., Dutt, P., & Adbi, A. (2021). Microfinance and entrepreneurship at the base of the pyramid. *Strategic Entrepreneurship Journal* (in press). Available at https://onlinelibrary.wiley.com/doi/10.1002/sej.1394.

Song, I., Lui, C., & Vong, J. (2014). Lowering the interest burden for microfinance. *International Journal of Process Management and Benchmarking, 4*(2), 213–229.

Stiglitz, J. E., & Weiss, A. (1981, June). Credit rationing in markets with imperfect information. *American Economic Review, 71*(3), 393–410.

Stiglitz, J. (1990). Peer monitoring and credit markets. *World Bank Economic Review, 4*(3), 351–366.

Thi-Hong, V. L., Vo, A. T., Nguyen, N. T., & Duc, D. H. (2021). Financial inclusion and economic growth: An international evidence. *Emerging Markets Finance and Trade, 57*(1), 239–263.

Vong, J., & Song, I. (2015). Mobility technology solutions can reduce interest rates of microfinance loans. *Emerging Technologies for Emerging Markets. Topics in Intelligent Engineering and Informatics, 11*, 11–24.

Williamson, O. E. (1979). Transaction-cost economics: The governance of contractual relations. *Journal of Law and Economics, 22*(2), 233–261.

Yunus, M., & Jolis, A. (1999). *Banker to the poor: Micro-lending and the battle against world poverty*. PublicAffairs.

Zetzsche, D. A., & Dewi, T. R. (2018, April 17). *The paradoxical case against interest rate caps for microfinance—And how FinTech and RegTech resolve the dilemma* (Working Paper no. 2018-003). University of Luxembourg Law. Available at https://ssrn.com/abstract=3159202.

CHAPTER 3

Microfinance Issues

The supply chain/business model canvas anticipated in the introduction is recalled in Fig. 3.1.

3.1 From Survival to Self-Sufficiency: How NGOs with a Social Vision Might Become Commercial Banks

MFIs generally operate according to one of the following three different evolutionary modes: bare survival, longer-lasting sustainability, or full self-sufficiency:

- in survival mode, institutions barely try to cover their running expenses, facing a progressive erosion of the startup sponsored capital, unable to generate any retained resources for future operations. These institutions, unless continuously sponsored, are condemned to death, explaining the great Darwinian selection and mortality of the sector, which burns out organizations, together with their goodwill, future programs, and expectations for the poor, generating dissatisfaction in the donors and dismay in the borrowers; opportunistic behaviors might also arise since if borrowers believe that a lender is not permanent or unwilling to impose sanctions, delinquency might increase;

R. Moro-Visconti, *MicroFinTech*, Palgrave Studies in Financial Services Technology, https://doi.org/10.1007/978-3-030-80394-0_3

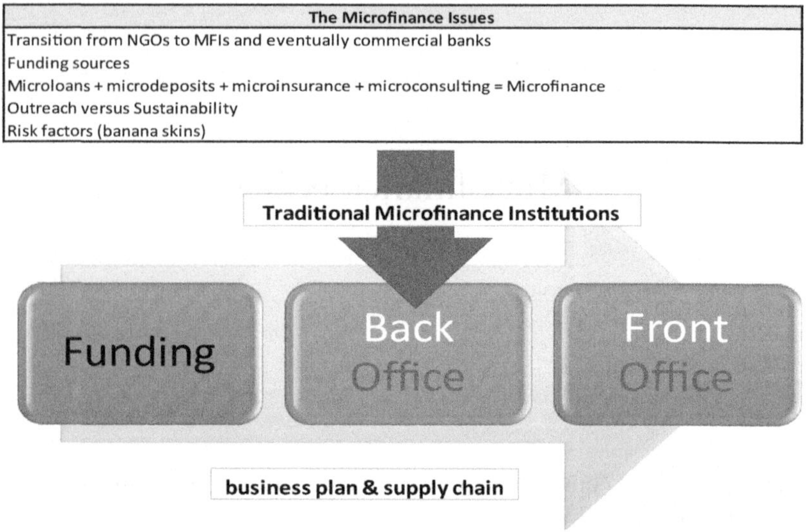

Fig. 3.1 Microfinance issues and the supply chain/business model canvas

- sustainability is concerned with the ability to secure a long-lasting survival, reaching, and keeping a break-even point between earned revenues and subsidies vs. fixed and variable running costs. Sustainable MFIs earn their cost of capital and can avoid cash- and equity-burnouts;
- self-sufficiency is an even greater standard, giving the possibility to increase the quality and the number of products—making the significant jump from lending-only micro-banks to overall MFIs (with deposits, insurances …)—while applying market prices that attract non-bankable but potentially viable borrowers; competition, not undermined by "addicted" subsidized institutions can also increase, with positive spillover (and some drawbacks[1]); full self-sufficiency facilitates the ability to raise capital from a variety of sources, while market competition prompts MFIs to control costs and to look for effectiveness gains.

[1] Increased competition reduces margins and decreasing crossed subsidies might harm the poorest.

The institutional life cycle theory[2] of MFIs' development describes an evolutionary pattern where most MFIs start as NGOs with a social vision, funding their operations with grants and concessional loans from donors and international financial institutions that provide the primary source of risk capital. This theory is consistent with the business cycle of both MFIs and their clients.[3]

A challenging step forward—a real jump of quality—is represented by the collection of public deposits before which the MFI has to accept formal banking regulation. This passage is usually accompanied by a reduction in subsidies and with targeted interest rate charges to borrowers that are consistent with the market rate remuneration of deposits and other funding sources, such as interbank loans.

The intensity of regulation is a long-debated issue: like a medicine, too much kills the patient and too little is useless. Advantages, costs, and enforceability of regulatory policies constitute a typical trade-off from a theoretical but also practical point of view, also considering the difficulties of less developed countries in efficiently controlling unsophisticated intermediaries; the Consensus Guidelines on MFI regulation take a balanced view, arguing that small-scale deposit-collecting should be allowed to go unsupervised, particularly in a closed context where depositors are only forced-saving borrowers, with a net debt toward the MFI.

The transition process from a non-profit organization or a credit cooperative to a profit-oriented firm is strongly advocated and considered "politically correct" since bigger and sustainable institutions have consistent advantages, particularly in terms of a cheaper and wider provision of capital; in severe imperfect markets, where most MFIs still operate, costs related to market contracts are, however, generally cheaper for non-profit institutions, that consequently seem still useful.

The macroeconomic context of the country and the development of its capital markets play a significant role not only in shaping the regulatory framework, increasingly sophisticated in the most advanced countries but also in the possibilities to access financial resources. The better the environment, the easier and cheaper is the funding.

Banks making small loans need a greater—more expensive—capital adequacy, setting aside greater provisions against the higher expected

[2] See Ashta (2018).

[3] See Tchakoute Tchuigoua et al. (2020).

losses from small loans, somewhat mitigated by the microfinance low delinquency rate.

Exclusive reliance on donors funding brings to well-known capital rationing problems, which prevent MFIs from meeting the enormous demand from the underserved, and might also avoid pressures to operate efficiently: commercially-funded MFIs have to survive in the market and have to cope with a daily pressure for revenues enhancing and cost-cutting, to keep survival margins, flexibly reacting to competitive market shifts (e.g., if market interest rates go down, the commercial institution has to follow the trend, otherwise it will sooner or later be abandoned by the clients).

Donor-backed MFIs may not fully respond to market pressures to operate efficiently or may deliberately choose to pursue other goals, such as outreach over effectiveness, by serving poorer or rural clients with greater delivery costs.[4]

The marginal involvement of poorer clients, although socially desirable, substantially increases the running costs of the institution, due to concomitant and interacting factors (lower loan sizes with decreasing economies of scale; greater unitary screening and monitoring costs; absolute lack of any worthy collateral; low cultural—entrepreneurial level …).

Cost–benefit analyses are significant to assess if and to which extent microfinance is efficient in respecting its goals and if it can have a better impact than other alternative methodologies or uses of funds. This is evidently of crucial importance for both donors and beneficiaries, with psychological as well as material good or bad consequences.

A correct assessment of the right objectives might seem trivial—although often forgotten or misunderstood—starting point but is essential since microfinance has never proven to be a remedy for all evils and is not a suitable tool for the satisfaction of many primary needs.

If subsidies must be sustainable and self-fulfilling, at least in the long period, then they have to be addressed to projects and investments that can generate positive cash flows, ideally consistent enough to repay the debts. However, if this is the context, then "cold projects," which generate very limited if any cash returns are automatically excluded, and only "hot projects" can conveniently be selected.

[4] Armendariz de Aghion and Morduch (2010).

As it happens with many selections, even this choice seems cruel and unfair since it discriminates not only "cold projects" of primary importance, such as hospitals, education, and schools, no-toll infrastructures, etc., but also "cold poor" (the marginal destitute) from "hotter" ones. However, also improper use of microfinance, even if with the best intentions, can lead to disastrous results.

Bad but instructing examples also concern government-subsidized agricultural credit, considered an appropriate development strategy to reach the poor during the post-colonial period. Relaxed requirements for collateral and subsidized interest rates represented a spoiling free lunch for many borrowers (and some cozy lender, often belonging to the same ethnic group), ending up in a costly and economically unbearable disaster made of higher transaction costs, interest rate restrictions, corrupt practices, and great default rates, which has unsurprisingly resulted in the phenomenal growth of informal financial markets.

Empirical evidence and statistics show that the vast majority of MFIs are tiny—and very few are large; dimensional growth is often not one of the main concerns—as it is for many businesses in other industries—of sponsored MFIs: the paradox is that to grow to a sustainable level they need additional "fuel" (subsidies) but exhausted donors might empty their pockets—pouring money into a bottomless pit—before reaching the magic threshold. Scarce donor funding has empirical evidence of being the principal factor in limiting growth (and consequent positive side effects, such as scaling, increased effectiveness, outreach, the attractiveness of private investors …) and donor-led models are hardly sustainable in the long run.

Moreover, the real effectiveness of foreign aid is strongly challenged by a harsh local environment where the cultural distance between donors and beneficiaries requires time and patience much more than money. Money is a double-sided weapon, easing poverty alleviation but at the same time corrupting the poor, with the risk of transforming them into permanent beggars. Self-esteem and the capability to solve internal problems can break the cycle of dependency for the poor living at the bottom of the social pyramid.[5]

Smart coalitions between various NGOs—actually too many and too small to survive—are feasible solutions to the problem and if they can

[5] See Prahalad (2006).

hurt the ego of lonely sponsors, they, however, prove very effective for the sometimes-forgotten real objective: sustainable outreach for the poorest!

The transformation of NGOs or other subsidized MFIs to commercial banks does not only require Central Banks authorizations but is also usually accompanied by the presence of new private and profit-oriented shareholders; changes in the objectives and the by-laws of the institutions generally foresee the ability to distribute profits, which do not necessarily have to be reinvested in the business. Donors can conveniently act as catalysts for subsequent professional and profitable intervention, "crowding in" funds and preparing the ground for self-sustainable MFIs.

Earning survival profits is quite different from adequate revenues to attract investors not concerned with social missions, maybe heartless and greedy but often necessary for a jump of quality, to approach otherwise unreachable international financial markets (like it or not, these are the rules of Capitalism and—among others—of listed companies).

Investors in MFIs might be attracted by low correlation to global capital markets but significant exposure to domestic GDP, with an attractive portfolio diversification for international investors but not for domestic investors lacking significant country risk diversification options.

MFIs can operate as non-governmental organizations (NGOs), credit unions, non-bank financial intermediaries, or commercial banks, according to their legal status. This classification might broadly describe the increasing pattern of sophistication that MFIs might follow in their development. The many players in the microfinance industry have various missions and agendas, creating a market segmentation that increases the borrowers' choices, even if the "not interesting" poorest might, unfortunately, be left aside.

3.1.1 *Microfinance Investment Vehicles: The Missing Link in the Demand–Supply Chain of Funding?*

The size of the demand for finance in underdeveloped countries is so significant that even microfinance, despite its astonishing merits, is far from getting to optimal outreach and probably only the commercial mainstream will be able to meet it.

Commercial viability (financial sustainability) of MFIs is a precondition to attract not-for-philanthropy investors and while they can choose to incorporate from scratch their own MFI (following a pattern like most

Table 3.1 Microfinance investment vehicles

1. *Registered mutual funds*, mainly concerned with fixed-income investments in MFI;
2. *Commercial fixed-income investment funds*, providing senior debt to high-growth MFIs;
3. *Structured finance vehicles,* which pool and repackage loans toward MFI (mainly Collateralized Debt Obligations), placing them as marketable securities;
4. *Blended value fixed-income and equity funds*, the most mission-driven MIVs, offering a mix of social and financial returns;
5. *Holding companies of microfinance banks*, established by leading microfinance consulting companies and Development Finance Institutions (DFIs) to provide subsidized startup equity finance;
6. *Equity funds,* represented by private equity and venture capital firms, offering a blend of equity and convertible debt to high-growth MFIs in emerging markets

NGOs), a typical, quicker, and safer solution is to invest in various and already viable MFIs, through an investment vehicle.

Microfinance Investment Vehicles (MIVs) are special purpose vehicles raising funds from commercial, private, institutional, or even social investors (endowment or pension funds, foundations ...) and run by professional managers to invest them in microfinance assets, creating an otherwise unthinkable bridge between international capital markets and financial entities located in underdeveloped countries. MIVs represent a privileged instrument for international commercial bank investments in the microfinance business.

MIVs might be classified into six categories (Table 3.1).

MIVs can be linked to innovative social network instruments like crowdfunding, which will be illustrated in Sects. 4.9.1 and 6.5.

Investment funds might also soften—with appropriate guarantees—MFI's access to domestic capital, free of currency risk,[6] easing linkages with local commercial banks or deposit mobilization from clients; provision of equity and subsequent capital adequacy are required for safe leveraging. In equity investments, local currency risk is borne by (foreign) shareholders, while in bond underwritings the risk is generally assumed by local MFIs. The fact that local currencies are typically nonconvertible in

[6] Most foreign debt for MFI is denominated in hard currencies (mainly the US$), so creating a currency risk (due to the imbalance between foreign currency liabilities and domestic currency assets) against which hedging proves challenging and expensive.

a greater inflation environment[7] does not help since hedging becomes more challenging (particularly if the currency is not pegged to the US$ or other strong currencies) and international coordination of monetary policies is harder and less efficient.

Underwriting of bonds issued by MFIs and securitization of the existing portfolios of MFIs are other complementary investment options for MIVs, while funds of funds can create further portfolio diversification for investors, albeit with increasing transaction costs.

Apart from money, MIVs can also provide wanted expertise, easing the adoption of new technologies and outreaching/cost-cutting innovations (such as Automated Telling Machines, computerized credit scoring systems ...), while helping to face industry typical risks, such as credit risk, country/political risk, currency risk, operational, reputational and liquidity risks.

Most MIVs are debt vehicles but it is only when they provide greatly wanted equity that they can strengthen the MFI's financial structure, and then they can also actively participate in its governance, being enabled to appoint directors that represent the fund.

A minimum break-even size is essential for the fund's profitability and critical for attracting underwriters, easing the development of upward share distribution—to investors—as well as downward investment distribution to the selected MFI.

Efficient reporting, considering economic and social returns, and using standard key performance ratios, although challenging to implement, is essential for adequate compliance and transparency toward investors, which might otherwise mistrust this unconventional form of investment, addressing elsewhere their savings.

Socially Responsible Investments are attracted by "double-bottom line" institutions such as MFIs and balancing social and financial returns is a crucial move toward sustainable outreach.

[7] Inflation and exchange rates are linked by the purchasing power parity theory, which uses the long-term equilibrium exchange rate of two currencies to equalize their purchasing power. Developed by Gustav Cassel in 1920, it is based on the law of one price: the theory states that, in an ideally efficient market, identical goods should have only one price and consequently price changes (inflation) and currency rates are linked.

3.1.2 Uncorrelated Investments, Risk, and Portfolio Diversification

To date, the microfinance sector has built a record of extremely low default rates despite rapid growth. This has been due to the close relationship with the clients, solid customer screening, and concentration in the poor market. The absence of a close relationship with the client (borrower) and the sophistication/opacity of derivatives and other toxic products are another remarkable disadvantage of so many once-upon-a-time successful products of mainstream banks.

All microfinance practitioners—investors, lenders, and regulators – should operate with caution to preserve this record to avoid the existence of exploitative practices by selfish practitioners like in the case of the subprime scenario. Careful underwriting, risk management techniques, and a strong focus on portfolio quality are critical to the impressive repayment performance of microfinance.

The success of the industry to date has depended on the relationship between lender and client,[8] built on the loyalty of borrowers traditionally neglected by traditional banks. Care must be taken to preserve this relationship. Commercial microfinance stands at the threshold of the capital markets. Success has accelerated in recent years with significant benefits to investors and with enormous benefits to the end clients (the entrepreneurs at the bottom of the economic pyramid[9]).

Globalization and international transmission of economic recession[10] can take place through financial, labor, and trading markets. Globalization has an impact on the economies of developing countries from three distinctive processes: trade in goods, flows of capital, and migration of people.[11]

Globalization (Sun & Liang, 2021) has always shown to have positive aspects in decreasing the international cost of equity capital for companies accessing international stock markets—but MFIs in developing countries have hardly been able to benefit from this (being too small, young, or neglected to be sufficiently attractive).

[8] See Godfroid (2019).

[9] See Prahalad (2006).

[10] See Soumaré et al. (2020).

[11] Collier (2007, p. 80). Physical borders for workers are still the hardest to trespass and mobility of capital is much easier than immigration.

The presence of financially strong shareholders is an important relief for MFIs. This is because most MFIs are privately held companies, with the main shareholders generally consisting of both for-profit and non-profit investors, who have a long-term strategic interest and are less driven by market forces. Therefore, the strong ownership structures, with owners who have financial resources and enough equity status and closely monitor MFIs, might act as an important shield against the economic crisis. Cooperatives where shareholders, lenders, and borrowers typically align their interests often prove elastic and flexible in hard times, being exempt from the market myopia typical of greedy stock market investors.

Microfinance shows a lower volatility pattern than equities or bonds quoted in emerging markets' Stock Exchanges since it is invested in instruments that are not yet listed and whose value is only partially influenced by unpredictable fluctuations in interest rates, credit spreads, and speculative transactions. Microfinance shows a weaker correlation to political or economic events since it belongs to the informal sector which is by its very nature a thriving source of new businesses, which are somewhat independent of the fate of the formal economy. Similarly, it is weakly correlated with global financial movements in major markets.

While in Western countries the 2008 recession—fuelled by global and integrated economies—severely hits the banking system, with immediate and painful consequences on households, a double safety net protects poor microfinance clients:

1. From a macro point of view, the financial and banking system of poor countries is less integrated to the Western markets and this segmentation acts as a protection from the recession contagion: some spillover is unavoidable but the impact is milder than elsewhere;
2. MFIs operating in poor countries are less integrated among them: while Western banks are increasingly interlinked, both internationally and locally, amplifying the mechanism of transmission of recession[12] through international capital markets and domestic ties, MFIs in developing countries are at the same time weakly linked to international markets and not so integrated among them, especially if we consider the difference between regulated and unofficial

[12] See Moro Visconti (2009, 2011).

intermediaries, which live together in less developed countries, while in Western countries moneylenders and other unregulated intermediaries are typically forbidden.

Funding capacity can resist if it is sufficiently insulated from a global recession and domestic savings from poor rural clients are the best source in hard times, also considering that:

1. they are denominated in the same local currency, so being exempt from foreign exchange risk;
2. savings and deposits from the same borrowers are a simple but effective form of guarantee, particularly precious under challenging times where other kinds of (external) pledges are more difficult to find and consequently more expensive;
3. Savings have shown to be even more important than loans for poor households and the attitude to save in poor countries seems marginally less affected than in richer ones, even because psychological pressures and media information are much less effective (Table 3.2).

Liquidity constraints increase risk and might also have unfavorable procyclical effects since lack of provision of adequate finance to borrowers can stop their investment plans and undermine their survival capabilities, preventing them to pay back their debt. Increasing default rates exacerbate liquidity constraints, with a spiral and self-fulfilling effect which might prove extremely dangerous, even from a psychological point of view. It takes years to build up trust and reputation whereas few weeks are enough to destroy both.

MFIs in developing countries are very different from Western banks or financial institutions, since they do not make use of derivatives and other toxic products or excess leverage and are much closer to the ultimate clients, being in direct touch with where risk is generated. The paradigm according to which in the last years many financial institutions that raise funds have got free of lending risk, repackaging, and selling it to a chain of intermediaries who in some cases barely know themselves, does not apply to unsophisticated MFIs, who do not suffer from the bad effects of full deregulation.

Table 3.2 Microfinance investment risks

Type of risk	*Description of risk*
Country risk	The likelihood that changes in the business environment will adversely affect operating profits or the value of assets in a specific country. Country risk includes the threat of currency inconvertibility, expropriation of assets, currency controls, devaluation or regulatory changes, institutional corruption, or instability factors such as mass riots, civil war, and other potential events. Failing states with bad policies and governance, especially if landlocked[a] by bad neighbors, unsurprisingly have a higher and more persistent country risk. In times of distress, the sovereign risk becomes effective; credit default swaps spreads "explode" and recovery value shrinks. Country debt restructuring might prove painful and with long-lasting reputation drawbacks
Political risk	Closely linked to country risk, political risk is a consequence of the complications that businesses and governments may face because of what is commonly referred to as political decisions or any political change that alters the expected outcome and value of a given economic action by changing the probability of achieving business objectives. This is the risk of a strategic, financial, or HR loss for a firm because of such non-market factors as macroeconomic and social policies (fiscal, monetary, trade, investment, industrial, income, labor, and developmental) or events related to political instability (terrorism, riots, coups, civil war, and insurrection)
Financial Market risk	The risk that the financial conditions will be adversely affected by the changes in market prices or interest rates, foreign exchange rates, and equity prices
Foreign exchange risk	The risk of losses due to unstable currency exchange rates and adverse changes, such as the devaluation of the local currency (if the debt is denominated in reevaluating hard and foreign currencies). MFIs face foreign exchange risk only to the extent that debt is denominated in hard foreign currencies; this is hardly ever the case in small institutions
Interest rate risk	The risk that changes in interest rates might affect the operating and net margins of the MFI. Interest rates increases raise the cost of collected capital and are not always transmittable to more expensive loans since borrowers might be unable to pay higher rates and their default risk might increase

Type of risk	*Description of risk*
Operational risk	This is a risk arising from the execution of a company's business functions. The risk of losses that arise directly from services and product delivery, resulting from human or systems errors. It involves fraud risks, legal risks, physical or environmental risks, etc. It is associated with human resources, governance, and information technology. In general, it considers the risk that operational costs are higher than revenues, with consequent negative margins (borrowing and running costs are higher than lending profits)
Credit (repayment or delinquency) risk	Credit risk applies to lending and investing activities and it considers the risk of financial losses resulting from borrowers' delay or nonpayment of loan obligations MFIs are institutionally more directly concerned about risk than other Western financial institutions, such as mainstream banks or—even more—hedge funds and other sophisticated and not-so-transparent intermediaries or products. Since repayment installments are weekly or monthly for MF clients, and the loan amounts are small, credit risk is typically lower than in healthy banks
Guarantee (collateral) risk	Strongly linked with credit risk since the lack of adequate guarantees can undermine the borrower's capacity or willingness to honor his debt Since guarantees are typically limited or nonexistent in MFI, from this point of view they are safer than mainstream banks and they have a competitive advantage
Gender risk	A traditionally burning question concerns gender risk: are women more discriminated when asking for money? It should not be so in microfinance, albeit for small loans empirical evidence shows that women are more trustworthy and have better repayment records

(continued)

Table 3.2 (continued)

Type of risk	*Description of risk*
Corporate governance risk	Corporate governance sets the rules of cohabitation and the behavior of the different stakeholders that pivot around the MFI (borrowers, lenders, shareholders, supervisory authorities …). Typical banking and specific microfinance risks include adverse selection (the difficulty in discriminating between good and non-trustworthy borrowers), moral hazard (the "take the money and run" option), and strategic bankruptcy (false information that the borrower gives about the outcome of the financed investment, to elude repayment). Information asymmetries are also part of the game. Corporate governance is also concerned with legal and compliance risk, which involves losses arising from failure to follow relevant legal and regulatory requirements. In unregulated MFI, the risk—if existent—is low but even the benefits of regulation and good governance are missing
Competition risk	Commercial banks have started downscaling to access the microfinance market The informal sector (money lenders) is most likely to provide stiff competition to microfinance as it is not affected by the economic turmoil
Mission drift risk	Not-for-profit MFI targeting the poor might transform in for-profit institutions aimed at maximizing returns
Reputation risk	The risk of earnings and capital arising from negative public opinion, which may affect the institutions' ability to sell products and services or access other funding
Liquidity risk	The risk of losses that arise from the possibility that the MFI may not have enough funds to meet their obligations or be unable to access adequate funding
Strategic risk	The risk to earnings or capital arising from adverse business decisions or improper implementation of strategies, due to mismanagement or organization fallouts. Reliable strategic goals, development of proper business actions, and deployment of adequate resources, and the quality of management reduce the risk
Inflation risk	Probability of loss resulting from erosion of an income or in the value of assets due to the rising costs of goods and services. The possibility that the value of assets or income will decrease as inflation shrinks the purchasing power of a currency A surge in inflation levels might bring to deposits withdrawals for survival needs

Type of risk	*Description of risk*
Capital adequacy risk	Capital adequacy risk refers to the possibility of losses resulting from the firm's lack of enough capital to finance business operations. With under-capitalization, a small adverse shift in circumstances can impair the solvency of the MFI, if bad loans erode the capital
Funding risk (credit tightening)	The risk of not finding adequate supplies of financial resources to meet the borrowers' needs
Savings risk	Strongly linked with funding risk, this risk has a direct impact on the licensed MFI's ability to collect deposits, which also represent a guarantee for loans to the same depositors
Concentration risk	Diversification of funding and lending sources improves the MFI's stability On the opposite side, concentration risk involves small MFI or NGOs, who do not collect deposits and rely only on one partner, who acts also as a depository bank, intermediating funds on behalf of the NGO
Default risk	The inability of the MFI to meet its obligations, unless occasional, brings it to bankruptcy. The risk can be considered an unlucky combination of some of the other risks described above, concerning operational, credit, and liquidity risk

[a]This expression is taken from Collier (2007), according to which countries are "landlocked" if they have no direct access to the sea and heavily depend upon their coastal neighbor for transport costs. Each country benefits from the growth of neighbors and this is particularly true for landlocked countries, even if wireless devices somewhat soften this dependence. Land-locked countries could serve as labor resource pools, rather than develop as independent national economies

Stress tests to which many ailing Western banks are now undergoing, to detect if and till which break-even point they can survive, might conveniently be adapted also to the MFI in developing countries, with different possible scenarios and following outcomes.

3.2 Funding Sources and Lending Structures: Should Finance for the Poor Be Subsidized?

At the center of the current debate about the future of microfinance, is the question of whether MFIs should be profit-oriented, privately funded, self-sustaining businesses or socially-minded, subsidized, non-profit organizations. This dilemma is still actual and can be reconsidered with technology, for instance applying result-based financing patterns to digital microfinance investments. Impact investing is part of this trendy scenario, where grantors are increasingly looking for real-time feedback.

Should MFIs be compared based on their profitability or based on their outreach, i.e., the extent to which they try to provide financial services to those that were previously deprived of these services? In the microfinance industry, there may be room for more than one business model. For-profit and non-profit firms coexist, and increasingly in the same (regional) market. The coexistence of these firms has shaped and will continue to shape the evolution of the microfinance industry.

As the microfinance industry has spread across the globe, both for-profit and non-profit MFIs are faced with the same questions: what is the optimal amount of outreach, and what is a proper yield on my loan portfolio? Some non-profit institutions have proven to be more profitable than their for-profit peers, while the latter sometimes outclass their non-profit peers when it comes to outreach, suggesting that microfinance accommodates not just very different business models (profit maximization, outreach maximization), but also different mixtures of these business models (Bos & Millone, 2015).

The thesis of this book is that technology-led economic and financial savings are precious for any business model and any profit/non-for-profit target. So, even if technology can have a different impact on heterogeneous MFIs, it is expected to be positive in any case.

Empirical evidence shows that the provision of financial services to the very poor requires subsidy (soft financing, consisting of subsidized loans), at least for the startup of simple and often informal banking activities, which can progressively transform themselves into regulated MFIs. Subsidies might well include grants for capacity building, audit, staff recruiting, office building, ICT investments, etc., as well as the financing of the transaction from NGOs to licensed banks. Funding strategies impact performance (Tchakoute Tchuigoua et al., 2017).

This was the case even for the well-known Grameen Bank paradigm, which is still subsidized,[13] to charge soft interest rates.

Subsidizing is an unavoidable but dangerous startup mechanism,[14] not only because it can spoil and humiliate the poor (being personal work and not external help the crucial source of self-esteem[15]), emptying the donors' pockets of the mainly foreign NGOs but also since it may damage and distort the regular and market-oriented workings of the microfinance industry for the not-so-poor, with side effects (corruption; circumventive and opportunistic behavior generating well-known problems such as rent-seeking or round-tripping; lack of transparency and meritocracy ...) that eventually damage also the real poor.

Even subsidized equity has an implicit (shadow) cost since the shareholders acting as sponsors must collect the money they put in the MFI, bearing market costs, and taking care of the loss for the missed potential return in profitable alternative investments.

Like for any young corporation, the mortality rate for new MFIs is high; a particular feature of sponsored entities is the impossibility of their survival without grants, particularly in the first years; but mismanagement and improper use of funds are widespread, particularly if sponsors are far away from a country that they superficially know and check, and these disappointing problems tend to have a catastrophic impact on donors, that feel cheated and betrayed and often react stopping further subsidies, so condemning the institution to an inglorious death.

The link and interactions with people belonging to various social classes have a great impact in depicting socio-economic conditions even following the "trickle-down theory," which describes economic policies perceived to benefit the wealthy and then "trickle-down" to the middle

[13] In the mid-1990s, the bank started to get most of its funding from the Central Bank of Bangladesh. More recently, Grameen has started bond sales as a source of finance. The bonds are implicitly subsidized as they are guaranteed by the Government of Bangladesh and still, they are sold above the bank rate.

[14] The subsidy trap is a well-known and documented danger.

[15] which the philosopher Rawls (1971) identifies as the most significant primary good.

and lower classes. As a consequence, even if microfinance is at first targeting the not-so-poor, there can be positive marginal side effects even for the poorest, which can eventually benefit from a general bettering of economic conditions, creating new jobs and entrepreneurs.

Credit is not the only or even the main financial service needed by the poor and subsidies might be better spent on savings and payment systems, creating a sound financial environment where savings can represent a parachute even for borrowers and an internal funding source for local banking intermediaries, following—albeit on a simpler and reduced scale—the simple mechanism of a standard bank that collects money from depositors and intermediates it with selective lending.

If the funding source and the lending structure are unbalanced, as it frequently happens for small MFIs that find it challenging to collect money at home—since local financial markets are underdeveloped and poorly regulated—then the whole system appears weak and exposed to currency risk and asymmetric shocks: for instance, a local crisis (frequent in locations where country risk is substantial and unpredictable) might severely damage the collection of funds from abroad, suddenly interrupting the source of finance.

International markets have the memory of an elephant and while it takes a long time to build up a respectable reputation, few weeks are enough to destroy it for ages.

The relationship between donors (from individuals to organized NGOs) and the poor is very complex, not only due to evident capital rationing problems—since resources generally fall short of the poor's endless needs—but also to motivational and psychological issues, somewhat harder to measure and detect but probably even more significant.

The heart of the donors sometimes goes beyond their pockets and a rational analysis of the situation often shows negative consequences that can overwhelm even the best intentions, damaging the poor and creating an ephemeral dependence. Some smart donors are thinking to use subsidies sparingly and only in the startup phase when institutions are too young to be able to walk with their legs. Everybody knows—particularly in richer countries—that children and teenagers cannot properly survive and develop without family "subsidies" (education, keeping, incentives …), which, however, in the long run, can severely spoil and affect them, with everlasting consequences on their adult life. Moreover, hardly anybody can afford to be … rich and stupid for more than a generation, this being a lesson that Western countries are painfully beginning to discover.

On the other side, free and easy money humiliates the poor, transforming them into permanent beggars, with no rescue possibilities. The psychological effect is frequently underestimated by distracted and superficial donors and is amplified by the natural shame of the poor, who often do not dare to ask and feel attracted but also humiliated by Western standards of living. There is no motivation without hope. Moreover, free money to the poorest—not used to it—is a particularly dangerous drug, which makes them addicted, keeping them artificially far from their real world.

Even if it is challenging to find a monolithic and inflexible solution to a broad range of problems, a general consideration, inspired to common sense, might prove useful: starting a self-fulfilling system—of an MFI or something else—is often harder than providing an immediate subsidy and proves more time consuming, with no or few short-term results that are so significant for the psychology of impatient and unwise donors.

Education to the development, responsiveness and accountability, rational use and sharing of resources are the crucial issues of a mind and cultural change that needs time—often measured in generations—and much more effort to grow with solid roots.

When a donor begins to understand that he is receiving more—much more—than what he gives and the poor understands that he can be useful even to the donor, the quality of the relationship consistently strengthens, and the results are astonishingly better and longer-lasting.

Donors can act as private sponsors and might be willing to accept a reduction in their expected returns in change for the satisfaction stemming from the financing of projects with a high social value, where the poor borrowers are actively involved, with positive psychological and motivational side effects (acquisition of self-confidence; the dignity that prevents poor to be ashamed of their condition; possibility to rescue from the misery trap …).

In microfinance, sustainability is permanence and unsustainable MFIs tend to inflict costs on the poor in the future far greater than the gains enjoyed by the poor in the present. MIFs' sustainability is driven by a combination of factors such as an excellent quality credit portfolio, coupled with the application of sufficiently high rates of interest—allowing for a reasonable profit—and sound management.

Financial sustainability is efficient for outreach because permanency leads to a structure of incentives and constraints that, if carefully dealt with, stimulates all the stakeholders (sponsors, MFIs, borrowers, and their families…) to increase the difference between social benefit and social cost and to align their interests, so reducing information asymmetries and governance problems.

Unsustainable MFIs might be particularly dangerous—particularly if they collect deposits and interbank loans—since they are part of banking and financial institutions, a very delicate sector where insolvencies propagate rapidly and can easily undermine even sound institutions.

Subsidized institutions might not harm market-driven intermediaries only if the financial market is well segmented and the former serve extremely poor clients that in any case would not have access to formal credit. When subsidized funds are available to micro-borrowers on a large scale, they might, however, practice a dumping policy that discourages unsubsidized institutions, creating entry barriers.

The weakness of banking regulation systems in underdeveloped countries is another crucial issue, with macro and systematic consequences on the overall day-to-day working and sustainability of MFIs, which need to reach enough critical mass, this being an easier task within a favorable environment. Even the relationship with financial and banking institutions of donor countries is—positively or negatively—affected by the overall quality of the domestic financial and credit market. Transparency and accountability, proper and efficient regulation, and compliance to international standards are increasingly significant in a global economy, and this golden rule also applies to the poorest, being—if missing—an important factor of marginalization.

Donations from Western countries are pro-cyclical and might sharply diminish in recession periods when they are most wanted (since recessions are increasingly global): from this undesired effect we might understand even more the importance of a properly rooted self-sustainability (Bhanot & Bapat, 2015; de Oliveira Leite et al., 2019; García-Pérez et al., 2020), actually, the best parachute during hard times, that in underdeveloped areas tend to be more frequent—if not permanent—and worse, due to local problems such as drought, famine, ethnic clashes, wars, or epidemic illnesses.

Cross-subsidies occur when the MFI can segment its clientele, discriminating between those who can afford to pay market rates and those who cannot; subsidizing can prove efficient, even if it might have, as usual, some potential drawbacks: the MFI should be able to keep a safe and sustainable equilibrium, otherwise, the game might once again not be long-lasting.

When competition between MFIs eliminates rents on profitable borrowers, it is likely to yield a new equilibrium in which poor borrowers are worse off. With a greater number of lenders competing in the same (not segmented) market, "impatient" borrowers have an incentive to take multiple loans, not always detected by a centralized interbank computerized system (with a track record of exposures, repayments, and delinquencies), still nonexistent in many developing countries. Screening can become more expensive, together with the growing unwillingness of competing MFIs to cooperate and share information.

The passage from an unregulated NGO to a public deposit collecting institution subject to banking regulation might originate a hybrid institution, where subsidized funding coexists with the market collection of capital (public deposits, interbank loans, issues of bonds or Certificates of Deposit ...) and—on the other side—subsidized lending to the very poor can cohabit with market-priced loans to those who can afford it.

To be or not to be a regulated entity is a hamlet doubt that must carefully consider pros and cons: regulation is expensive and requires more rigorous liquidity, capital adequacy, and reporting standards, bearing extra operating costs that might not always be fully recovered with effectiveness gains and lower cost of collected capital, particularly for small MFIs in contexts where savings pool is small or caps on lending rates are set by the local Central Bank.

Cross-subsidies might play a role in such a situation, which requires constant monitoring, due to its delicate and intrinsically unstable mixture of non-profit and profit objectives; collusive behavior of borrowers who might take profit from this somewhat ambiguous subdivision (trying to jump on the cheapest side ...) and corruption within the lending staff also must be taken into careful consideration.

The transition to a regulated bank might prove challenging and expensive in the short run requiring additional capital, technical requirements, compliance adequacy, and professional staff. NGOs generally accompany the growth and transformation of the MFI to a regulated bank, providing the necessary capital and skills.

Regulated institutions can raise funds at lower rates, so reducing their cost of capital, with a positive side effect on lending costs. Deposits are generally the cheapest and most stable source of financing for MFIs with banking licenses and access to capital markets can further reduce financing costs, prolonging the maturity of debt, and strengthening the financial structure of MFI.

Gains in effectiveness and cost-cutting, if achievable, might conveniently be transmitted, at least partially, to clients (that might otherwise address themselves elsewhere), reducing interest rates and being able to readdress subsidies, if still existent, to specific targets, segmenting the clientele (the poorest from the relatively wealthier ...) or the products (e.g., business loans might be charged market interest rates, while school fees loans could be subsidized).

Most of the population benefits from microfinance directly and indirectly. The welfare gains are larger for the poor and the marginal entrepreneurs, although higher interest rates in general equilibrium tilt the gains toward the rich (Buera et al., 2021).

Subsidies and donations are veritable tools that are supposed to engender effective performance in microfinance institutions. On the face value, subsidies seem to be very positive, but they can be counterproductive when related to their effects on performance, efficiency, and self-sustainability of the microfinance institutions (Emengini, 2019).

3.3 The Interaction Between Microloans, Microdeposits, and Microinsurance

In the synergic interaction between microloans, microdeposits, microinsurance (examined in Sect. 2.3.2), loans are usually the first product offered, even if the poor often have a priority for savings. Microinsurance typically follows loans and deposits since it is perceived as a more sophisticated—and less "primordial"—service, and it may be provided internally by the same MFI or, more frequently and especially when numbers and complexities grow, by specialized insurance companies, in accordance with the MFIs and sharing with them the retail network and facilities.

The capital structure represented by the partitioning between financial debt and equity within the liabilities may impact the overall profitability (Abrar & Javaid, 2016; Adeyeye & Oyetayo, 2016; Almansour et al., 2020; Parvin et al., 2020). Commercialized MFIs have an incentive to adopt international accounting principles (IFRS), as shown by Tchakoute Tchuigoua and Pignatel (2020).

Looking for innovative products that are increasingly interdependent, the synergic interaction among microdeposits, microloans, and microinsurance is depicted in Fig. 3.2.

Small not deposit-taking MFIs typically get funded with sponsored debt from NGOs or charities.

When the MFI is enabled to take deposits, being supervised by the local Central Bank, it is typically broad and sound enough to provide more loans, extending its outreach. More significant sources of funds make the MFI more stable (Fig. 3.3).

When microinsurance products are available and provided to needy clients, they synergistically interact with loans and deposits (Fig. 3.4).

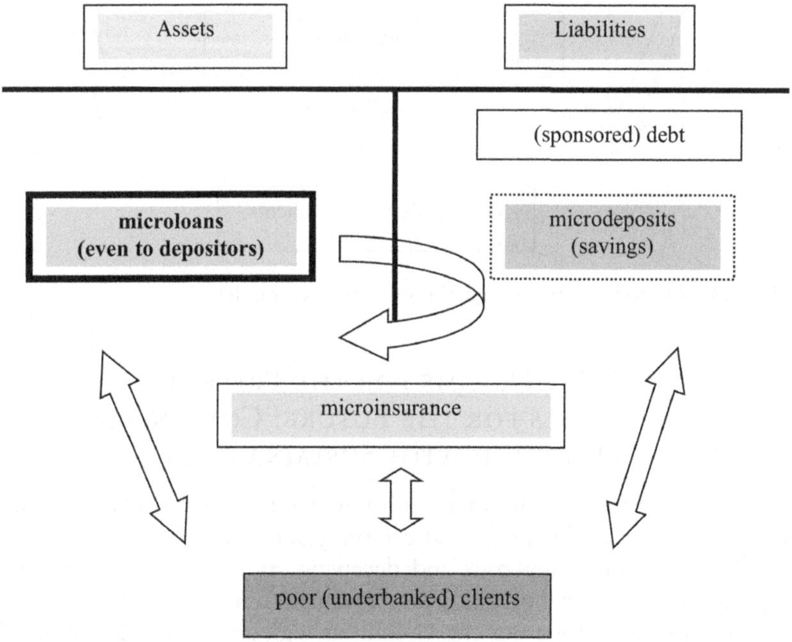

Fig. 3.2 Microloans igniting the microfinance model

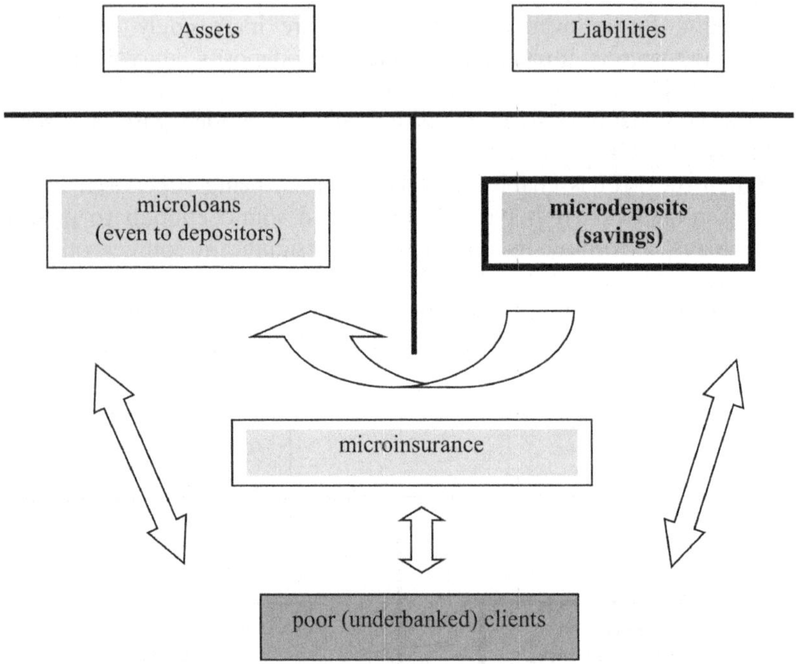

Fig. 3.3 Microdeposits igniting the microfinance model

3.4 Dreams for the Present and Goals for the Future: Combining Outreach with Sustainability

The success of microcredit does not imply that it can solve all the existing socio-economic problems that affect the poor: this false and simplified conviction is both dangerous and deceiving, as it generates exaggerate expectations that are not going to be satisfied. Microfinance is neither the philosopher's stone nor the Columbus' egg and is also not what the poorest primarily need.

As anticipated, microfinance is not the right device to provide direct financial coverage to "cold" investments, which cannot repay themselves generating adequate cash flows. Examples range from hospitals to schools to tribunals or toll-free infrastructures. However, linkages with "hot" projects, such as businesses that are (at least potentially) able to generate

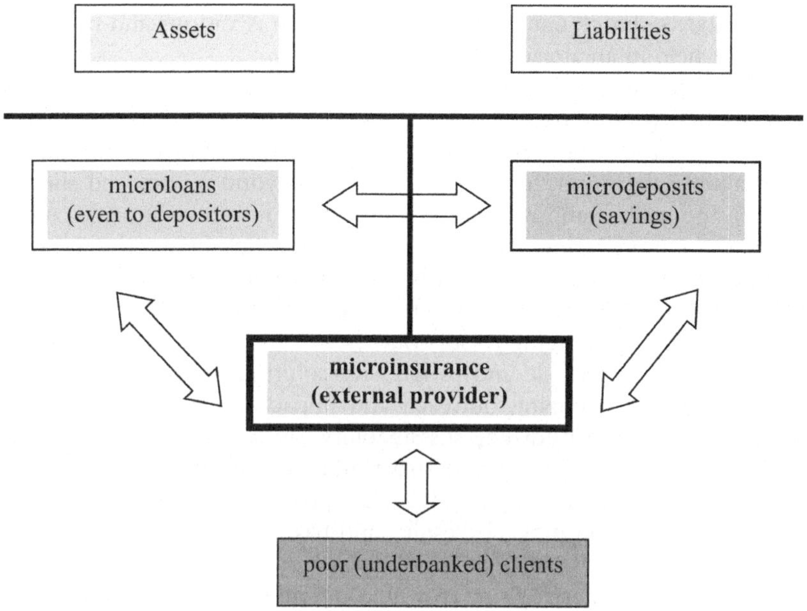

Fig. 3.4 Microinsurance interacting with microloans and microdeposits

enough cash to service the debt, are so strict and evident (illiteracy and illnesses are significant obstacles to economic activity and might inhibit survival ... an obvious physical prerequisite for repayment) that they cannot be simply dismissed or underestimated. So, a systemic and micro–macro approach to the problem is much wanted.

MFIs are limited in their ability to serve the poorest (this being a significant practical but also a theoretical obstacle to optimal outreach), for many complementary reasons such as the poorest natural unwillingness to borrow—life is already risky enough without taking on debt—or exclusion (often self-exclusion) from group members. The poorest also desperately need primary goods and services such as food, grants, or guaranteed employment before they are in a position to make good use of financial products.

Highly subsidized safety net programs are what the destitute at the bottom of the economic ladder primarily need. MFIs can cooperate and interact beyond a certain level, even if their job is various and confusion does not help in an already messy environment.

The microfinance business is often unprofitable or—in the luckiest cases—offering only decent returns and consequently it does not easily attract ambitious and profit-maximizing managers unless they have a charitable background, looking for "values" beyond money and success; greater and well-established MFIs, transformed into formal banks, might generally be more seductive but the problem is to let them arrive at such a level; good strategic management is strongly needed even in this complex field, where poor management is often offered to indigent clients, creating a vicious circle challenging to sort out.

The key for a feasible and progressive solution of the main microfinance target—maximizing outreach and impact while preserving long-term, possibly unsubsidized, sustainability—is to insist on the search for financial innovation, to find smart and unconventional solutions to unorthodox problems. This strategy has proved successful in the past, allowing to reach unthinkable results, and has to be followed even in the future.

Some hints can derive from growing on-field experiences and research, which are increasingly showing that while some main features are replicable in various environments,[16] flexibility and adaptation to local conditions are actively wanted since what is successful in a context might not be conveniently exported and replicated elsewhere.

Changing sizes in target groups, various loan maturities, individual rather than group lending, feasible ad hoc forms of guarantee (forcing deposits from retained earnings; pledging notional assets psychologically worthy for the borrower …), frequency of repayment installments, synergies between financial products (e.g., loans linked with deposits and insurances), specific methods of monitoring (from basic rural supervision to technology-driven devices) are only some of the interchanging examples of financial flexibility and innovation.

Tailor-made *ad-hoc* products are hugely requested in various social, economic, and cultural contexts, considering that the segmentation factors between several types of poor tend to be higher than those

[16] Environmental factors are a key issue in explaining variations among countries and include the regulatory environment; macroeconomic stability (country and political risk); competition from other financial intermediaries (subsidized by the government; private …); income level of clients, etc.

usually affecting wealthier borrowers around the world: while the latter are certainly more sophisticated, they respond and adapt more quickly to converging standards, driven by globalization pressures and incentives.[17]

Cultural changes and improvements are by far the most challenging and longest to look for since they entail a change of mentality process that needs plenty of time—often measured by generations—to develop solid roots. The frantic and increasingly interlinked world we live in might speed up the process, but velocity tends to go along with superficiality and long-lasting deepness requires time. The tortuous and painful evolution of the European cultures might teach us something—*historia magistra vitae*—about this hard process. No durable results are possible without grieving perseverance.

Client education might represent something more than the standard marketing device for customers' attraction; client-retention and business training to teach entrepreneurship is a strategy that a growing number of NGO-driven MFIs is trying to follow, with an interdisciplinary approach to a complex and interacting problem such as poverty alleviation has shown to be.

The pitfalls and problems of subsidies are too well-known not to raise a simple—somewhat embarrassing—question: are they really necessary for better and deeper outreach of the poorest?

The available empirical evidence does not provide clear-cut answers, even if it seems to suggest that sponsorship is unavoidable for startups and useful for a deeper and broader outreach of the destitute,[18] which do not represent an attractive target for commercial banks.

For-profit institutions usually target wealthier clients—from the not-so-poor onwards—and are generally able to increase the average size of their loans, so decreasing operating costs and consequent interests charged to clients (who become increasingly demanding and have a wider set of opportunities, stimulating competition from the supply side). However, client selection is unfortunately strongly linked with discrimination and

[17] E.g., international accounting standards or European directives, which aim to harmonize legislation, to favor comparison-driven competition. The risk for those who do not comply to international standards is to be emarginated from a global market, which sets for everybody the rules of the game: those who do not accept them are simply not admitted playing.

[18] Subsidies are generally beneficial when assuming a non-flat distribution of social weights, a demand of credit which is elastic to interest rates, adverse selection effects and positive spillover of microfinance credits on other lenders.

unprofitable women, albeit recording better repayments than men, are frequently left aside.

The threshold to profitability can be measured by accounting and financial indicators such as the "financial self-sufficiency ratio," which calculates the ability to generate enough revenues to cover the running and fixed costs. Institutions serving particularly poor customers, if compared with those serving better-off clients, charge greater interest rates and have fewer default rates, even if operating costs are consistently higher as it is their cost of collected capital.

The trade-off between the depth of outreach versus the strife for financial sustainability has given rise to a debate between the *financial systems* approach (which emphasizes the importance of financially sustainable microfinance programs) and the *poverty lending* approach (focused on subsidized credit to help overcome poverty). The most recent microfinance paradigm seems to favor the financial systems approach since it is the only one with long-term sustainability.

A subtler discussion might embrace the kind of MFI and its product design: individual-based MFIs seem to perform better regarding profitability (envisaging a mission drift from poor to richer clients), whereas group-based institutions serve better the poorest (and the most discriminated, such as women).[19]

In recent years, financial interests have increasingly influenced MFIs, with financial gain overshadowing service to the poor. This phenomenon, which we can term mission drift, has caused apprehension among academicians as well as policymakers, for its negation of the fundamental social ethos of MFIs and the mandate of sustainable financial inclusion (Mia & Lee, 2017; Mia et al., 2019; Milana & Ashta, 2020).

Goals to pursue and—possibly—achieve are focused around the above-mentioned trade-off and might consider the following hints:

- To improve outreach, one of the key drivers is to reduce the cost of debt (interest rates), with a market—unsubsidized—progressive approach: improving cash flow predictions, ensuring borrowers, easing deposit collection for collateral and saving purposes, building data banks for credit and delinquency records are just examples of what MFIs should hardly try to do, together with their clients, while

[19] See Wellalage and Thrikawala (2021).

environmental and macroeconomic issues—essential to provide the right framework for development—go beyond their forces but can receive a push from the bottom of the social pyramid;

- MFIs can conveniently reduce the cost of their collected capital, being so able to cut their borrowing costs and to transfer at least part of the benefit to clients, with a dimensional growth, easing economies of scale and reaching a regulated standard, being enabled to collect deposits and to access cheaper sources of funds from domestic and international capital markets;
- Improvements in corporate governance issues (transparency, accountability, minimization of conflicts of interest …) are fundamental for any MFI that wants to collect funds, either from sponsors or private investors or from clients-depositors (or even shareholders, applying the efficient model of credit cooperatives). No trust, no money;
- Technological improvements can be of great help, easing communication and circulation of information; wireless devices can cut physical distances, computerized records can ease delinquency and market statistics, etc. Nowadays, operational effectiveness and cost-cutting cannot be pursued without technology;
- Subsidies can undercut both scale and effectiveness and smart grants should always be transparent, rule-bound, and time-limited, possibly following donor guidelines;
- Targeting the model of mainstream banks, even if challenging and somewhat inappropriate to the particular context, is, however, a significant strategic goal, to be followed by common sense, realism, and flexibility, adapting the business to the circumstances; progressive compliance to international standards is a necessary condition for access to international capital markets, particularly in an increasingly global and competitive world; competition needs comparability and those who live in an Ivory tower are definitively out of the game;
- Measuring the social impact of microfinance is a hot and still mysterious issue: does it contribute to alleviating poverty and promoting development and emancipation? The answer to this question—embarrassing for the microfinance idealists and enthusiasts—is hopefully positive but empirical evidence is mixed and further research, using more computerized databases, wherever available, is strongly needed;

- Love for the poor—an invisible state of mind and heart—is not part of a pure capitalistic Decalogue but seems essential in a field where even the most successful MFIs hardly prove lucrative. Intangible benefits can, however, more than compensate some economic sacrifice, at least for the luckier who understand that they need the poor at least as how the poor need them. Easy moneymaking objectives should more conveniently be addressed elsewhere, real happiness maybe not.

The classical trade-off between outreach and sustainability stands as a crucial point in microfinance issues. If maximum outreach and the potential involvement of as many as possible between the poorest is, of course, a primary goal, sustainability is an unavoidable element of its persistence over time (length of outreach). Wideness/breadth and depth, quantity and quality are different sides of the same medal.

The joint maximization of outreach and sustainability (Awaworyi Churchill, 2020) is probably every microfinance practitioner's secret fancy. However, the dream might become a nightmare since these key parameters/objectives often prove antithetical; outreach is an uneasy self-sustained process, which might need severe subsidies, at least during its startup. Decreasing repayment marginality, driven by growing outreach, is a typical microfinance dilemma. Stamina and endurance to pursue these goals are greatly wanted.

According to Rawls (1971), the well-being of society coincides with that of the unluckiest individual—a demanding inspiration for the good-hearted who are looking for the extreme boundaries of outreach.

3.5 Microfinance Banana Skins (Outreach and Sustainability Bottlenecks)

Microfinance is a risky activity for all the stakeholders that pivot around an institution (its shareholders and bondholders; employees, borrowers, depositors, the Central Bank …) and an analysis of the main elements of uncertainty is useful both for their detection and their mitigation.

Risk has an asymmetric impact on the various stakeholders:

- shareholders, being residual claimants, accept to put completely in danger their capital, whose value has unlimited upside potential even if it is the last claim to be paid back, and only to the extent that some funds are still available. Shareholders, if foreigners, are also exposed to currency risk. The patient capital money is limited and unwillingness to refinance an MFI after its equity burnout severely threatens its survival. The exchange rate is not only a synthetic measure of the local currency's purchasing power against other countries, but it is also a numerical symbol of soft values, such as country's international reputation and a comparative barometer of its standing;

- debtholders are fixed claimants, who are entitled to receive back their credit and periodic interests before the shareholders but generally after other creditors such as workers. If the loan to the MFI is denominated in a hard-foreign currency, it is the MFI that is exposed to foreign exchange risk, while if the investor has invested in the local currency of the MFI the risk—potentially mitigated by appropriate coverage—belongs to the investor. To the extent that the risk is born by the MFI, it can affect even the same debtholders, if the institution burns the money kept for their repayment, and in most cases, it has a significant impact on residual equity-holders;
- employees may not receive regular payroll from an ailing MFI and their risk exposure is likely to increase if they also have invested in the institution (being depositors, bondholders, or equity-holders ...), without a safer diversification strategy;
- depositors may have their funds in danger if the MFI is unable to pay them back—triggering a run-to-deposits panic strategy—and if the local Central Bank does not correctly intervene as a lender of last resort. Partial insurance of the deposited money is frequent, as a percentage of the total or up to fixed amounts, and it should cover most of the lent funds, particularly if their nominal amount is small and fragmented;
- borrowers do not risk their own money since they are in the condition to pay back what they owe to the MFI that, however, may be asked to return the funds with little or any notice—depending on their contractual agreements—with potentially destabilizing effects. They also may lack a future source of funding, being forced to choose an alternative that is hardly viable if the crisis is systemic;
- the government is formally an external stakeholder, interested in the tax revenue that it may get from the MFI—and in this sense, it is a privileged creditor—but in reality, it is also concerned about the social impact of the MFI's potential distress. The Central Bank,

depending on the Government, is even more directly involved in the matter, particularly if the failing institution is deposit-taking and/or if it has commercial links (debits and credits) with other banks, reminding how likely and devastating a domino effect may be.

Among the biggest microfinance risks there are over-lending to delinquent clients, lack of adequate IT processes, excessive geographical concentration, and exaggerate product concentration.

The microfinance risk matrix considers not only the contingent impact of adverse events on the different stakeholders seen above but also the type of risk that is originated by different states of the world. The risk is generally misunderstood and often underpriced—since the likelihood of events is neglected and underestimated—unless when calamities occur.

To the extent that professional and specialized intermediaries deal with risk—and MFIs are better candidates than their indigent clients—an essential step toward risk mitigation is its transfer to those who can better diversify it. This statement holds for what concerns microinsurance.

One of the main questions for microfinance—as for any other market product—is concerned with its costs, explicitly referring to the cost of accessing microcredit. These costs, which can be explicit or implicit, depending on several factors—such as the nature of contracting and the intrinsic characteristics of the market and its players—that contribute to shaping the microfinance industry risk. Access to credit depends on many interrelated factors, consisting of hard issues such as the product's price—interest rates—but also related to less evident aspects such as availability and necessity of funds that all contribute to shaping the market's demand and supply.

Different contracting methods are legally deputed to mitigate risk, even if a substantial part of it rests untouched by market frictions and imperfections, such as poor governance, weak institutions, and a primitive and failing judicial system. They all contribute to the overall systematic risk, which shapes the environment where MFIs are located and deemed to prosper, survive, or simply die.

Country and political risk, analyzed in Table 3.2 are the first factors to be considered by any potential foreign investor, whose asset allocation is influenced by their perception of a target country, possibly never underestimating the probability that investment funds may not be (fully) repatriated. Ailing and undemocratic governments, with weak governance, love indeed to attract foreign funds but also to keep them indefinitely.

Examples of country risk are both painful and frequent and they range from the country defaults, which are likely to sweep away also financial institutions (MFI included) to specific policies aiming to block or limit repatriation of funds or to attack the microfinance industry.

Risks can also be macro- or microeconomic, being reflected again in overall political or country risk and ranging from strong and hardly controllable volatility of key economic parameters—such as foreign exchange or interest and inflation rates, linked by well-known arbitrage relations[20]—to smaller micro-effects (operational or credit risk …). Country risk can be very disturbing for foreign investors, up to the point of discouraging them from coming in or inducing them to exit. It is a fly-to-quality strategy that may endanger many developing countries, which are even unrelated among them if the whole segment is indiscriminately perceived as dangerously unstable.

Country risk is also relevant to detect the environmental context within which any MFI operates, raising some delicate questions when sharp contrasts come to evidence: can good MFIs survive and prosper in an ailing country? The contrary may not be disturbing since small inefficient MFIs are too tiny to have a country-wide impact, while the national macroeconomic context is likely to be more troubling, particularly in the long-term or if the MFI largely depends on foreign funding. Local funding with deposit collection stabilizes MFIs, reducing dependence on volatile foreign capital.

Information asymmetries, which are enhanced by distance and difficulties of comprehension of different realities, substantially bias the foreign perception of country risk, while locals simply know it better.

Like in a Shanghai game, where an improper movement of one stick may cause an uncontrollable effect on the others, in risk analysis an unwanted occurrence may have sequential effects that are hardly foreseeable. Early detection and mitigation may have a substantial impact on limiting unwanted perverse effects and their always dangerous contagion.

[20] Such as the purchasing power parity, according to which exchange rates adapt to inflation differentials, or the interest rate parity, which recognizes the positive effect of higher (real) interest rates on a currency appreciation or the spot forward parity, linking the spot with the forward market.

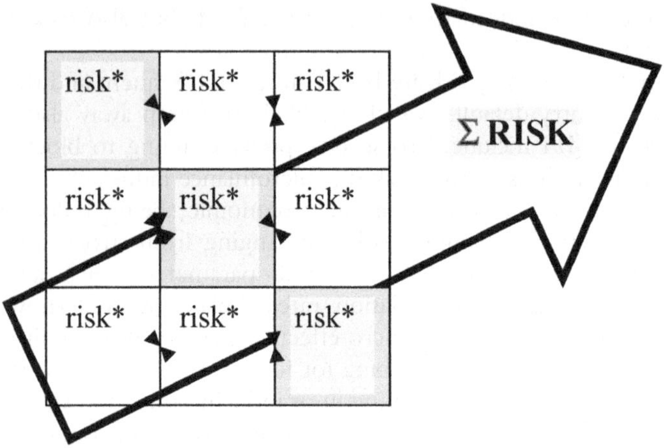

Fig. 3.5 Interactive risk matrix

Since banks and financial institutions are closely linked—and tied together by a further systemic reputation risk—this domino effect may well affect MFIs, particularly if they are of significant dimensions and deposit-taking. Smaller and informal institutions are less contagious, even if their greater number makes them hard to check and monitor—and most of them live unsupervised. International contagion is also damaging, particularly if it concerns sophisticated institutions with complex synthetic products—such as greatly leveraged derivatives as the global recession of 2008–2009 has shown. Small MFIs located in developing countries are generally poorly integrated into international financial markets, so benefiting from a natural shelter,[21] even if the credit crunch has affected all the economies, with a damaging growth downturn—market economies tend to shrink as credit dries up.

A theoretical example of an interactive risk matrix is represented in Fig. 3.5, whereas Table 3.2 contains a detailed description of the principal risks.

The microfinance banana skins surveys explore the risks that the worldwide microfinance industry faces, considering both the current hazards and their trends (fastest rising risk factors).

[21] See Moro Visconti (2009).

Table 3.3 Microfinance banana skins[22]

Biggest risks	*Fastest risers*
1 Credit risk (1)	1 Competition (3)
2 Reputation (17)	2 Credit risk (1)
3 Competition (9)	3 Reputation (11)
4 Corporate governance (7)	4 Political interference (7)
5 Political interference (10)	5 Mission drift (13)
6 Inappropriate regulation (13)	6 Strategy (-)
7 Management quality (4)	7 Staffing (20)
8 Staffing (14)	8 Unrealizable expectations (17)
9 Mission drift (19)	9 Profitability (9)
10 Unrealizable expectations (18)	10 Inappropriate regulation (22)
11 Managing technology (15)	11 Corporate governance (12)
12 Profitability (12)	12 Management quality (18)
13 Back office (22)	13 Ownership (16)
14 Transparency (16)	14 Liquidity (5)
15 Strategy (-)	15 Product development (24)
16 Liquidity (2)	16 Macroeconomic trends (2)
17 Macroeconomic trends (3)	17 Managing technology (23)
18 Fraud (20)	18 Interest rates (10)
19 Product development (24)	19 Fraud (14)
20 Ownership (17)	20 Transparency (21)
21 Interest rates (11)	21 Back office (19)
22 Too much funding (25)	22 Too much funding (25)
23 Too little funding (6)	23 Too little funding (6)
24 Foreign Exchange (8)	24 Foreign Exchange (8)

A table with the microfinance banana skins can help to have a first glimpse on the issue (for an update, with specific reference to Africa, see Moro Visconti, 2012) (Table 3.3).

Although these banana skins statistics are outdated,[22] they still represent a reference point of the main risk components that affect MFIs.

[22] See also https://www.centerforfinancialinclusion.org/microfinance-banana-skins-2014-the-csfi-survey-of-microfinance-risk.

3.6 Poverty Traps and Microfinance: From Financial Inclusion to Sustainable Development

The idea behind this study is that microfinance, if considered alone and detached from a broader vision of poverty and underdevelopment, may be either useless or even dangerous since a poor guy may become, because of microfinance, an indebted destitute ..., with no improvements and further problems!

We need a holistic approach, tackling the poverty traps comprehensively and then using microfinance, within a bigger puzzle.

Microfinance is a successful financial innovation to help the poor to sort out credit exclusion,[23] which is one of the poverty traps that prevent billions of underserved, particularly women, from escaping atavistic misery. Interconnected poverty traps range from misuse of natural resources (from blood diamonds to the oil curse) to conflict traps, demographic booming, being landlocked with bad neighbors, or exposed to unfreedom. Other traps concern cultural backwardness, unsafe drinking, and sanitation, food shortage up to starvation, illnesses, or climatic shocks, causing mass migrations and unfair globalization.

- Microfinance, a grass-roots movement to provide credit to the neediest, can considerably help to dismantle at least some of these poverty traps, and thousands of mostly small institutions are competing in a market where demand from the poorest for financial services is potentially unlimited—while supply is not.
- While the success of microfinance, often ignited by foreign aid funding, has gone beyond any expectation, enormous problems are still on the ground. The road toward what is now considered microfinance's optimal goal—maximization of outreach to the poorest, combined with financial self-sustainability—is still full of obstacles.

Poverty goes beyond social inequalities and it is concerned with the failure of the underserved, due to their social condition and to asset deprivation, to acquire and maintain a minimum set of core capabilities—such as nutrition, instruction, clothing, housing needs, basic

[23] See Habib and Jubb (2015).

healthcare—that prevent the poor from fully participating in labor and credit markets—hence the importance of microfinance.

Dehumanizing poverty goes also beyond low levels of current income and consumption, being concerned with the inability to access freely the market economy. Social exclusion from the benefits that others can enjoy is generally an enduring phenomenon, which is hard to eradicate, together with vulnerability to adverse shocks, due to the absence of social safety nets.[24]

The "poverty soup" is a cocktail of various—generally not tasty—ingredients, which compose the multicolored and unstable condition of the poor, like a kaleidoscope where various interacting colors mix and split, simply fine-tuning its detecting lenses.

Abandoned, withdrawn, and forgotten poor are daily frustrated and humiliated by their hard and starless hell-on-earth life and they constantly have to fight through eccentric and not conformist choices against colorless resignation and desperation, which derives from the perception that the world is hardly likely to change, and there is no perspective, despite one's—useless?—efforts. Living in empty and paralyzing darkness, the resigned, voiceless, and apparently (e)motionless poor show a fantastic talent for endless waiting.

Maladaptive and unhealthy behaviors, so common for many emarginated poor, cause personal distress and social impairment, destroying self-motivation and reinforcing misery. Such misery—with its social and anthropological interpretation—has a deep impact on the psychology of the poor, who are often deluded, depressed, not empathetic, and vulnerable. The poor also show disorganized behavior (evident in their dressing, body posture, personal hygiene ...) that segregates them from any wealthier status and prevents any clear life goal, bringing to boredom, monotony, and hopelessness. Extreme poverty is a dreamless mental status, silently breathing and whispering its feelings while mirroring a self-image of destitution. Self-reliance and motivation, albeit being a crucial ingredient of development, are hardly present in the "diet" of the poor.

Quintessential poverty is the living state for the majority of the world's and nations' people, and it may so tend to be confused with the study of humanity. Chronic, stubbornly persisting and path-dependent poverty

[24] Mookherijee in Banerjee et al., (2006, p. 234).

brings to vulnerability, which can trap in its intricate maze entire nations and social groups, with durable social inequalities, due to a destabilizing wealth gap. Diffidence against an unforgiving external world can bring fear and aggressiveness while pain quickly becomes an integral part of life.

Persistent pockets of severe poverty are untouched by worldwide development and created by an ill-conceived social system and they shamefully resist in a ruthless and selfish world—either we forget that others are suffering, or we decide to open our heart to love and longing for the poor, unlocking it from its prison of selfishness. Much is possible for those who love, going beyond the idolatry of reason, and they do not need to measure the result of their efforts, remembering that the opposite of love is indifference, not hate.

Many factors are crucial to understanding the reason people are poor and multivariate and interdependent analysis of multifaceted poverty seems necessary, with an anthropological holistic and poor-centric approach to intertwined poverty issues—always remembering that one-size-fits-all development strategies do not work. Trying to link and to distill largely disconnected disciplines is a hard but fruitful effort and it requires a mastering of complexity, digging inside the intricate array of connected poverty issues, and favoring an inspiring vision of the question. Everybody—rich or poor—represents many various things, inside and altogether, with his predictable irrationality and various tastes. As Voltaire said in 1750 "minds differ more than faces".

According to Sen (1999, p. 126) "The case for taking a broad and many-sided approach to development has become clearer in recent years, partly as a result of the difficulties faced as well as successes achieved by various countries over the recent decades". The Nobel Prize winner also suggests a "comprehensive development framework", rejecting a compartmentalized view of the process of development, avoiding the search for a single all-purpose remedy, which has proved largely inefficient in the past.

The link between the poverty traps and microfinance may be summarized here (Table 3.4).

3.7 Green Microfinance and ESG Compliance

Microfinance is increasingly involved with long-term issues, consistent with the Sustainable Development Goals (https://sdgs.un.org/goals).

Table 3.4 Poverty traps and (microfinance) mitigation strategies

Poverty trap	*Description*	*Connections with other traps*	*Mitigation strategies*	*Impact of microfinance*
Land-lockedness	Characteristic of countries with no direct access to the sea hampered in their development by isolation, bad neighbors, significant transportation costs	The conflict trap, fixing borders and blocking trade, exacerbated the problems of landlocked countries	Airplane connections. ICT and other technological and virtual communications Friendship treaties with bordering coastal countries	Negligible since microfinance cannot reshape borders. It may soften micro-problems of claustrophobic economies, as it is positively showed in landlocked countries such as Bolivia
Natural resources curse	Due to the improper and unfair exploitation of oil, gas, or mineral resources, to the advantage of local crooks and foreign multinationals but to the detriment of poor indigenous	The conflict trap since oil revenues may finance wars and cause conflicts for geopolitical reasons	International treaties and Western and domestic public opinion pressures. Competitive "beauty contest" among various exploiters. Fair and democratic disclosure and subdivision of proceeds	Negligible since extractive industries are capital intensive and so intrinsically unfit for microfinance schemes
Demographic growth	The poorest tend to over-reproduce them, sometimes beyond the survival threshold	The illiteracy trap, particularly concerning women: the more they are illiterate, the more they are induced to procreate	Literacy and instruction, emancipation, and job opportunities	Being a pro-women instrument, microfinance can considerably contribute to their emancipation, with an indirect impact on limiting excess fertility

(continued)

Table 3.4 (continued)

Poverty trap	*Description*	*Connections with other traps*	*Mitigation strategies*	*Impact of microfinance*
Conflict trap	Civil wars and conflict, with likely relapses, block development, destroying the economy	Natural resources, even exploitation, overpopulation, unfreedom may all interact, igniting or prolonging conflicts	Foster development, squeezing inequalities, promoting pluralism and reconciliation	Fostering micro-development, microfinance may give a (small) contribution to appeasement Supporting microfinance in devastated and fragile communities can be successful when donors work in concert, select qualified partners, are patient, are willing to take risks, and are prepared to pay greater costs. Efficient microfinance can create the foundation for a fully integrated financial sector and fuel reconstruction

Poverty trap	*Description*	*Connections with other traps*	*Mitigation strategies*	*Impact of microfinance*
Hunger and Malnutrition	The poor are often hungry; undernutrition and/or bad food quality brings illnesses, up to death	It reduces school attendance and learning capacity (illiteracy trap), hampering employment possibilities, particularly for discriminated girls, who are overexposed to ill-being, rising child mortality. It brings to desperate and unsustainable depletion of natural resources, reducing capacity to address market opportunities	Improve agricultural production; educate people upgrading hygienic standards; stress the importance of better nutrition	Economic progress, thanks also to microfinance, improves economic capacity and softens revenues volatility
Water shortage	Limit or block economic activity, up to death	It may bring to conflicts. Lack of regular rainfall exacerbates hunger, illnesses, and child mortality	Development and improvement of distribution systems	Implementation of small economic activities, backed by microcredit, can soften these typical underdevelopment problems
Illiteracy	Analphabetism completely blocks instruction, keeping the poor segregated from a knowledge economy	Demographic overgrowth	Capillary investments in education, from core levels to academic ones	Social gatherings such as group lending and microfinance returns may promote development and resources for school fees

(continued)

Table 3.4 (continued)

Poverty trap	*Description*	*Connections with other traps*	*Mitigation strategies*	*Impact of microfinance*
Climatic changes	Increase of the world temperature, with more extreme and volatile weather	Both drought and floods become more common, with potentially severe side effects on health and nutrition	Cutting CO_2 emissions and deforestation, using renewable sources of energy	Microfinance, like everything else, will not be spared. The increasing emphasis on responsible finance has added environmental impact to the factors considered as measures of success for a MFI
Language trap	Languages spoken by small and isolated ethnic groups, isolating them from the rest of the world	Being a linguistic land-lockedness, it can interact with the geographical one, increasing isolation	Education, introducing a second spoken language, possibly English, acting as a lingua franca	No impact
Property trap	The poor live in properties with no legal titling, so being unable to sell them, inherit or transmit and use them as a guarantee for mortgages	This invisibility trap is linked with the educational trap since illiterate poor are likely to have no real estate properties	Expand the cadastral system and record property borders, solving land disputes with equanimity	Housing microfinance can soften the problem
Educational trap	Illiterate poor are stuck in a growing misery status, particularly in a global knowledge economy	Illiterate poor generally do not have any property titling and are subject to the demographic trap, particularly if illiteracy concerns fertile women	Invest in education, a long-term strategy with no immediate proceeds	Proceeds from activities backed by microfinance can be conveniently spent in education

Poverty trap	*Description*	*Connections with other traps*	*Mitigation strategies*	*Impact of microfinance*
Foreign debt trap	Underwriting of debt, financed by foreign countries	Interacts with the development aid, being a part of it when debt is forgiven. Its rescheduled repayment or cancelation is conditional upon strict fiscal measures to cut the deficit, so shrinking public spending for the poor	Avoid over-indebtedness, relying on internal funding, and developing a taxation system that allows public spending to be covered locally	While foreign debt is a macro country-to-country arrangement, microfinance works on a micro-level. While being mostly unable to affect foreign debt choices, it can help to make dependence on foreign funding less impellent

Sustainability is often declined in its three main dimensions (economic, social, and environmental). While the socio-economic aspects are embedded in the microfinance business model, environmental concerns have hardly been appreciated, because bottom-of-the pyramid unbanked households who struggle for bare survival have little time to dedicate to green criticalities. But this is no longer the case, and growing concern over environmental sustainability, from climate change to pollution, represents a global threat, with little if any social distinction.

Figure 3.6 shows the interaction between microfinance and the three main sustainability dimensions.

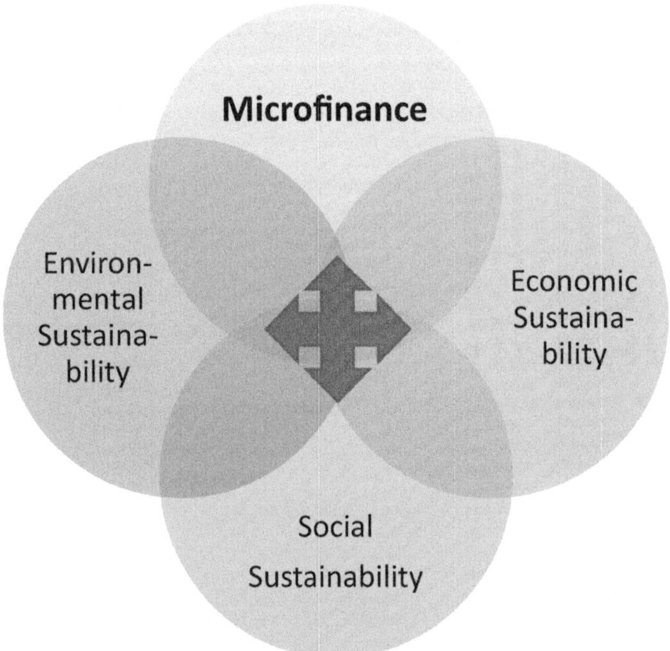

Fig. 3.6 Microfinance and sustainability

In recent years, development practice has seen that microfinance institutions (MFIs) are starting to consider their environmental bottom line in addition to their financial and social objectives.[25]

Assessing whether investments result in the desired non-financial performance is a key concern in the fast-growing field of impact investments, including microfinance. The social performance of the institutions that offer financial inclusion services to underprivileged populations has come under increasing scrutiny, whereas the social performance of the investment vehicles that in turn finance these institutions is researched less.[26]

The linkage between the financial performance of microfinance institutions (MFIs) and comprehensive ESG (Environmental,[28] Social, and Governance) performance has been ignored by researchers till date albeit this tie may serve as a primary objective for MFIs.[29]

References

Abrar, A., & Javaid, A. Y. (2016). The impact of capital structure on the profitability of microfinance institutions. *South Asian Journal of Management Sciences, 10*(1), 21–37.

Adeyeye, P., & Oyetayo, O. (2016). Balance sheet management and outreach success for microfinance banks in Nigeria. *International Journal of Economic Development Research and Investment, 7*(1), 473–499.

Allet, M., & Green, H. M. (2015). Microfinance: Characteristics of microfinance institutions involved in environmental management. *Journal of Business Ethics, 126*, 395–414.

Allet, M., & Hudon, M. (2015). Green microfinance: Characteristics of microfinance institutions involved in environmental management. *Journal of Business Ethics, 126*, 395–414.

Almansour, A. Y., Alrawashdeh, N., & Almansour, B. Y. (2020). The impact of capital structure on the performance of microfinance institutions. *Management Science Letters, 10*(4), 881–888.

[25] Allet and Hudon (2015).

[26] Meyer and Krauss (2021).

[22] Data for year 2011 (2009 in brackets). *Source* http://www.cgap.org/gm/document-1.9.49643/Microfinance_Banana_Skins_2011.pdf.

[28] See Allet and Green (2015).

[29] Tauhidul Islam (2017) and Tanin (2017).

Armendariz De Aghion, B. A., & Morduch, J. (2010). *The economics of microfinance*. MIT press.

Ashta, A. (2018). *Lessons from microfinance for social entrepreneurship theory: The life cycle of the social enterprise*. Available at SSRN: https://ssrn.com/abstract=3136710

Awaworyi Churchill, S. (2020). Microfinance financial sustainability and outreach: Is there a trade-off? *Empirical Economics, 59*(3), 1329–1350.

Banerjee, A. V., Bénabour, R., & Mookherjee, D. (2006). *Understanding poverty*. Oxford University Press.

Bhanot, D., & Bapat, V. (2015). Sustainability index of micro finance institutions (MFIs) and contributory factors. *International Journal of Social Economics, 42*, 387–403.

Bos, J. W. P., & Millone, M. (2015). Practice what you preach: Microfinance business models and operational efficiency. *World Development, 70*, 28–42.

Buera, F. J., Kaboski, J. P., & Shin, Y. (2021). The macroeconomics of microfinance. *The Review of Economic Studies, 88*(1), 126–161.

Collier, P. (2007). *The bottom billion: Why the poorest countries are failing and what can be done about it*. Oxford University Press.

de Oliveira Leite, R., dos Santos Mendes, L., & Sacramento, L. C. (2019). To profit or not to profit? Assessing financial sustainability outcomes of micro-finance institutions. *International Journal of Finance & Economics, 24*(3), 1287–1299.

Emengini, E. S. (2019). Subsidy/donation and performance of microfinance institutions. *Asian Journal of Economics, Business and Accounting, 13*(1), 1–12.

García-Pérez, I., Fernández-Izquierdo, M. Á., & Muñoz-Torres, M. J. (2020). Microfinance institutions fostering sustainable development by region. *Sustainability, 12*(7), 2682.

Godfroid, C. (2019). Relationship lending in microfinance: How does it impact client dropout? *Strategic Change, 28*(4), 289–300.

Habib, M., & Jubb, C. (2015). Poverty alleviation with microfinance: Bangladesh evidence In A. Heshmati, E. Maasoumi, & G. Wan (Eds.), *Poverty reduction policies and practices in developing Asia*. Springer Verlag.

Meyer, J., & Krauss, A. (2021). The social performance of microfinance investment vehicles. *Journal of Sustainable Finance & Investment, 11*(2), 163–186.

Mia, M. A., & Lee, H. (2017). Mission drift and ethical crisis in microfinance institutions: What matters? *Journal of Cleaner Production, 164*, 102–114.

Mia, M. A., Dalla Pellegrina, L., Van Damme, P., & Wijesiri, M. (2019). Financial inclusion, deepening and efficiency in microfinance programs: Evidence from Bangladesh. *European Journal of Development Research, 31*(4), 809–835.
Milana, C., & Ashta, A. (2020). Microfinance and financial inclusion: Challenges and opportunities. *Strategic Change, 29*(3), 257–266.
Moro Visconti, R. (2009). Are microfinance institutions in developing countries a safe harbor against the contagion of global recession? *International Finance Review, 10*, 389–438.
Moro Visconti, R. (2011). Global recession and microfinance risk governance in developing countries. *Risk Governance and Control Journal, 1*(3), 17–30.
Moro Visconti, R. (2012). Is African microfinance different? Evidence from banana skins. *African Journal of Microfinance and Enterprise Development, 2*(2), 25–45.
Parvin, S. S., Hossain, B., Mohiuddin, M., & Cao, Q. (2020). Capital structure, financial performance, and sustainability of micro-finance institutions (MFIs) in Bangladesh. *Sustainability, 12*(15), 6222.
Prahalad, C. K. (2006). *The fortune at the bottom of the pyramid*. Wharton School Publishing.
Rawls, J. (1971). *A theory of justice*. Harvard University Press.
Sen, A. (1999). *Development as freedom*. Oxford University Press.
Soumaré, I., Tchakoute Tchuigou, H., & Hessou, H. T. (2020). Are microfinance institutions resilient to economic slowdown? Evidence from their capital ratio adjustment over the business cycle. *Economic Modelling, 92*, 1–22.
Sun, S. L., & Liang, H. (2021). Globalization and affordability of microfinance. *Journal of Business Venturing, 36*(1), 1–18.
Tanin, T. I. (2017). *Does environment, social and governance (ESG) drive the financial performance of microfinance institutions? A cross-country panel analysis* (Master dissertation). INCEIF, Kuala Lumpur. Available at https://ikr.inceif.org/handle/INCEIF/2637.
Tauhidul Islam, T. (2017). *Does environment, social and governance (ESG) drive the financial performance of microfinance institutions? A cross-country panel analysis*. INCEIF, Kuala Lumpur. Available at https://ikr.inceif.org/handle/INCEIF/2637.
Tchakoute Tchuigoua, H., & Pignatel, I. (2020). Microfinance institutions and International Financial Reporting Standards: An exploratory analysis. *Research in International Business and Finance, 54*, 101309.
Tchakoute Tchuigoua, H., Durrieu, F., & Kouao, G. S. (2017). Funding strategy and performance of microfinance institutions: An exploratory study. *Strategic Change, 26*(2), 133–143.

Tchakoute Tchuigoua, H., Soumaré, I., & Hessou, H. T. (2020). Lending and business cycle: Evidence from microfinance institutions. *Journal of Business Research, 119*, 1–12.
Wellalage, N. H., & Thrikawala, S. (2021). Bank credit, microfinance and female ownership: Are women more disadvantaged than men? *Finance Research Letters* (in press).

CHAPTER 4

The Impact of Technology on Microfinance

The supply chain/business model canvas anticipated in the introduction is recalled in Fig. 4.1.

4.1 Leveraging Financial Inclusion with Digital Technology

Technology and innovation are believed to be the key factors for economic growth. The effect of technological solutions has been assessed within the developed framework for stakeholders and industry drivers specifically in financial services. We are continuously examining how technology can be better used to solve the problems of microfinance by increasing sustainability and outreach to the poor.

Technology is rapidly changing how individuals access financial services[1] and interact with financial service providers. Agent networks and other technology-enabled businesses allow people to conduct many basic transactions, such as person-to-person payments, bill payments, deposits, and more, to take place without stepping inside a bank branch. As a result, it is acknowledged that most of the microfinance growth during the last decade has been attributed to the existence of strong technology platforms. At the advent of technology financial institutions along with

[1] Mia (2020).

R. Moro-Visconti, *MicroFinTech*, Palgrave Studies in Financial Services Technology, https://doi.org/10.1007/978-3-030-80394-0_4

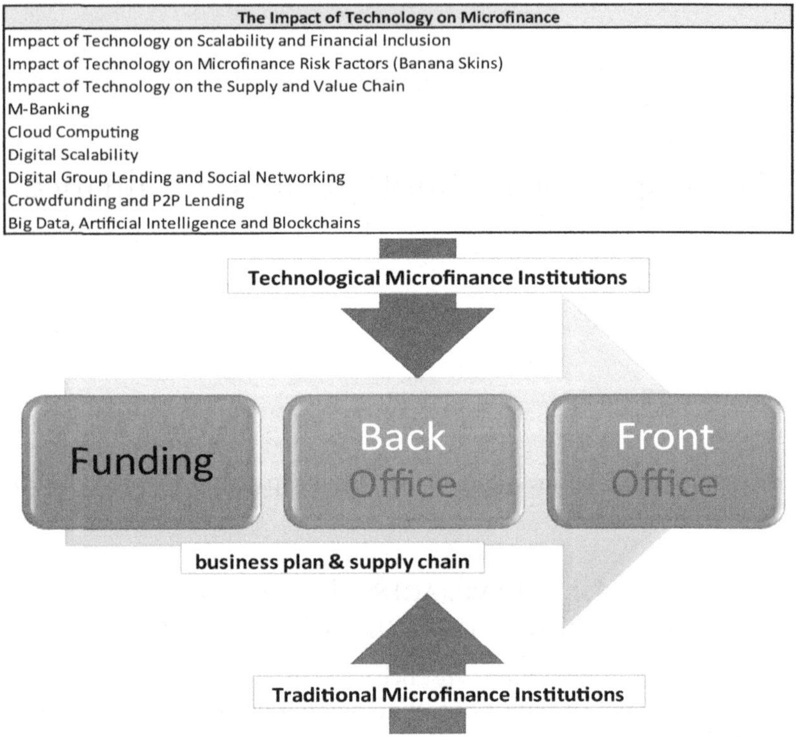

Fig. 4.1 The impact of technology on microfinance

MFIs found it easy to reduce the operating costs and increased outreach and penetration. Management Information Systems (MIS), branch office franchise model, Internet Banking, Electronic Fund Transfer at Point of Sale (EFTPOS), Automatic Teller Machines (ATMs), Interactive Voice Response (IVR) systems, and smart cards are among the major technologies that have entered microfinance over the years from the formal financial sector. Additionally, MFIs are also considering investing in cloud-based computing Systems (CBS), which enable regulators to pull sector-related data further by reducing reporting time and cost of the institution (Usman et al., 2018).

Information and communication technology (ICT) is an important driver in the maturing microfinance industry (Ashta, 2011; Budampati, 2018; Gutiérrez-Nieto & Serrano-Cinca, 2019; Riggins & Weber, 2016). Microfinance providers, both non-profit MFIs and for-profit banks, provide financial services to the poor that are critical for eradicating poverty and promoting economic development in developing nations. As the industry matures, MFIs face an increasingly competitive environment forcing them to balance the dual goals of outreach and sustainability. Interestingly, ICT may be both the instigator of this new environment and the potential solution to MFI survivability (Kauffman & Riggins, 2012).

The ICT dimensions when used as instruments for financial inclusion accelerate economic growth and reduce poverty and inequality. Therefore, policies to promote information and communication infrastructure could stimulate financial inclusion by promoting digital finance. Moreover, better collaboration between ICT and the financial sector will likely advance digital financial inclusion that could help to bridge the financial infrastructure gap (Mushtaq & Bruneau, 2019).

Most of the MFIs employ ICT platforms such as computers, the Internet, Web sites, LAN, mobile, and fixed phones to perform daily operations and enhance access to financial services to clients. Apart from carrying out a business process, ICT plays a key role in financial service delivery to clients via electronic delivery channels. Hence, services are normally available to clients regardless of location and time. The use of mobile phones and the Internet is essential for communication between MFIs and clients. Clients can enquire about the availability of financial services offered by MFIs through sending SMS or making telephone calls to the MFIs personnel. Besides, clients can browse on the Web site to understand available financial services and information and download forms for a membership account and borrowing money (Mwashiuya & Mbamba, 2018).

Technology is reshaping the banking industry mainly since the advent of IT applications as home banking. Spillover effects on microfinance are re-engineering old-fashioned business models and, in some cases, MFIs are pioneering change, as it happens for M-banking. Whereas technology typically originates in Western countries and then trickles down in poorer areas, with microfinance, emerging markets represent a pioneering lab for financial innovation (Sharma & Al-Muharrami, 2018).

Even if technology has many different applications, some strands are predominating the actual landscape. IT applications through the digital web are the bridging platform where technologies converge. This is the case for M-banking, social networks, FinTech applications, etc.

The impact on the different stakeholders, starting from the micro-borrowers, is meaningful, mainly because they face a transition from an oral to digital culture. In many backward environments, the oral tradition is seldom complemented by a written culture that is nowadays incorporated in a digital environment where data are created and stored. This cultural leap forward has profound, albeit under-investigated, socio-economic implications. And the very fact that technology has nonrival characteristics eases its spread and simultaneous use, boosting scalability and economies of experience.

Technology is possibly the most potent transmittable tool within a globalized world, subject to unprecedented movements of capitals, goods, people, and their know-how, a common denominator which represents the "software" behind any "hardware" transfer, with a demiurgic impact that makes it a cornerstone of internationalized economic value.

Technology is also introducing new stakeholders as TLC operators or social networks, who respectively carry and intermediate data. Digital information is exchanged through web platforms and data carriers are becoming the dominant player, with possible abuses (threatening privacy, overcharging their services with the extraction of monopolistic rents, etc.).

In the globalization trend, technology is easier to spread than other factors, as it represents a cultural bridge among different experiences. An example is given by the penetration rate of smartphones that are readily accepted everywhere, much more than cultural differences in food, dressing, religion, etc.

The most common microfinance processing tasks, such as credit analysis, recording disbursements, payments, and monitoring, can be positively affected, and re-engineered by ad hoc technology.

Innovation can concern either back-office or front-office activities. While the former involves the inside organization of the MFI, the latter interact with the end users, typically with a mobile phone and connected digital platforms.

Technology can be easily customer-tailored, and its client-centricity attitudes are crucial in microfinance, driving value co-creation that levers both sustainability and outreach.

The poor are typically isolated, lacking opportunities and being deprived of necessary developmental assets such as proper communication and networking.

Network theories may thus act as an original starting point for interpreting issues of poverty, which can be alleviated by combining basic technology with affordable funding programs such as microcredit.

Value-adding technology, levered by microfinance, may then be sequentially added to the development paradigm.

To the extent that technology and microfinance can be suitably combined, they may lever scalable productivity, in a way similar to Metcalfe's exponential upsides for networking organizations.

This may happen for instance with M-banking, within a "digital culture" environment, and with viral social networks, such as Facebook or Twitter, or Mobile Apps.

Social media represent the gathering interaction among members of the web where they create, exchange, and share information and ideas in virtual communities. They expand social networks between individuals or groups and can be categorized as "relational goods." Creation and bridging, bonding and maintenance of social capital are for instance eased by Facebook or LinkedIn. The potential of the virtual sharing economy (concerning car-pooling, accommodation sharing, etc.), where access overcomes property, is still mostly unknown and unexploited.

Evidence shows that backward environments are characterized by cultural segmentation factors, such as local idioms and oral traditions (unfit for codified recording and transmission of information), which slow down the diffusion of social media. Lack of access to technology preserves rural environments from contamination but also segregates digital leftovers, preventing intangible-driven development. Assimilation of new technology depends on the technological level of the country, and the absence of education leads to poverty traps and economic stagnation of innovation laggards.

Communication and the networking enabled by information and communication technologies (ICT) are proving to be economically, socially, and politically transformative. The spread and appropriation of ICT have been a critical aspect of globalization and these technologies have central roles in openness and multi-task innovation.

The most remarkable change has been explosive growth in mobile phone access, giving ubiquitous access to people at the "bottom of the pyramid" using very low-margin, high-volume business models.

Innovation, initially stimulated by selfish monopolistic returns, eventually trickles down to the benefit of larger social networks, inspiring unprecedented business models.

Technology levers product and process innovation that jointly creates scalable value, combining new devices with a re-engineering of the supply and value chain.

Though several microfinance institutions (MFIs) have made forays into digital technologies, they still resort to manual interventions for most frontend cash-based transactions of disbursements and repayments.[2]

4.2 Technology and Microfinance Risk Factors

Technology has an impact not only on the economic marginality of the MFI (increasing revenues and reducing costs) but also on the resilience of its supply chain that becomes less volatile and so less risky. This is for instance due to the impact of big data that provide instant feedback about the dynamic evolution of lending activities, reducing information asymmetries between the MFIs and its borrowing clients.

Microfinance providers are taking progressive steps to embrace digital finance, often starting with the digitization of existing products, services, and operations, either by using mobile devices, partnering with a digital financial service provider, or developing a proprietary agency network. Although this trigger benefits for both clients (convenience, security, faster transactions, and creation of a digital footprint) and microfinance providers (increased operational efficiency, diversification of customer base with value-added products, rural outreach at a lower cost), digital finance comes with certain challenges and risks, and can sometimes represent a threat if not leveraged appropriately (AFI, 2018).

Microfinance risk considers possible unpleasant events that may prevent the MFI from achieving its goals, up to the point of threatening its going concern continuity. Technology has an impact on the risk that can be either mitigated or exacerbated by innovation.

According to CSFI (2011), "the problem of getting the technology right is moving up the risk scale. MFIs face tough decisions on the management of their IT systems and their delivery strategies soon. Do they have the know-how and resources to get them right? Some of our

[2] Srinivas and Mahal (2017).

respondents thought these were among the most difficult issues facing MFI today: failure could put an MFI out of business. A microfinance analyst said it was a case of "Invest in technology or cease to exist in five years."

The impact of technology on the main microfinance risk factors is summarized in Table 4.1.

4.3 The Impact of Technology on the Supply and Value Chains

A microfinance supply chain is a network between the ultimate client and its suppliers to distribute microloans (or to get microdeposits), representing the steps it takes to get the service to the customer.

The value chain of microfinance typically consists of four levels: investors, microfinance funds, MFIs, and micro-entrepreneurs (Fanconi & Scheurle, 2017).

Technology-driven sustainability of the MFI value chain contributes to reshaping the supply chain leveraging outreach. The specialization of intermediaries increases the offer of financial products that accompanies multi-stage growth, following a developmental pattern that has already occurred in Western countries.

Figure 4.2 shows the evolution of the microfinance providers that goes together with the technology-driven upgrade of the clients. This evolution is consistent with the theory that larger MFIs can distribute their fixed costs better, requiring lower interest rates (de Oliveira Leite et al., 2019).

An optimized supply chain results in lower costs and higher operational efficiency. Technology can help re-engineer the supply chain, making it shorter (with fewer intermediating passages) and more resilient to external occurrences. Efficiency gains can save costs, increasing the marginality of the MFI and its outreach potential.

The supply chain can be represented even in terms of the value chain (Fanconi & Scheurle, 2017, chapter 3), whereas each stakeholder (investors; microfinance fund; MFIs; micro-borrowers) presides over a segment of the chain and extracts value from it.

Funding investors are essential to subsidize MFIs, not only in their startup stage but also later, till they are unprofitable. Equity-holders may not seek economic returns if they have philanthropic targets that are less subject to mission drift temptations. Table 4.1, consistently with Table 3.2, shows the impact of innovation on microfinance risk.

Table 4.1 Impact of innovation on microfinance risks

Microfinance Biggest risks	*Impact of innovation and management technology*
Credit risk	IT technology can have a significant impact in detecting and monitoring credit quality, with credit scoring and sharing of information. Credit scoring algorithms based for instance on social media footprints can be used to optimize lending
Competition	Technology creates a digital divide between haves and haves-not; competition increases with comparability, speediness, and other innovative products and processes. Early innovators get a competitive lead and may disrupt older players
Management quality and staffing	Technology increases skills and productivity, improving HR quality and reducing time and cost-absorbing routine tasks
Mission drift	The temptation to reach wealthier clients may increase with the digital divide
Profitability	Technology and digital procedures may actively contribute to making the business model more scalable, cutting variable costs (with an increase in fixed IT costs, which may raise the break-even point), and easing monitoring; productivity should also improve
Back office	The "dirty job behind" is likely to be profoundly changed by technology and computerized systems of recording; it may also be centralized and dematerialized, with economies of scale and experience
Transparency	Written and recordable paperless IT procedures are a key starting point for transparency and softening of information asymmetries
Strategy	Technology and innovation may have a profound impact on management, reshaping and rethinking strategies, reconsidering the whole value chain, target products, and clients, etc
Liquidity	Technology improves awareness and accountability, with a potential impact even on liquidity, which may be better handled and foreseen

(continued)

Table 4.1 (continued)

Microfinance Biggest risks	*Impact of innovation and management technology*
Fraud	Fraud is linked to (lack of) transparency and may be more easily detected with IT procedures, allowing for better monitoring. As mentioned earlier, the speed of movement of money may make fraud detection more difficult and too late. Blockchains may soften transaction recording concerns
Product development	New products and especially innovative product delivery (e.g., M-banking and its by-products) may be conceived because of innovation
Interest rates	They do not depend on technology but again may be better detected and handled. If costs reduce, NGO MFIs, at least, may cut interest rates, driving down industry rates

Incentives to adopt technology are vital for its successful implementation and so need to be properly activated. Resistance to innovation adoption is normal, especially from consumers (see Reinhardt et al., 2019) or unskilled employees of the MFI that are afraid of being replaced by automation.

Motivation so needs to involve all the stakeholders that preside over the supply and value chain:

- Equity-holders that are often frustrated about negative returns and unsustainability of the business model that may bring dissatisfaction; the central thesis of this study is that innovation can help to cut costs, reach an economic break-even, and then broaden the client base, targeting sustainable outreach;
- Employees of the MFI can upgrade their skills and replace routine activities with smarter tasks, for which they need proper training;
- Customers can improve their value for money, getting better services at lower costs.

The adoption of technology needs to be subsidized and may follow results-based financing strategies where payments depend on performance (P4P—pay for performance). This strategy largely developed in

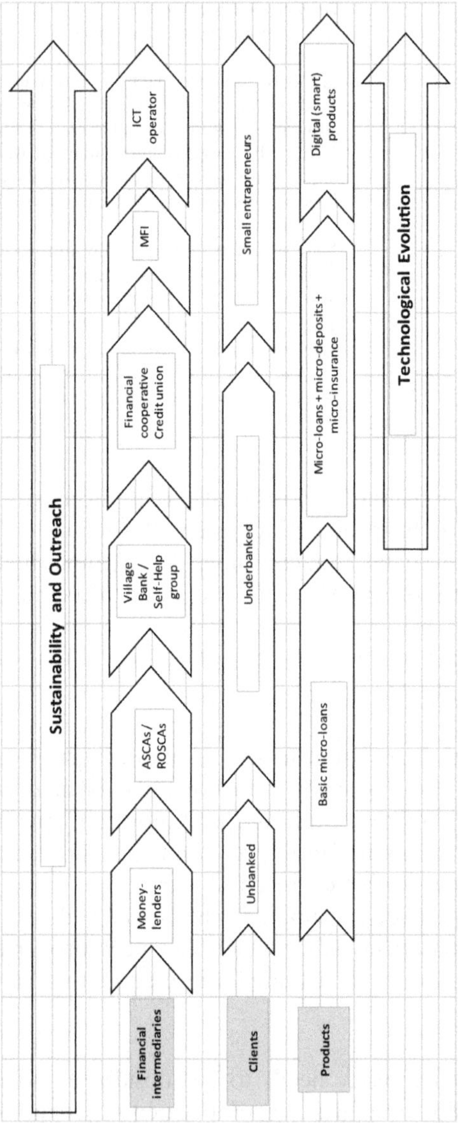

Fig. 4.2 Technology-driven microfinance development

the healthcare industry (Paul et al., 2018), may well be adapted even to microfinance.

Intermediation of funds along the supply/value chain adds value in terms of economic marginality, and this effect is represented in the income statement of the MFI if economic and financial margins are positive.

Being the supply chain a network, it can be represented even in terms of the network theory that technology makes digital, with Internet platforms where stakeholders virtually meet to exchange information, goods, and services.

The impact of technology across the supply/value chain must consider not only the transformations in the business model of the MFI but also the access of borrowers to innovation. This may represent a bottleneck if the underserved micro-borrowers do not possess digital devices (a mobile phone with a decent network coverage is the entry-level instrument).

4.4 Credit Scoring with Electronic Payment Records

A credit score is a numerical expression based on a level analysis of a person's credit files, to represent the creditworthiness of an individual. A credit score is primarily based on credit report information typically sourced from credit bureaus.

Lenders, such as banks and credit card companies but also MFIs, use credit scores to evaluate the potential risk posed by lending money to consumers and to mitigate losses due to bad debt. Lenders use credit scores to determine who qualifies for a loan, at what interest rate, and what credit limits. Lenders also use credit scores to determine which customers are likely to bring in the most revenue. The use of credit or identity scoring before authorizing access or granting credit is an implementation of a trusted system.

This standard framework must be adapted to the microfinance industry and environment, where credit scoring is still embryonic, and many transactions are not digitally recorded. Technology represents even here a big leap forward, enabling the adoption of best practices that are routinely adopted in the banking industry.

A cultural bottleneck is represented by the very fact that in many backward environments, where microfinance is mostly needed, oral culture is still widespread. The traditional passage from oral to written to digital habits that is taking place in Western countries is eased by the circumstance that a written culture is well established, whereas in remote areas we often assist to a sharp discontinuity from an oral to a digital world. Many poor are mostly analphabet, but they are increasingly able to use unsophisticated mobile phones, exchanging messages, and talking.

The very fact that underbanked households use M-banking enables them to circulate financial information that can be stored (typically in cloud servers), interpreted, and analyzed even with artificial intelligence patterns. Digitalization of transactions matters and represents an input factor for credit scoring.

Benefits of appropriate credit scoring techniques are evident even in developing environments: they improve the overall financial and banking system, easing lending risk assessment, avoiding multiple borrowing temptations (being transactions recorded and matched, MFIs and other financial intermediaries can check the borrower's identity and status).

The most important benefit is, however, represented by the possibility to build up a credit history track record of any borrower, simply keeping and processing a digital record of her or his transactions. This scoring may well be extended to group lending, identifying a responsible household.

Credit scoring is strongly influenced by technology, using big data as an input factor and artificial intelligence (machine learning) in the valuation process.

According to Bazarbash (2019) "one of the core strengths of FinTech credit is the use of machine learning techniques and big data analytics to promote credit scoring. Among the strengths of machine learning in promoting financial inclusion, it could particularly facilitate the low-cost automated evaluation of small borrowers that would be otherwise left out of the traditional credit market. By turning soft information into hard information, machine learning allows for incorporating a wide range of information from various sources and structures. Moreover, machine learning can capture nonlinearities in the relationship between risk drivers and credit risk outcomes substantially beyond traditional models. These strengths could enable machine learning to mitigate the information asymmetry problem that is at the heart of lending, particularly to small borrowers with a short history of formal financial reports. However, machine learning has certain weaknesses that should be taken into consideration when applying for credit risk assessment. Heavy reliance on learning from data, particularly in a context where the size of the sample is considerably larger than traditional ways of credit scoring, could result in noisy information playing a role in driving results of credit analysis and leading to financial exclusion of creditworthy applicants. The bias in the sample should be identified and avoided by analysts as much as possible to avoid digital financial exclusion."

Credit scoring is also essential to consider non-performing loans (NPL), which represents a major concern for both traditional banks (especially during and after cyclical recessions) and MFIs.[3] Small NPLs, referred to micro-borrowers, are even more difficult to deal with, as their unitary amount is negligible and reinforcement is difficult and, in most cases, unprofitable. Even in this case, technology may help, improving the soring mechanism, and easing the monitoring phase.

4.5 M-banking and Point-of-Service Payment Technologies

Mobile phones are nowadays spreading everywhere, with increasing network coverage that is progressively reaching even isolated rural areas. They represent the first bridging device between the digital MFI and the client. Mobile phones need to be cheap and user-friendly, with customized functions, like Mobile Apps that interact with the MFI and facilitate basic operations (microloans, microdeposits, remittances, up to preliminary e-commerce functions) that are digitally recorded within the MFI, fuelling big data sourcing and artificial intelligence processing (Kaicer, 2020).

According to Global Findex,[4] 1.7 billion adults do not have an account at a financial institution or through a mobile money provider. Vast disparities exist between high-income economies and developing economies, with the latter having lower inclusion rates. A significant gender gap also persists in financial account ownership in emerging economies, currently standing at an average of 9%, leaving around 980 million women without an account. Unbanked adults are disproportionately young, demonstrating an age inequality in financial inclusion around the world. Despite these inequalities, mobile money continues to play a significant role in driving financial inclusion with over 866 million registered accounts

[3] See Zamore et al. (2021).

[4] See Demirguc-kunt et al. (2018).

across 90 countries, transforming the financial services landscape in many developing markets (GSMA, 2019).

Table 4.2 shows the main financial access indicators, evidencing a progressive worldwide improvement in most parameters, which however still far from reaching a comfort zone. Mobile money indicators on average grow more than commercial bank parameters.

Other financial data statistics are available from IMF sources (https://data.imf.org/).

The increasing use of mobile phones and the use of the Internet has changed many industries, including banking. Mobile banking has advanced to today's payment with the help of mobile phones anywhere and anytime, and mobile phone manufacturers have had to meet the growing needs of users for simpler and easier banking transactions. A

Table 4.2 Financial access survey[5]

Key indicators	*2013*	*2014*	*2015*	*2016*	*2017*
Automated Teller Machines (ATMs) per 100,000 adults	0.71	0.76	0.93	1.07	1.27
Branches of commercial banks per 100,000 adults	2.28	2.33	2.19	2.14	2.14
Depositors with commercial banks per 1,000 adults	157.39	174.90	183.57	184.60	174.58
Borrowers at commercial banks per 1,000 adults	3.77	3.03	2.96	3.05	3.30
Outstanding deposits with commercial banks (% of GDP)	18.34	19.02	19.30	19.29	20.44
Outstanding loans with commercial banks (% of GDP)	4.14	3.76	3.70	3.12	3.23
Outstanding loans with comm. banks: of which SMEs (% of GDP)	0.26	0.16	0.17	0.20	0.18
Mobile money agent outlets: registered per 1,000 km^2	1.17	1.65	2.35	2.19	2.98
Mobile money accounts: registered per 1,000 adults	81.49	79.28	12.02	21.35	27.42
Mobile money transactions: value (% of GDP)	0.31	0.33	0.34	0.69	1.09

[5] Source: International Monetary Fund—http://data.imf.org/

revolutionary step forward in this area was the production of smartphones, which made contactless payments. The development of mobile technologies has thus modified banking operations, with the primary goal of providing new distribution channels for banking services. All this led to intensive cooperation between mobile operators and banks. The lower costs of mobile banking, as well as more accessible services in time and place of banking transactions, have contributed to the number of users of mobile banking services constantly increasing in the world (Tomic & Stojanovic, 2018).

Many MFIs are experimenting with innovative delivery channels to reduce costs, facilitate greater outreach to hard-to-reach areas, and increase customer value for money. Mobile phones could be used to reach many more customers at a lower cost than any other delivery channel, introducing a branchless banking strategy. M-banking is also potentially ubiquitous, operating anywhere and anytime. Since transactions are digitally recorded, they fuel a big database that can be used to create a history tracking of payments and provide other useful information.

M-banking, shortening the organizational chain with its space-less and timeless virtual branches, stands out as an exciting device to soften the human resources bottleneck, tackling technological risk, even if it needs a substantial investment background and cooperation with ICT actors.

Substantial penetration of mobile money accounts presents opportunities for innovative MFIs to explore expansion in areas including alternative lending, cross-border transfers, personal finance, and remittances. Collaboration with local financial players can help FinTechs navigate this market (Ernst & Young, 2019).

Synergies between microfinance and M-banking have proved difficult since inception: "there are fundamental reasons why MFIs are generally not positioned to get into m-banking early on. Most m-banking deployments provide transfers, a service that very few MFIs provide. Indeed, MFIs and successful m-banking businesses occupy different worlds today. The MFI world is focused on credit and maybe some savings, while the m-banking world is focused on transfers and payments. The MFI world largely uses unsophisticated backend systems while the m-banking world uses some of the most sophisticated backend systems we know today (even better than some banks). The MFI world focuses on creating low-cost, human-driven infrastructure, while the m-banking world is tied into and uses payment systems infrastructure. It is not surprising then that these two worlds have not yet aligned" (Kumar et al., 2010).

Statistics of M-banking[6] show the potential for a catch-up and outreach.

Key M-banking statistics[7] for a reference country like the US are the following:

- 79% of smartphone owners have used their device for online purchase in the past six months.
- 86.5% of Americans used a mobile device to check their bank balance in 2020.
- The total value of payments made using mobile devices reached $503 billion in 2020.
- In 2021, there are 5.22 billion unique mobile users worldwide.
- Bank of America continues to be an industry leader with 30 million mobile active users.
- Mobile App fraud transactions have increased by over 600% since 2015.
- 89% of digital fraud losses are due to account takeovers.
- About one in every 20 fraud attacks is associated with a rogue Mobile App.
- Mobile fraud losses totaled more than $40 million across 14,392 breaches in 2019.

Mobile banking is changing traditional microfinance models[8] and probably represents the most successful innovation in the field.

Looking at what has happened in the banking industry in the last 25 years and to the massive impact of digitalization (with home banking; branchless solutions, etc.), the ongoing trend in microfinance[9] is far from being surprising.

Mobile or "branchless" banking (m-banking) is the delivery of financial services outside conventional bank branches through mobile phones and non-bank retail agents. M-banking technologies include smart cards

[6] See https://blogs.imf.org/2019/02/14/fintech-in-sub-saharan-africa-a-potential-game-changer/.

[7] .https://dataprot.net/statistics/mobile-banking-statistics/#:~:text=Key%20mobile%20banking%20statistics&text=86.5%25%20of%20Americans%20used%20a,billion%20unique%20mobile%20users%20worldwide.

[8] See Dorfleitner et al. (2017).

[9] See Banerjee et al. (2015) and Sundaresan (2009).

and mobile phones (increasingly, smartphones) that can conduct financial transactions. M-banking has developed rapidly as a service that allows the unbanked to access financial services with their mobile devices.

Whereas home banking is mostly diffused in Western countries where desk computers or laptops are ubiquitous, M-banking is unsurprisingly more spread in catching up economies where electronic devices are less sophisticated, although the penetration rate of mobile phones is impressive—and growing—even in backward areas.

M-banking follows an impressive growth in mobile phone user penetration.

Some technical features make m-banking particularly attractive:

- The service is ubiquitous (if there is proper network coverage) and can take place at any time, so avoid spatial and temporal barriers that hamper the usefulness of physical bank branching;
- Money does not physically move, with important safety consequences;
- Electronic transfers are immediate;
- Digital recording of operation permits proper accounting for statistics, credit scoring, etc.

Safety reasons are particularly important in poor environments, where custody of cash (under the pillow … or in other unsafe places) is uneasy and thefts are frequent.

If these are the pros, there are also some pitfalls, for instance, connected to cyber-crimes or phishing.

In the mobile banking industry, a pivotal role is operated by TLC companies, who provide the "air" (Internet connection), making the transactions possible. This role is so important that in some cases TLC operators could become a sort of shadow bank if they absorb credit operations within their business model. TLC operators may also be equity partners and co-investors of MFIs, providing the physical TLC backbone and building up a revenue model where data transferred through the web represent, more than "voice," an increasingly valuable asset.

According to Ashta (2012), technology companies are realizing that if the poor can use telephones, then that is sufficient for them to get into the field and provide them micro-services which make it possible to lower transaction costs in dealing with them.

Sided applications concern the use and sale of these (confidential) data to advertising companies or other users. This practice, diffused in the social media industry, may have severe privacy implications, especially if the data provider (the ultimate customer) is unaware of their extended use and does not participate to value co-creation and sharing.

Whereas in the Western world these malpractices are increasingly scrutinized by public authorities, in catching up environments there is a lower awareness.

4.6 Geolocation of Clients and Branches

Geolocation is the identification or estimation of the real-world geographic location of an object, such as a radar source, mobile phone, or Internet-connected computer terminal. In its simplest form geolocation involves the generation of a set of geographic coordinates and is closely related to the use of positioning systems but its usefulness is enhanced by the use of these coordinates to determine a meaningful location, such as a street address.

The word geolocation also refers to the latitude and longitude coordinates of a particular location.

In the microfinance industry, the geolocation of the current and potential clients (to improve outreach) is an essential component of a comprehensive strategy. The establishment of physical branches that complement M-banking may become necessary—and profitable—in areas where there is enough concentration of clients. This is typically the case in urban areas, where the density of the population is much higher and physical distances lower.

Physical branches and M-banking do not necessarily represent two distinct business models and they may coexist, as they do in many traditional banks with complimentary delivery platforms.

Branches are useful especially where and when customers look for unconventional services whose degree of standardization is unfit for web applications. An example is given by micro-consultancy that is typically tailor-made or by loans that exceed the standard features of microcredit.

Geolocation strategies can be designed and implemented considering the existing mapping of a selected territory, with Geographic Information System (GIS) techniques that map the area and identify, for instance, the concentration and distribution of key parameters as population, penetration rate of ICT devices, TLC antennas, etc.

4.7 Digital Scalability and Cloud Computing

Scalability indicates the ability of a process, network, or system to handle a growing amount of work. Scalability fosters economic marginality, especially in intangible-driven businesses where variable costs are typically negligible. Massive volumes may offset low margins, producing economic gains. Digitalization is defined as the concept of "going paperless," the technical process of transforming analog information or physical products into digital form. Digital scalability operates in a web context, where networked agents interact to generate co-created value.

Economic and financial margins that represent a primary parameter for valuation are boosted by cost savings and scalable increases of expected revenues. Digitalized intangibles synergistically interact through networked platforms that reshape traditional supply chains (Moro Visconti, 2020, chapter 3).

In broader terms, scalability means flexibility, which allows to better address and achieve the specific needs of customers, which are never static. People's interests and tastes, as well as environmental conditions, change continuously over time. Scalability is therefore vital as it contributes to competitiveness, efficiency, and quality. Scalability helps the system to work gracefully without any undue delay and unproductive resource consumption while making good use of the available resources (Gupta et. al., 2017).

Since scalability depends on the capability of a business to profit from the addition of (internal and/or external) resources, these latter can fall either into the "vertical" or "horizontal" category and generate two different types of scalability.

Vertical scalability (scaling-up) corresponds to the ability to increase the capacity of existing hardware or software by adding more resources to the single system node. For instance, we can add processing power to a server to increase its speed. In the same way, we can scale a system vertically and expand it by providing more shared resources such as processing, main memory, storage, and network interfaces to the main node to be able to satisfy a greater number of requests per system (Gupta et al., 2017).

By contrast, horizontal scalability (scaling out) refers to adding more nodes to the same system, thus impacting and modifying the supply chain. A real case could be adding computer workstations to a network, meaning to connect multiple computers to accomplish more work in less time.

This method allows the system to work as a single logical unit, increasing overall efficiency.

Digital business models are usually designed for rapid growth, and the recent advances in digital technologies continue to create new possibilities to scale up and reach a global scale. As described by Gander (2015) the drivers by which digital business models may attempt to gain scale are analyzed in Table 4.3.

Digitization is the process of changing from analog to digital form, for instance converting handwritten or typewritten text into the digital form. This process is nowadays increasingly replaced by a direct recording of data in digital forms, even using artificial intelligence devices.

Digitalization represents a step forward and is concerned with the use of digital technologies to change a business model and provide new revenue and value-producing opportunities.

Digitalization is increasingly linked to cloud computing, a storage system where inventory space is potentially unlimited, physical location is irrelevant, and usability is guaranteed everywhere, through a web connection (and enabling passwords).

Today, cloud computing enables financial institutions to significantly reduce their IT expenses by "delocalizing the IT infrastructure" outside of the company and reduce excess staff (Vandeputte & De Toffol, 2017).

Both digitalization and cloud computing are essential components of a supply chain that is populated by big data (and the Internet of Things sensors) and operated with artificial intelligence patterns.

According to Pythowska and Korynski (2017), while there is widespread recognition of the need to use digital solutions to a larger degree, the ability and willingness of MFIs to do that vary greatly. Small institutions claim lack of financial resources as the main challenge in bringing technology to their organizations. The most useful digital services are those related to the automation of loan applications and management of the related documentation. The small-scale operations of most MFIs in Europe are a barrier to the introduction of FinTech solutions. The results also show that MFIs are cautious about not losing their competitive advantage of a personal relationship with their clients. FinTech and digitalization solutions should be applied based on a rational calculus of costs and benefits, in line with the mission of the organization and the needs and capabilities of the clients.

Cloud computing potentially has a role to play in a wide variety of international economic development contexts, but two prominent areas

Table 4.3 Scalability drivers

Scalability driver	*Characteristics*	*Criticalities*
Learning by using	The greater the scale of a technology's use, the more its users learn about its features, strengths, and weaknesses (also using SWOT analysis)	Disseminate learning between users may be costly and may require managerial attention and resources
Networking (Network externalities)	"Scalability becomes supercharged with network effects" (Haskel and Westlake, 2018). A network is scalable if it can cope with the existing demands placed upon it but also can be flexibly expanded to meet future demands. Network externalities occur when the value obtained by using products or services increases with its greater diffusion among populations of users	Reputation and know-how to manage and disseminate value created by customers' customization and to orchestrate ecosystems
Scale economies	Supply-side effects of scale can include economies of production and distribution. With large output quantities, the unit cost of each product or service encounter falls, due to the possibility of spreading fixed costs, advertising budgets, and research and design costs across a larger quantity of products	Conceive and maintain a generic platform; resources to prevent non-scalable features from becoming part of the ecosystem
Information returns	Reduction in users' perceptions of the risk of adopting a product or service following its use by others. The more widely adopted technology is, the better it is understood, and the less risky it appears	Conforming to other people's preferences and perceptions about a product or service does not necessarily lead to better technology adoption, since others' preferences may not in some cases correspond to an individual's personal actual preferences
Technological interrelatedness	The more a technology is adopted, the greater the number of supporting sub-technologies that are developed and become part of its infrastructure	Costly and complex to support as the number of product configurations grows with each customer

(continued)

Table 4.3 (continued)

Scalability driver	*Characteristics*	*Criticalities*
Distributed sourcing	The way resources are decentralized across value chains and ecosystems. The distributed design enables the rapid growth in the use of a product or service without sacrificing performance or causing congestion in the system which degrades the customer experience	Potential for congestion due to overloading of capacity following a rapid, unanticipated, and sizeable increase in user numbers, which may result in service failure
Economies of experience	Economies in which products or services are sold emphasizing their effects on people's lives and actions, to create "memorable customers' experiences"	Costs and new know-how to acquire for turning from product to service/experience orientation. Change of customers' expectations and managers' strategies
Real options	Options available to managers concerning either business investment opportunities, or projects involving tangible assets versus financial instruments	Difficulties in estimating the precise value of real options
Blitzscaling	Specific techniques allowing companies to achieve massive scale at incredible speed. When a company grows at a rate that is much faster than its competitors, this might make the company feel uncomfortable with the context of operation	Possibility for disrupting startups to exploit network externalities to create digital monopolies. Size is increasingly valued but economic profitability may be neglected

Source Moro Visconti (2020), chapter 3

of development focus provide important illustrative examples of both the promise and perils of cloud-based services. Emerging cloud-based services now offer applications for portfolio management and accounting otherwise unaffordable for most MFIs. In another case, the powerful software platforms that power mobile money services are now emerging as cloud-based hosted services. This introduces an important third partner into the system, operating between the mobile network operators and the banks holding trust accounts.[10]

[10] Barnett (2011).

While the advent of cloud services has created opportunities for new companies, it has also created new opportunities for established organizations in the microfinance industry. Utilizing this type of model, a traditional microfinance association, acting on behalf of its members, can offer sophisticated back-office software that would otherwise be unaffordable to those institutions on an individual basis.

4.8 Digital Group Borrowing (Lending) and Social Networks

Group lending is a much-celebrated idea to overcome the lack of collateral, which represents one of the biggest obstacles to credit access for the poor. MFIs generally lend a small individual loan to a household belonging to a group of usually 5–20 people that guarantee for him and intervene in the case of delinquency. Group lending with joint liability is the standard contract used by MFIs (Altinok, 2018).

Transaction cost is incurred in forming the group, and so group lending has emerged as a useful tool in reducing this cost by transferring its burden on the group (Sharma et al., 2017).

Should the individual borrower prove reliable, the MFI might extend credit to other members of the group. The essence of group lending is to transfer responsibilities from bank staff to borrowers, who contribute to the selection and monitoring of debtors, helping in the enforcement of contracts. In exchange, customers get otherwise inaccessible loans.

Group lending with joint liability is seen as an effective instrument to circumvent information asymmetries because it incentivizes group members to use their social ties to screen, monitor, and enforce loan repayment on their peers. The social relations embed social capital and facilitate the collective actions of group members, allowing them to coordinate their repayment decisions and cooperate for their mutual benefit (Postelnicu et al., 2014).

A robust internal incentive for monitoring within the group arises in collective lending, even if this cannot prevent any problem; social sanctions hardly prove efficient outside small rural areas where everybody knows others, and this problem grows along with the urbanization process that is taking place almost everywhere. However, even in small villages, the threat of social sanctions between close friends and relatives is hardly credible (Armendariz De Aghion & Morduch, 2010). Attending and monitoring group meetings can prove expensive in dispersed areas;

frequency of meetings is another implicit cost. Borrowers' behavior might also prove collusive against the bank, undermining its ability to exploit social links as proper collateral.

Groups are efficient if not correlated among them—since they allow for risk diversification and reduction—but do not work well when a generalized systematic crisis occurs (such as the periodical floods which devastate Bangladesh and have masterminded the first Grameen bank model).

This background describes traditional group lending, a key aspect of microfinance that can be revolutionized by technology.

Social networks acting through digital platforms reshape the composition of the group and its operativity. Members can be in touch in real-time through dedicated chats via WhatsApp or other applications, and they can exchange information or financial services. M-banking can be used collectively through digitalized group-lenders and borrowers, with benefits that range from immediacy to traceability and savings in transactions. Digital platforms enhance virality and consequent scalability of operations.

Social networks are based on network theory that studies graphs as a representation of (a)symmetric relations between discrete objects. In computer science and network science, network theory is a part of graph theory: a network can be defined as a graph in which nodes and/or edges have attributes (e.g., names). An interdependent network is a system of coupled networks where nodes of one or more networks depend on nodes in other networks. Developments in modern technology enhance such dependencies. Networks represent a fundamental characteristic of complex systems whose connected structure may give an innovative interpretation of the interactions among (linked) stakeholders like MFIs and micro-borrowers.

A graphical representation of group lending shows how they can be intuitively linked to networks. Whereas traditional group lending shows limited links between each group member and the group leader who acts as a hub connected to the MFI, in digital group lending patterns linkages increase and the disintermediation directly connects each member to the MFI, so decreasing the role of the group leader.

Figure 4.3 does not show the full dynamics of the digital interactions that work everywhere on a 7/24 basis (seven days a week, all day long), whereas traditional group lending faces consistent physical barriers. Enhanced connectivity among different nodes increases the overall value of the network, leveraging both sustainability and outreach.

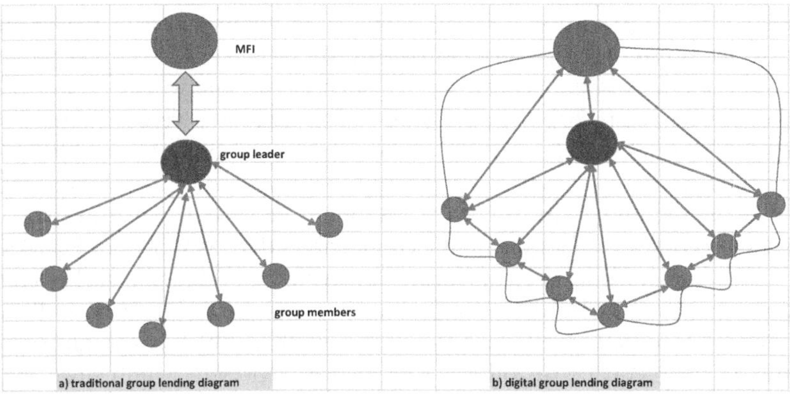

Fig. 4.3 Traditional versus digital group lending

Social networks represent a digital base for peer-to-peer (P2P) lending or (more intermediated) crowdfunding. Micro-equity stakes levered by collective lending can usefully complement microloans, supporting startups and digital entrepreneurship.

Group lending strategies (Shah et al., 2019) transfer monitoring to borrowers, where joint liability ensures strong incentives to members to help their peers succeed.

Group lending represents a fundamental characteristic of microfinance, complementary to individual lending (which shows gains in privacy and time saving, although it lacks shared guarantees).

Technology can revolutionize traditional group lending activities, linking it to social networks and other equity sources like crowdfunding (see Sarkar & Alvari, 2018) or peer-to-peer (P2P) lending, as shown in Sect. 4.9 and 6.5.

Digitalization of group lending activities[11] with virtual platforms also enables proper recording and storage of the transactions.

A social network is a social structure made up of a set of social actors (such as individuals or organizations), sets of dyadic (bilateral) ties, and other social interactions between actors. Social networks are increasingly digitalized, whenever they are intermediated through digital platforms that exchange and record data in real-time. Assortative mixing of network

[11] See Agrawal and Sen (2017).

members is a prerequisite for an equilibrated composition of the group that needs internal harmony and cohesion.

Social networks represent a subset of networks. Network theory (Barabási, 2016) is the study of graphs as a representation of either symmetric relations or asymmetric relations between discrete objects.

Each household (microfinance customer) represents a vertex that is linked to other vertices through a connecting edge, as shown in Fig. 4.4.

Whereas dyads show bi-univocal links (typically bi-directional) between two vertices, tryads are concerned with a triangular interaction. Paraphrasing George Orwell, we may say that vertices are all equal, but some are ... more equal than others. Key vertices represent a hub since they are at the center of stronger links among other connecting vertices, as it happens for main airports. This representation is consistent with group borrowing, where there is a leading interface between the group and the MFI (Fig. 4.5) that represents the connecting hub between two (dyad), three (tryad) or more clients.

Members of a group lending entity represent a social network that is normally hierarchical since there is one vertex that represents the corresponding entity between the group and the MFI.

Relationships among the members of the network are shaped by social ties but can also be expressed with the use of geometry, namely topology.

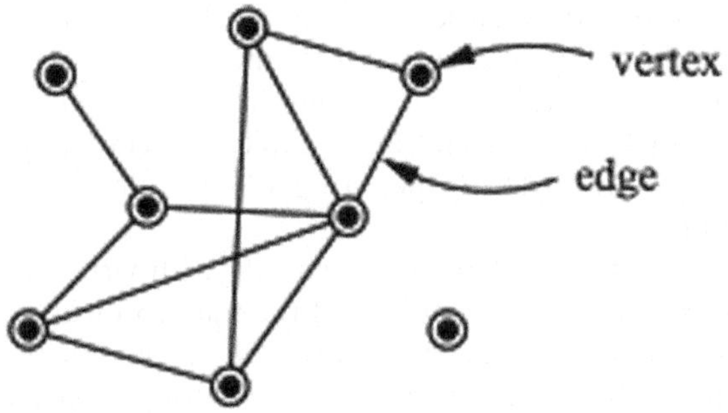

Fig. 4.4 Vertices and edges forming a network

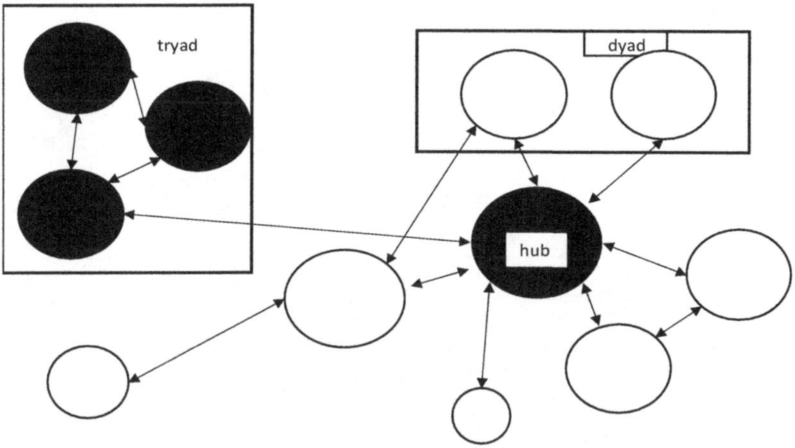

Fig. 4.5 Dyads, Tryads, and Hubs

Digitalized social networks of group lending (or borrowing) exchange information (financial data; credit histories; track record of payments, etc.) through the web.

Applications to microfinance products start from primordial SMS exchanges and are now increasingly replaced by more modern techniques like chats forming a group of adherents with a common purpose.

Networks can be much broader than the one graphically represented in Fig. 4.6 as shown in the following representation (see Fig. 4.6).

Network data analysis can ease the detection of the efficiency of MFIs (Nourani et al., 2020).

4.9 Crowdfunding and Peer-To-Peer Innovations Linked to Group Borrowing

Crowdfunding is the practice of funding a project or venture by raising small amounts of money from many people, typically via the web. Crowdfunding is a form of crowdsourcing and alternative finance.

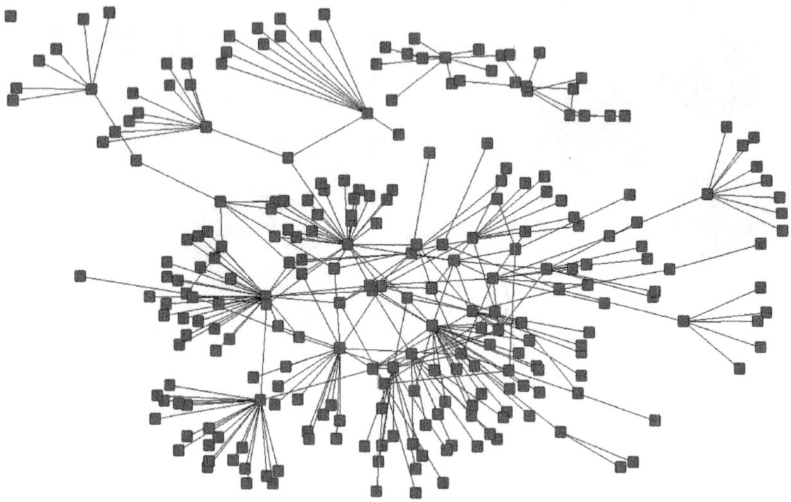

Fig. 4.6 Example of random network

Even if crowdfunding is mainly diffused in developed countries where microfinance is not widespread,[12] its links with traditional microfinance seem evident, although they deserve further scrutiny.

The main difference between crowdfunding and microlending is that the former is concerned with equity stakes, whereas microloans are represented by debt, being somewhat more like peer-to-peer (P2P) lending.

P2P is the practice of lending money to individuals or businesses through online services that match lenders with borrowers. Since peer-to-peer lending companies offering these services generally operate online, they can run with lower overhead costs and provide the service more cheaply than traditional financial institutions. This consideration—lower costs for those who intermediate funds through the web—is the main thesis of this study and provides the rationale for cost-cutting strategies through technology.

Crowdfunding, P2P lending (borrowing), and digital group borrowing (lending) show important differences but also some common denominator, mainly represented by their linking technology (a digital platform

[12] See Pedrini et al. (2016).

always connected to the web) and the very fact that they are all part of similar social networks.

Borrowing and lending digital platforms bypass financial intermediaries like MFIs and so allow for cost savings and promptness. Financial disintermediation is a natural consequence of this process that affects the supply and value chain.

Social networks interacting through digital platforms may so represent the bridging technology that connects microfinance (group borrowing/lending) to crowdfunding and P2P lending.

Differences but also a continuity thread are represented by an evolutionary pattern, starting from the very base of the social pyramid, where the unbanked poor may start climbing the social ladder accessing microfinance through relational group borrowing, and then proceed to P2P borrowing and lastly to equity crowdfunding.

Three main types of crowdfunding can interact with microfinance:

1. *Reward crowdfunding* is when people offer money in exchange for a tiered system of rewards. Even though this method offers backers a reward, it is still generally considered a subset of donation-based crowdfunding since there is no financial or equity return.
2. *Donation crowdfunding* is when people donate money, with no expectation of reward or equity.
3. *Equity crowdfunding* allows investors to become shareholders.

According to the European Commission (2020), for microfinance, two areas of technological innovation are most relevant: payments and borrowings. The important innovations in the payments sphere relate to remittances, mobile payments, mobile points of sale, peer-to-peer (P2P) payments, and B2B transactions. When it comes to borrowings, non-bank microfinance providers are increasingly applying credit risk assessment, Internet-based platform lending, crowdfunding, and auto-underwriting (technology-driven underwriting process that provides a computer-generated loan decision).

4.9.1 *Crowdfunded Digital Platforms Interacting with Microfinance Institutions*

The interaction between crowdfunded platforms and MFIs, already anticipated in the literature review, can be tentatively synthesized in Fig. 4.7.

While there are many possible business models, the core interaction is between the crowdfunded platform (2) backed by its investors (1) and the MFI (3) with its traditional clients (4) that can become digitized (5). FinTech-driven innovation inspires the top-down workings of crowdfunded platforms (1) but is also influenced by bottom-up feedbacks of digitized micro-borrowers (5), intermediated by the MFI (3), making the whole process circular and self-fulfilling. Crowdfunded platforms can contribute to the globalization and affordability of microfinance (Sun & Liang, 2021).

4.10 Big Data and Artificial Intelligence

The relationship between microfinance and big data/artificial intelligence is still unusual and hardly present in the academic debate, with little if any practical application.

A perspective outlook should, however, consider that the pervasive diffusion of both big data and artificial intelligence (that often operate jointly since big data provide input data for artificial intelligence patterns) will soon cross the microfinance industry, with practical applications and pollination of ideas that now seem futuristic but may soon become a commodity.

Before entering further details, a short definition of the main characteristics of both big data and artificial intelligence will be provided.

Big data is the term for any gathering of large-volume information sets from multiple sources and is so expensive, fast-changing, and complex that can become hard to process. The difficulties incorporate investigation, catch, duration, inquiry, sharing, stockpiling, exchange, perception, protection infringement, and quantification of financial value. The explosive growth of data in almost every industry and business area is driven by the rapid development of the web, Internet of Things (IoT), and cloud computing (Jin et al., 2015).

Whereas data have always existed, big data represent a novelty that has seldom been associated with microfinance. Big data represent an unprecedented informative set that can be used for many applications, as credit

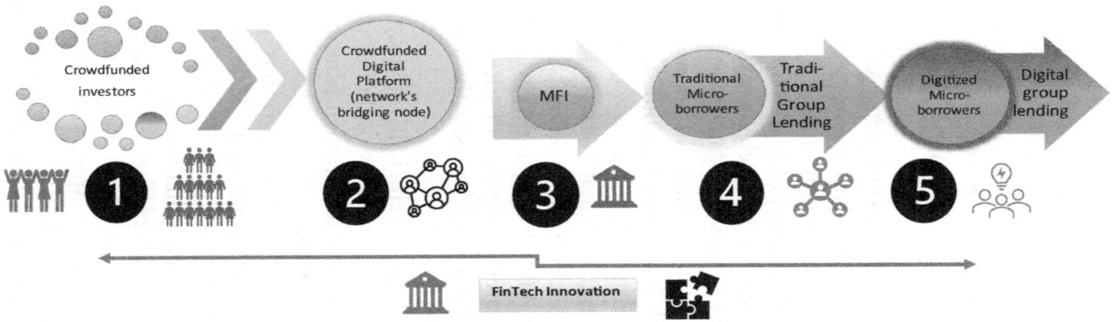

Fig. 4.7 From crowdfunded investors to digital group lending

scoring (learning from credit history and current trends, to extrapolate payback patterns) or customer habits, captured through SMS, chats or other social network applications.

Big data are exchanged primarily through digital platforms, the virtual marketplace where buyers and sellers exchange products and services, often through B2B, B2C or C2C e-commerce transactions. As such, digital platforms are the virtual places where data are traded and collected, thus feeding the high volume of information that will be analyzed with data mining.

Social networks or Mobile Apps mainly represent the digital platforms that are consistent with the microfinance framework.

Big data and IoT sensors are closely linked to artificial intelligence, the theory, and development of computer systems able to perform tasks usually requiring human knowledge, such as visual perception, speech recognition, decision-making, and translation between languages. Big data feed artificial intelligence with timely and massive information that is consequently processed with a machine learning approach.

Data are increasingly considered as a worthy asset: as African economies become increasingly "digital," data will become a source of power in economic governance. African citizens may benefit from their data as a source of revenue, knowledge, and power (Mann, 2017). Data appropriation from digital intermediaries and social media data intermediaries have however become a concern (see the Facebook/Cambridge Analytica data scandal of 2018).

ICT and data analytics help in efficiently tracking the demand for microfinance products. MFIs can so focus on better demand forecasting, using artificial intelligence patterns for optimal planning and probabilistic reasoning (Russel & Norvig, 2015).

Digitalized microfinance produces an enormous and continuous flow of data that can be collected and processed. Whereas big data represent the input source, artificial intelligence presides over the processing of data that are increasingly perceived as a valuable asset.

Traffic among different websites fuels big data creation with file sharing, streaming media through social networks, interacting devices such as IoT sensors, use of Mobile Apps, science data, eMails, digitalizers, texts, geometries, sounds, antennas, voice data, videos, posts, blogs, and other connecting sources through several different devices. Combinations of different data sources are also relevant as they add value through data fusion. A networked domino effect, driven by scalable data systems connected through digital platforms, spreads information in real-time.

Big data ignite value and supply chains that preside over value co-creation among composite stakeholders. Value creation is again consistent with the main thesis of this study, according to which value created through cost-cutting technology improves microfinance sustainability and boosts outreach.

As Moro Visconti et al. (2017) show: "a big data-driven value chain is represented by several consequential steps such as data creation, search and capture, storage, querying, analysis, sharing and transfer, visualization, customization. Each step, codified by software algorithms, is part of an incremental and flexible value chain. Every step adds up a value that must be shared among its contributors (providers, intermediating platforms, users, etc.), which participate to value co-creation. This chain produces different stages of information that are embedded in traditional value chains that so become big data-driven."

Big data value chain is based on the following strategic steps, synthesized in Fig. 4.8:

1. Creation (data capture)
2. Storage (warehousing)
3. Processing (data mining—fusion and analytics)
4. Consumption (sharing)
5. Monetization

Each step of the value chain is linked to big data 5Vs (volume—velocity—variety—veracity—value). What most matters is, however, the interaction of the 5Vs, whose impact along the value chain changes from step to step as shown in Fig. 4.1 using more " + " for higher impact.

Figure 4.8 shows an impact decrease along the value chain for the early Vs (volume, velocity), and a correspondent increase for last V (value). Variety and Veracity acquire importance with the processing phase and their impact is optimized (with data mining-fusion and data visualization and sharing) and then transferred to maximize value during monetization.

Larger quantities of data are routinely produced from an increasing number of sources. At this stage, big data value is low because they are unstructured, uncorrelated and the stakeholders deemed to capture data have low capacity to evaluate their veracity.

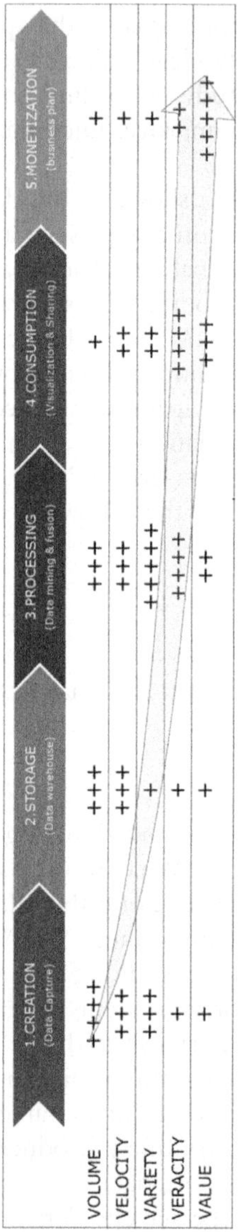

Fig. 4.8 Big data value chains

Data warehousing hardly increases big data value because it is concerned with storing data regardless of their type (the variety with only one +) and validity of big data. Several data processing resources are allocated to drastically solve issues on data volume (mining only the essential data) and variety (fusing several types of data). Although processing increases big data value, its outputs are not yet ready for immediate use.

The fourth stage of the value chain addresses the exchange of big data processing outputs adopting communication (sharing platform) and representation (data visualization) technologies. Here, volume, velocity, and variety are already simplified; however, the veracity is still partially unsolved. Finally, the last stage of the value chain maximizes value through a synthesis of the first four Vs.

Therefore, big data drive value generation that can be revealed by:

- (Radical) innovation;
- Market expansion (new products or services toward new markets);
- Differentiation/branding (optimization);
- Shortened supply chain, processing speed and thus favoring cost reduction;
- Better forecasting and consequent risk reduction.

Cost reduction is caused by many factors and in different phases of the product/service lifecycle, like optimized logistics or just-in-time production, and stock management. For manufacturing, IoT can have a tremendous impact on cost reduction, for example lowering maintenance costs for tools and machines, higher product conformity, production cycle optimization, etc. Risk reduction is also significantly impacted by big data analysis, which better defines key elements of business planning such as production processes or sales and marketing strategies."

Artificial intelligence is intelligence demonstrated by machines, in contrast to the natural intelligence displayed by humans and other animals. In computer science, artificial intelligence research is defined as the study of "intelligent agents": any device that perceives its environment and takes actions that maximize its chance of successfully achieving its goals. The term "artificial intelligence" is applied when a machine mimics "cognitive" functions that humans associate with other human minds, such as "learning" and "problem-solving" (Russel & Norvig, 2015).

The traditional problems (or goals) of artificial intelligence research include reasoning, knowledge representation, planning, learning, natural language processing, perception, and the ability to move and manipulate objects. While robotic applications, self-driving cars, or image recognition (for medical scans, etc.) represent applications that are currently far from the microfinance perimeter, other accomplishments seem closer to a common goal.

Among the possible applications of big data-nurtured artificial intelligence to microfinance, we may tentatively quote the following:

- Strategic planning, where big data are collected through digital platforms, stored in the cloud, interpreted with artificial intelligence algorithms, and eventually used to improve forecasts and fuel machine learning patterns;
- Natural language processing, where messages exchanged through digital platforms can be interpreted and used;
- Credit history patterns, to extrapolate trendy behaviors for optimal scoring. Credit history is still problematic in countries where financial transactions are hardly digitized and not always properly recorded.

The relationship between microfinance and big data, fostered by digitalization,[13] is still largely unexplored.

In more general terms, it may be evidenced that big data's impact on the microfinance ecosystem is still obscure. Whereas its importance seems evident, the declination of the impact deserves further scrutiny. Big data applied to a mass of unbanked potential clients may reveal powerful information, for instance being inspired by the financial diaries of the poor, examined in the following sub-section.

These data are still hardly digitized and so their extraction, storing, and interpretation are challenging. But thanks to mobile phones and other technological advances, the outlook is rapidly changing and upgrading.

[13] Pythowska and Korynski (2017).

4.10.1 *Financial Diaries and Social Habits of the Poor: A Digital Collection Matching Top-Down Budgeting with Bottom-Up Evidence*

MFIs typically follow traditional top-down budgeting procedures, according to which hypotheses about trendy patterns are stated by the management, and the contact with the underlying reality is often filtered through unchecked expectations.

In small MFIs, budgeting is an academic exercise, and hypotheses are seldom backed by strategic assumptions.

Innovation has an impact on this dirigistic process, and it operates in several aspects that mainly concern:

- The possibility to use big data, collected in real-time, to continuously refresh hypotheses, matching the top town approach with bottom-up empirical evidence;
- The use of an analytic collection of habits of the target clients (economic and financial diaries,[14] showing how they collect, store, and use money; social and consumption behaviors, etc.) that interact with the MFI through digital platforms, realizing useful information used by social media or TLC corporations for marketing purposes (digital advertising; customer segmentation, etc.).

The economic life of the poor changes substantially according to their social condition—ranging from the chronically vulnerable poorest of the poor, who are daily engaged with hand-to-mouth survival, to those who are painfully approaching, step after step, middle-class social status.

A key problem in developing countries is that many poor people can provide only their work. Since complementary assets require outside financing (being savings not existent or not properly ›stored‹), the lack of finance (together with lack of education, State aid, infrastructures ...) is an obstacle to the birth of entrepreneurship, with negative side effects on employment.

Yunus and Yolis (1999) show that if the poor are provided access to finance, they might startup microenterprises, building up a virtuous cycle and transforming underemployed laborers into small entrepreneurs.

[14] Collins et al. (2009).

The poor who live in a permanent state of need are different from wealthier individuals, even from a psychological perspective—those who live in the margins, see themselves and the others, while those who live isolated and surrounded by their selfish wealth, just see themselves. Poverty is transcendent, and it goes beyond material deprivation, involving states of mind, aspirations, need to be considered and taken care of.

When financial and economic flows add up, they are transformed into accumulated capital and wealth, which represent storage for future consumption and starting sources for investments. Long-term wealth accumulation, so important for igniting development and keeping it alive, is however a target well beyond the capabilities of the abject poorest. This point is due also to credit constraints, which are particularly binding for the poor with no collateral since they constrain small enterprises' development and lock the underserved in their poverty traps.

Both economic and financial flows and accumulated wealth need to be financially intermediated, so to make safe storing possible, to allow people for lending and borrowing, to leverage up capital, matching asynchronous financial maturities, hedging against risk, and providing emergency capital, in case of need. Proper financial instruments can so soften pervasive insecurity. If these are some of the main basic functions of financial markets, other more sophisticated necessities are sometimes needed, even if they are seldom provided to the poor.

For roughly two-thirds of the world population, simply there are not financial institutions and life has to be designed in another—unpleasant—way. When opportunities are denied, it proves difficult to get out of poverty, considering that the world works with money and everybody needs the first coin to catch the second one—in many cases, it is just a starting problem, likely to be solved if only properly addressed.

The poor are often considered being completely unaware of the financial mechanisms, which are so pervasive in the capitalistic culture. On the one side, this point is true regarding the most sophisticated products, which are totally—and luckily—unheard of in most poor environments, but on the other side, through a simpler perspective, many poor are astonishingly very familiar with basic financial aspects, counting every penny they earn and trying to make the most out of it—a matter of survival, under a continuous stimulus of permanent need.

Basic forms of informal saving and borrowing are much diffused, since they are an answer to day-by-day problems for the poor who need to store up money, to normalize and match volatile cash inflows with often unpredictable outflows, in an environment where personal or impersonal emergencies (sickness, injury, unemployment versus natural disasters ...) are endemic. A basic survival strategy becomes coping with risk—traditionally higher in poor environments—and putting in place appropriate mitigation measures against endemic emergencies.

Income shocks, which occur when poor households receive less than expected, are typically combined with disgraceful events such as illnesses, livestock death, natural calamities, which derail households from their envisaged accumulation pattern, making the poor even more vulnerable.

Unlucky events may cause a "last straw" threshold effect if they are the last inauspicious event of a long sequence of ominous happenings.

Financial instruments and markets in poor environments—making basic financial intermediation feasible and possible—have huge potential, for a variety of complementary reasons, as:

- need for simple but vital financial products to manage and intermediate money-saving, borrowing, depositing, preserving, transferring, and repaying;
- lack of suitable financial services, since the existing ones are typically expensive—often unaffordable—unreliable, unregulated, and poorly designed, and they make the poor even more vulnerable and unable to choose among different competitive options;
- need to intermediate funds, to match different maturities, to smooth volatility, mitigate risk, and store savings in a safe place. Volatility tends to be negatively skewed, since improvements are typically gradual, while declines are more sudden and severe;
- need for formal and institutional markets, complementary to unofficial financial services.

Financial intermediation, based on money as a conventional system of payment and exchange for goods and services, goes beyond a barter economic system and it allows people to store, transfer, and transform fungible wealth, conventionally represented by a currency. Money is a tangible and psychological metaphor for the price of things, within a set of opportunities represented by the market.

Monetary savings are a cornerstone within the financial system, even in its embryonic phase, and they can help the poor, who live on an income that is small, but also uncertain, volatile, and unpredictable. One never knows what may happen tomorrow, especially if living with no safety nets, apart from the solidarity of the family clan. It is astonishing to see how even the poorest can save and intermediate cash—and those who do not have social security nets need to save more.

The poor do need to intermediate, to hold cash reserves, and to get survival bridge-financing in the form of little lump sums of money, often with little notice, when cash inflows are late and income patterns are volatile, to smooth the ups and downs of household consumption[15]. Such a necessity is carried through with a network of typically informal relations, ranging from the family and the ethnic clan to neighbors, friends, local saving clubs, or greedy moneylenders.

The network may have an increasing pattern of formality, becoming semi-formal or even formal. In such an evolution, microfinance can help. The poorest may however be intimidated by contact with formal banking institutions, unfit for their needs.

4.10.2 Survival Cash Flow Management

Uneven cash inflows are irregular, unpredictable, typically low, and often seasonal since they are awkwardly timed, especially in the countryside—peaking in harvest times and drying up in other "hungry" periods. The systematic risk of the businesses (from volatile agricultural outputs to uncertain trading results) has a strong impact on incomes—to be consumed for survival but also stored for deferred use. Financial intermediation is a necessity, not just an option, even if it is unsophisticated and concentrated on short-term liquidity management.

Financial products are typically highly flexible, and their intermediation can bring many different possible outcomes, even in unsophisticated and backward environments. Need is a powerful engine behind innovation and creativity whereas the demand for financial products, including microfinance, is particularly strong at the base of the social pyramid, also because of the increasing purchasing power of the poor. Successful examples may conveniently be replicated over a larger number of poor borrowers and depositors.

[15] See Collins et al. (2009, p. 14).

Informal reciprocal lending and borrowing among the poor are highly diffused, typically exchanging little sums of money for short time horizons, and they normally take place within the extended family network, being acquaintance, confidence, and trust fundamental aspects of unregulated exchanges. Interest rates are often forgiven, to the extent that loans are short-termed and reciprocal, balancing fluctuating states of need, where today's lenders are likely to be tomorrow's borrowers.

The poor have unsophisticated primary needs for basic survival and complicated products are not suitable and dangerous for them, even if the world they live in is not less complicated or variegated than that of wealthier households—as already mentioned, the problems of the ant are not smaller than those of the elephant.

As Rajan says[16]:

> People, poor and rich, need reliable financing so that their ideas can be brought together with assets to generate long-run sustainable growth. The two key ingredients to a well-functioning market economy are competition and access - competition so that performance keeps improving and access so that everyone has a chance to participate, and nobody's talents are wasted [...] we will focus on access to finance, for, after all, people, poor and rich, need reliable financing so that their ideas can be brought together with assets to generate long-run sustainable growth.

There are human events that are relatively impermeable to the level of wealth, such as births, marriages, or funerals. If little choice is attributed to the last sad event, which democratically occurs to both the rich and the poor, birth and weddings are influenced by the level of wealth only to a very little extent, poor spouses make even more children than richer couples, whereas most people long for getting married anyway, irrespectively of their financial means and romantically trying to be poor but happy.

The financial life of the poor is very much concerned with these basic choices and happenings and it moves around the key and unsophisticated events, following the ordinary life cycle. Wealth matters more—and makes the difference—in other complementary aspects, such as the standard and quality of living or the possibility to build up entrepreneurial activity, for which some initial money is gratefully needed.

16 http://www.yearofmicrocredit.org/pages/whyayear/whyayear_quotecollection.asp.

Challenges, events, and opportunities always have a financial side, which is important but rarely decisive. The financial psychology of the poor—concerned about how they perceive money and attribute a symbolic value to it—also matters, to understand their cultural values and to foresee their needs and behavior.

Big data can ease the detection and monitoring of cash flow patterns, providing useful information to MFIs and customers that can improve the matching of their reciprocal targets.

4.11 Agency Banking and Biometrics

Banking intermediation models coexist in many different forms, providing to customers a variety of options and solution that is proportional to their sophistication and needs. Agent bankers are authorized by Central Banks to offer selected bank products and specific services on behalf of a specific bank. Customers will be provided the opportunity to access financial products and services at the closest location. This breaks down geographical barriers and eases financial inclusion cutting costs and improving accessibility. This model is native to Kenya, the country where M-Pesa[17] the most successful mobile bank, was born and is operating with more than 8 million clients.

Agency banking is based on a business model that indirectly tries to shape a bridge between physical bank branching and bankless M-banking. Both strategies have pros and cons and tend to coexist, especially in sophisticated environments where choice is wider.

Agents can help MFIs operate more efficiently and increase their customer outreach if managed well.[18] A publication from the International Finance Corporation[19] based on its work with nine MFIs in Africa shows the cost of handling transactions via agents is about 25% lower than through branches.

Whereas M-banking is a strategy that is closer to the main thesis of this study—cutting costs and improving sustainability and outreach with innovation—physical branching is not, per se, a wrong or old-fashioned

[17] See Sect. 6.9.

[18] http://www.cgap.org/blog/6-ways-microfinance-institutions-can-adapt-digital-age.

[19] https://www.ifc.org/wps/wcm/connect/67a1ee9e-9f95-4baa-8430-2a101ca77a9e/MFI+Digital+Strategy+Field+Note_8.pdf?MOD=AJPERES.

strategy, and in some cases (e.g., professional loans, international operations, etc.) it may offer the necessary infrastructure for upgrading basic financial services.

Biometric identification cards lower barriers to account ownership (World Bank, 2017, p. 91).

4.11.1 Blockchains

The blockchain is a decentralized and distributed digital ledger that corresponds to an open database with a pattern of sharable and unmodifiable data that are sequenced in chronological order.

Practical applications go well beyond the controversial cryptocurrencies, even thanks to smart contracts and the digital scalability of innovative business models. Blockchain technology can be used for e-commerce or for the recording of copyright data or to track digital access.

Through the Internet of Value, transactions can be carried on without intermediaries, exploiting digital networks where different players interact, contributing to value co-creation.

The legal nature of the blockchain (public, private, or consortium) and its revenue-driven business model are prerequisites for the appraisal. Utilization value for adopters (regarding lower costs, higher reliability of data, etc.) should also be considered.

Blockchain[20] is a consequential list (chain) of blocks (records), linked using cryptography. Each block contains a cryptographic hash of the previous block, a timestamp, and transaction data (generally represented as a Merkle tree root hash[21]).

Blockchain could be regarded as a public ledger, in which all committed transactions are stored in a chain of blocks. This chain continuously grows when new blocks are appended to it. Blockchain technology has characteristics as decentralization, persistency, anonymity, verifiability,

[20] https://www.economist.com/briefing/2015/10/31/the-great-chain-of-being-sure-about-things. See also Mattila (2017).

[21] In cryptography and computer science, a hash tree or Merkle tree is a tree in which every leaf node is labeled with the hash of a data block and every non-leaf node is labeled with the cryptographic hash of the labels of its child nodes. Hash trees allow efficient and secure verification of the contents of large data structures. A Merkle tree is recursively defined as a binary tree of hash lists where the parent node is the hash of its children, and the leaf nodes are hashes of the original data blocks (https://en.wikipedia.org/wiki/Merkle_tree).

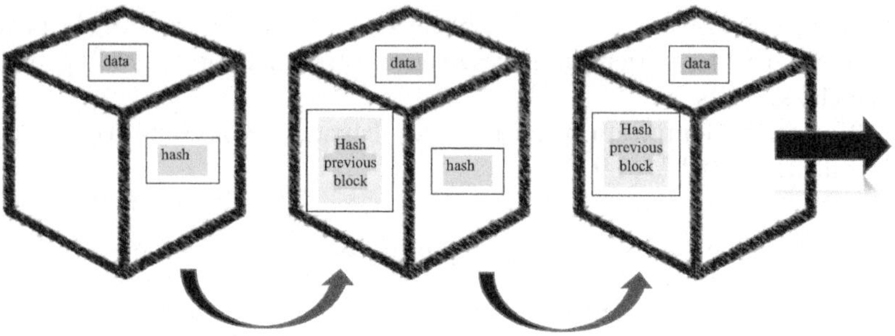

Fig. 4.9 Blockchain as a sequential chain of data

and auditability. It can be utilized to ensure the authenticity, reliability, and integrity of data and business activities. Blockchain can work in a decentralized environment, which is enabled by integrating several core technologies such as cryptographic hash, digital signature (based on asymmetric cryptography), and distributed consensus mechanism. With blockchain technology, a transaction can take place in a decentralized fashion. As a result, blockchain can greatly save the cost and improve efficiency (Figs. 4.9 and 4.10)[22]

The main chain (black) consists of the longest series of blocks from the genesis block (green) to the current block. Orphan blocks (purple) exist outside of the main chain.

A blockchain belongs to the distributed ledger (database) technologies and represents a process where many subjects share IT data to make a virtual database available to a community of users. In most cases, this database is public, and the community is open, even if there are examples

[22] https://www.henrylab.net/wp-content/uploads/2017/10/blockchain.pdf.

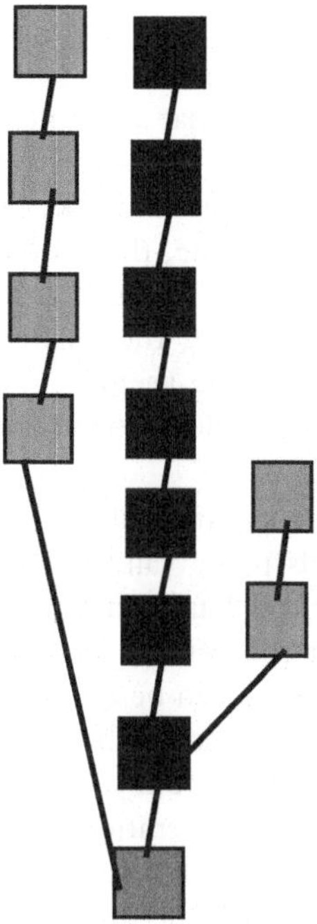

Fig. 4.10 Blockchain formation

of private[23] implementations where each participant has a copy of the data.

[23] There are different types of blockchain: some are open and public, and some are private and only accessible to people who are permitted to use them. A public blockchain is an open network. Anyone can download the protocol and read, write, or participate in the network. A public blockchain is distributed and decentralized. Transactions are recorded as blocks and linked together to form a chain. Each new block must be timestamped and validated by all the computers connected to the network, known as nodes, before it is written into the blockchain. All transactions are public, and all nodes are equal. This means a public blockchain is immutable: once verified, data cannot be altered. The best-known public blockchains used for cryptocurrency are Bitcoin and Ethereum: open-source, smart contract blockchains. A private blockchain is an invitation-only network governed by a single entity. Entrants to the network require permission to read, write or audit the blockchain. There can be different levels of access and information can be encrypted to protect commercial confidentiality. Private blockchains allow organizations to employ distributed ledger technology without making data public. But this means they lack a defining feature of blockchains: decentralization. Some critics claim private blockchains

A blockchain is mainly an open and distributed ledger that can memorize encrypted digital transactions (peer-to-peer)[24] between two counterparts in a secured way that is verifiable and permanent. Once recorded, the data within a block cannot be retroactively altered without any modification of the subsequent blocks. Due to the nature of the protocol and the validation scheme, this would require the consensus of most of the network participants (Norman et al., 2018), and this hypothesis is practically unfeasible, being the participants many, exponentially growing and hardly related among them.

In summary, blockchain has the following key characteristics[25]:

1. Decentralization. In conventional centralized transaction systems, each transaction needs to be validated through the central trusted agency (e.g., the Central Bank) inevitably causing cost and performance bottlenecks at the central servers. Differently, a transaction in the blockchain network can be conducted between any two peers (P2P) without authentication by the central agency. In this manner, blockchain can significantly reduce the server costs (including the development cost and the operation cost) and mitigate the performance bottlenecks at the central server.
2. Persistency. Since each of the transactions spreading across the network needs to be confirmed and recorded in blocks distributed in the whole network, it is nearly impossible to tamper. Additionally, each broadcasted block would be validated by other nodes and transactions would be checked. So, any falsification could be detected easily.
3. Anonymity. Each user can interact with the blockchain network with a generated address. Further, a user could generate many addresses to avoid identity exposure. There is no longer any central

are not blockchains at all, but centralized databases that use distributed ledger technology. Private blockchains are faster, more efficient and more cost-effective than public blockchains, which require a lot of time and energy to validate transactions (https://www.intheblack.com/articles/2018/09/05/difference-between-private-public-blockchain).

[24] Electronic money transfers made from one person to another through an intermediary, typically referred to as a P2P payment application. P2P payments can be sent and received via mobile device or any home computer with access to the Internet, offering a convenient alternative to traditional payment methods.

[25] https://www.henrylab.net/wp-content/uploads/2017/10/blockchain.pdf.

party keeping users' private information. This mechanism preserves a certain amount of privacy on the transactions included in the blockchain. Note that blockchain cannot guarantee perfect privacy preservation due to intrinsic constraint.
4. Auditability. Since each of the transactions on the blockchain is validated and recorded with a timestamp, users can easily verify and trace the previous records by accessing any node in the distributed network. In Bitcoin blockchain, each transaction could be traced to previous transactions iteratively. It improves the traceability and the transparency of the data stored in the blockchain.

The valuation shares similarities with other digital intangibles (database, Internet of Things, big data, etc.) and is primarily founded on the cost savings that derive from the use of blockchains. The valuation of blockchains can so be complemented with an estimate of the incremental value that they confer to traditional assets.

Technology can create a digital identity and provide efficient payment of microloans with smart contracts.[26] The storage of information that easily becomes big data is another property of blockchain technology. Transparency through distributed ledgers where each stakeholder democratically participates to value co-creation minimizes corruption with automation and digitization.

No physical branch presence is needed for blockchain to work. Since blockchain operates on a distributed network, there is no need for a complex and expensive private infrastructure to run. This saves on the costs that banks and telecom companies pass on to users through fees and other charges when using bank accounts or performing mobile transactions.

Secure identification of the lending and borrowing identities is another well-known property of blockchain technology. Such blockchain-based digital identities will allow borrowers to build their economic histories and credit profiles, even if they are invisible to the legacy banking system.

Blockchains can be linked to FinTechs and, eventually, to more basic microfinance activities,[27] contributing to fight poverty.[28]

[26] World Bank (2020).

[27] Davradakis and Santos (2019) and Fosso Wamba et al. (2020).

[28] Kshetri (2017).

4.11.2 *Internet of Value*

Innovation is a key element for the differentiation strategies of a company that contributes to making it unique, adopting Porter's competitive advantage that can bring to monopolistic rents.

With the Internet of Value, a value transaction can happen instantly, just as how people have been sharing words, images, and videos online for decades. And it is not just money. The Internet of Value will enable the exchange of any asset that is of value to someone, including stocks, votes, frequent flyer points, securities, intellectual property, music, scientific discoveries, and more.[29] Until now, selling, buying, or exchanging these assets has required an intermediary like a bank, marketplace (physical or digital), credit card company, or third-party booking service. Blockchain technology allows assets to be transferred from one party directly to another, with no middleman. The transfer is validated, permanent, and completed instantly.

Blockchain contributes to a new generation of web patterns (Internet of Value) that consist of a digital network that transfers value, being built on open standards.

The corporate use of blockchains contributes to product and process innovation, with a positive impact on the supply chain (Saberi et al., 2018; Korpela et al., 2017; Dujak & Sajter, 2019), exploiting the big data.

The blockchain can also generate a value increase of the digital platforms (B2B, B2C ...), through its secured transactions, so representing an e-commerce facilitator.

The intangibles linked to physical objects through the Internet incorporate a higher added value, since they can exploit their digital networking attitudes. The connectivity among different and heterogeneous objects, even though the network-web as a virtual platform of exchange, represents leverage for value creation especially if the intangibles synergistically interact within an Intellectual Property (IP) portfolio.

The sharing economy is an economic model often defined as a peer-to-peer (P2P)-based activity of acquiring part, providing, or sharing access to goods and services that are facilitated by a community-based online platform. Information is exchanged through (virtual) communities that exchange data mainly through digital platforms linked to social networks.

[29] https://ripple.com/insights/the-internet-of-value-what-it-means-and-how-it-benefits-everyone/.

Monopolies dominate the current sharing economy, and markets like this are ripe for disruption. The emergence of blockchain cuts out middlemen so savvy startups can create headaches for the likes of Uber and Airbnb.[30]

For what concerns the intangible capital, one area that seems particularly promising for blockchain is represented by value co-creation and open innovation.

There are meaningful correlations between the blockchains and the FinTech applications or artificial intelligence that influences the workings of blockchains and payment systems with its machine learning patterns.

4.11.3 Linking Blockchains to Social Networks and P2P Lending

Blockchains can be ideally linked to social networks that interact and fuel them with information. Network structures are variegated and only the sequential network resembles the pattern of a blockchain.

Networks can be centralized, decentralized, or distributed. Decentralization is a property of public blockchains (Fig. 4.11).

Blockchain lending essentially builds on the timeless peer-to-peer model, making the entire process more seamless and reducing the amount of time the process takes. The middleman (a bank) is cast aside, and individual borrowers or businesses are connected directly to willing lenders. The great value of such decentralized lending is that with a single request, a borrower can access very competitive financing, as geography is not constrained on a blockchain platform, lenders from all over the world can bid to provide the loan. Thanks to smart contracts and oracle technology, lenders can validate transactions, verify the legitimacy of counterparties, and perform routine account administration tasks almost momentarily, reducing costs and accelerating the process.[31]

Blockchain technology provides decentralized consensus and potentially enlarges the contracting space using smart contracts with tamper-proof and algorithmic executions (Cong & He, 2018).

[30] https://coincentral.com/sharing-economy-companies-are-set-to-be-disrupted-by-blockchain/.

[31] https://medium.com/trivial-co/lending-and-borrowing-on-the-blockchain-should-banks-be-scared-e0a01c857c43.

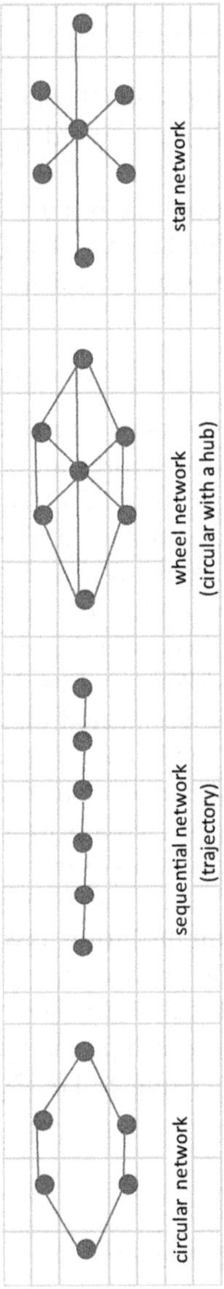

Fig. 4.11 Network structures

A blockchain oracle[32] is a third-party information source that has the sole function of supplying data to blockchains which permits the creation of smart contracts. A smart contract at a fundamental level is simply a self-executing piece of code; smart contracts evaluate incoming data from an oracle and initiate a flow of execution depending on the information received.

4.12 The Intangible Portfolio

Big data, blockchains, artificial intelligence, and digital networks represent complementary trendy intangibles that rotate around microfinance, FinTech, and MicroFinTech applications.

They form a comprehensive intangible portfolio, with interactions and synergies (represented in Fig. 4.12.) that are still largely unexplored.

Synergies are enhanced by the networking digital platform that brings together the information vehiculated by big data, certified by blockchains, and interpreted with artificial intelligence patterns.

4.13 Startup Microfinancing

Startup activities represent the base of microenterprises. Access to capital is traditionally difficult for startup initiatives and is increasingly so when collateral assets do not exist, track record of credit history is missing, and short-term repayment installments traditionally used in microfinance do not match for longer-term business needs.

Despite these difficulties, startup microfinancing is looked for by young entrepreneurs. Traditional MFIs may be complemented by other specialized investors, such as:

[32] Oracles (https://www.mycryptopedia.com/blockchain-oracles-explained/) provide additional functionality to smart contracts by providing a means for them to communicate outside of a decentralized blockchain network. Blockchain oracles can take on numerous forms, some of those forms include but are not limited to:

- Software oracles;
- Hardware oracles;
- Inbound oracles;
- Outbound oracles;
- Consensus-based oracles.

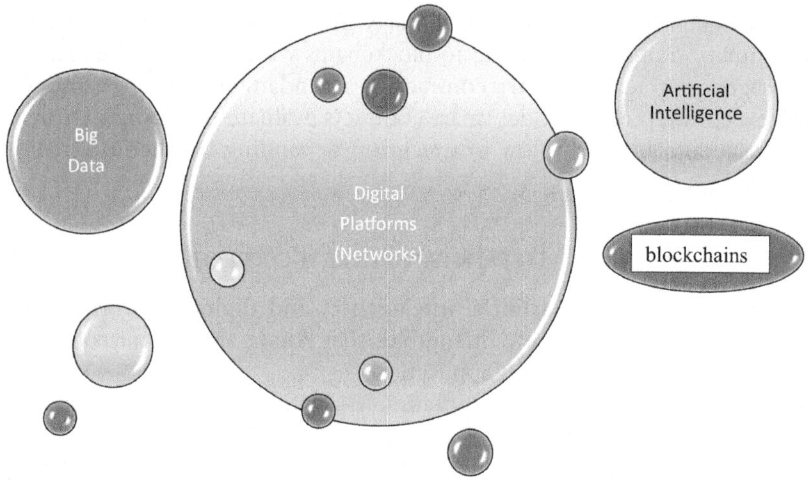

Fig. 4.12 The synergistic intangibles portfolio

- Crowdfunding platforms that may provide equity and, later on, debt;
- Incubators and mentors;
- Venture capitalists and private equity funds, after the early stage.

Figure 4.13 shows a possible evolution of the business and its financial backers.

Startups are typically debt-free since they are unable to produce positive cash flows or to provide adequate asset-backed guarantees in the first years of their life. Raised capital is so mainly represented by equity, and its

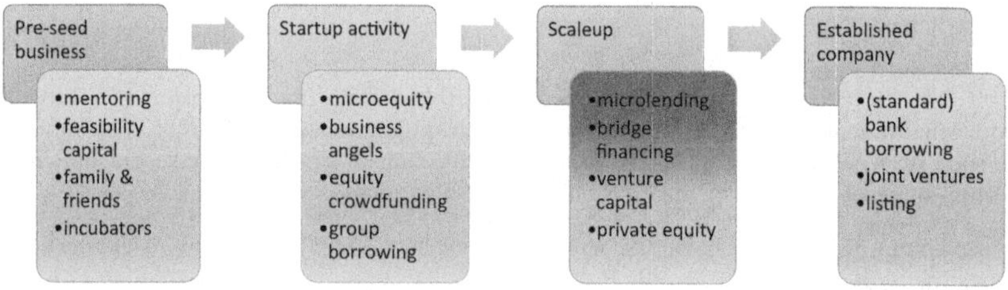

Fig. 4.13 Business evolution and financial investors

monetary component is the cash reservoir that keeps the firm alive until it reaches a liquidity surplus.

As shown in Moro Visconti (2021), debt-free startups have some peculiarities in their accounts:

- in the balance sheet raised capital (funds) tend to coincide with equity;
- in the income statement, EBIT is similar to the net result (considering that interest rates are nonexistent, and taxes also, due to a negative tax base);
- in the cash flow statement, the operating cash flow tends to coincide with the net cash flow;
- In the absence of the cost of debt, the cost of capital (WACC) coincides with the cost of equity.

The difference between a traditional firm and a startup economic, financial, and balance sheet system can be represented in Fig. 4.14.

This representation may be considered too sophisticated for small and informal newborn businesses with no accounting backbone, but still constitutes a benchmark and a mighty target that can inspire new entrepreneurial activities.

Cash flow forecasting is crucial to estimate the financial breakeven (runway cash flow), combining the EBITDA generated (or absorbed) by the startup with its change in net working capital and CAPEX.

Whenever the microenterprise grows and passes from the startup to the scaleup phase, equity injection can be accompanied by debt that becomes sustainable thanks to the self-generated internal liquidity, proxied by a positive EBITDA.

Seasoning startups can afford to collect debt whenever they start creating positive cash, build up worthy collateral assets, and soften information asymmetries.

Technology can represent a growth catalyzer, easing business plan simulation, and providing cost-cutting solutions.

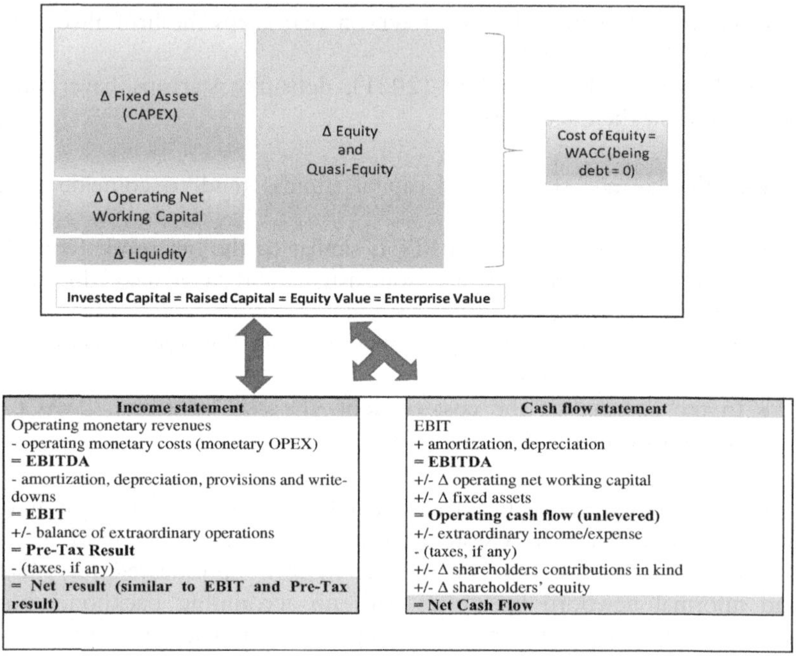

Fig. 4.14 Interactions of income statement and variations of the balance sheet to produce the cash flow statement in a debt-free startup

References

AFI. (2018). Digital transformation of microfinance and digitization of microfinance services to deepen financial inclusion in Africa. Available at https://www.afi-global.org/publications/2830/Digital-Transformation-of-Microfinance-Digitization-of-Microfinance-Services-to-Deepen-Financial-Inclusion-in-Africa.

Agrawal, P., & Sen, S. (2017). Digital economy and microfinance. *The MIBM Research Journal*, *5*(1), 27–35.

Altinok, A. (2018). *Group lending, sorting, and risk sharing*. Available at https://www.researchgate.net/publication/324953074_Group_Lending_Sorting_and_Risk_Sharing.

Armendariz De Aghion, B. A., & Morduch, J. (2010). *The economics of microfinance*. MIT press.

Ashta, A. (Eds.). (2011). *Advanced technologies for microfinance*. IGI Global.

Ashta, A. (2012). Co-creation for impact investment in microfinance. *Strategic Change, 21*, 71–81.

Banerjee, A., Duflo, E., Glennerster, R., & Kinnan, C. (2015). The miracle of microfinance? Evidence from a randomized valuation. *American Economic Journal: Applied Economics, 7*(1), 22–53.

Barabási, A. (2016). *Network science*. Cambridge University Press.

Barnett, B. (2011, October). *Cloud computing & financial services for the poor*. Usaid. Available at https://Www.Microfinancegateway.Org/Sites/Default/Files/Mfg-En-Toolkit-Cloud-Computing-Financial-Services-For-The-Poor-Primer-Procurement-Guidance-Oct-2011.Pdf.

Bazarbash, M. (2019). *FinTech in financial inclusion: Machine learning applications in assessing credit risk* (IMF Working Papers, Wp/19/109). Available at https://www.imf.org/en/Publications/WP/Issues/2019/05/17/FinTech-in-Financial-Inclusion-Machine-Learning-Applications-in-Assessing-Credit-Risk-46883.

Budampati, S. (2018). Impact of Information technology on microfinance industry. *Advanced Science and Technology Letters, 150*, 116–121.

Collins, D., Murdoch, J., Rutherford, S., & Ruthven, O. (2009). *Portfolios of the poor: How the world's poor live on $2 a day*. Princeton University Press.

Cong, L. W., & He, Z. (2018, April). *Blockchain disruption and smart contracts* (NBER Working Paper no. 24399).

CSFI. (2011). *Microfinance banana skins 2011*. Available at www.cgap.org/p/site/c/template.rc/1.9.49643/.

Davradakis, E., & Santos, R. (2019). *Blockchain, FinTechs and their relevance for international financial institutions* (EIB Working Papers no. 2019/01). European Investment Bank.

de Oliveira Leite, R., dos Santos Mendes, L., & Sacramento, L. C. (2019). To profit or not to profit? Assessing financial sustainability outcomes of microfinance institutions. *International Journal of Finance & Economics, 24*(3), 1287–1299.

Demirguc-Kunt, A., Klapper, L., Singer, D., Ansar, S., & Hess, J. (2018). *The Global Findex Database 2017: Measuring financial inclusion and the FinTech revolution*. Available at http://documents1.worldbank.org/curated/en/332881525873182837/pdf/126033-PUB-PUBLIC-pubdate-4-19-2018.pdf.

Dorfleitner, G., Hornuf, L., Schmitt, M., & Weber, M. (2017). *FinTech in Germany*. Springer Verlag.

Dujak, D,. & Sajter, D. (2019). *Blockchain applications in supply chain*. Springer Verlag.

Ernst & Young. (2019). *FinTech ecosystem playbook*. Available at https://www.ey.com/Publication/vwLUAssets/EY-fintech-ecosystem-playbook/$FILE/EY-fintech-ecosystem-playbook.pdf.

European Commission. (2020). *Microfinance in the European Union: Market analysis and recommendations for delivery options in 2021–2027*. Available at https://ec.europa.eu/social/main.jsp?catId=738&langId=en&pubId=8347&furtherPubs=yes.

Fanconi, P., & Scheurle, P. (2017). *Small money—Big impact: Fighting poverty with microfinance*. Wiley.

Fosso Wamba, S., Kala Kamdjoug, J. R., Bawack, R., & Keogh, J. (2020), Bitcoin, blockchain, and FinTech: A systematic review and case studies in the supply chain. *Production Planning and Control, 31*(2–3), 115–142.

Gander, J. (2015). *Designing digital business models*. Kingston University.

GSMA. (2019). *Mobile money: Key success factors of a National Financial Inclusion Strategy*. Available at https://www.gsma.com/mobilefordevelopment/wp-content/uploads/2019/03/GSMA_Key-Success-Factors-of-a-National-Financial-Inclusion-Strategy-1.pdf.

Gupta, A., Christie, R., & Manjula, R. (2017). Scalability in internet of things: Features, techniques and research challenges. *International Journal of Computational Intelligence Research, 13*(7), 1617–1627.

Gutiérrez-Nieto, B., & Serrano-Cinca, C. (2019). 20 years of research in microfinance: An information management approach. *International Journal of Information Management, 47*, 183–197.

Jin, X., Wah, B. W., Cheng, X., & Wang, Y. (2015). Significance and challenges of big data research. *Big Data Research, 2*(2), 59–64.

Kaicer, M. (2020). Information technology performance management by artificial intelligence in microfinance institutions: An overview. *International Journal of Computational Intelligence Studies, 9*(3), 186–189.

Kauffman, R. J., & Riggins, F. J. (2012). Information and communication technology and the sustainability of microfinance. *Electronic Commerce Research and Applications, 11*(5), 450–468.

Korpela, K., Hallikas, J., & Dahlber, T. (2017). *Digital supply chain transformation toward blockchain integration*. Paper presented at the 50*th* Hawaii International conference on system sciences (p. 4182).

Kshetri, N. (2017). Potential roles of blockchain in fighting poverty and reducing financial exclusion in the global South. *Journal of Global Information Technology Management, 20*(4), 201–204.

Kumar, K., McKay, C., & Rotman, S. (2010). *Microfinance and mobile banking: The story so far*. Available at https://www.cgap.org/sites/default/files/CGAP-Focus-Note-Microfinance-and-Mobile-Banking-The-Story-So-Far-Jul-2010.pdf.

Lui, P. T., (2016). *Medical record system using blockchain, big data and tokenization*. Paper presented at the Information and Communications security: 18th International Conference (pp. 254–261).

Mann, L. (2017). Left to other peoples' devices? A political economy perspective on the big data revolution in development. *Development and Change, 49*(1), 3–36.

Mattila, J. (2017). *The blockchain phenomenon. The disruptive potential of distributed consensus architectures*. Available at https://brie.berkeley.edu/sites/default/files/juri-mattila-.pdf.

Mia, M. A. (2020). Technological change and innovations in microfinance institutions: What matters? *Global Business Review, 17*(5), 1179–1195.

Moro Visconti, R. (2020). *The valuation of digital intangibles. Technology, marketing and internet*. Palgrave Macmillan.

Moro Visconti, R. (2021). *Startup valuation*. Palgrave Macmillan.

Moro Visconti, R., Larocca, A., & Marconi, M. (2017). Big data-driven value chains and digital platforms: From value co-creation to monetization. In A. K. Somani & G. Deka (Eds.), *Bigdata analytics: Tools, technology for effective planning*. CRC Press.

Mushtaq, R., & Bruneau, C. (2019). Microfinance, financial inclusion and ICT: Implications for poverty and inequality. *Technology in Society, 59*, 663–686.

Mwashiuya, H. T., & Mbamba, U. O. L. (2018). Relationship between information communication technology adoption in microfinance institutions and access to financial services. *International Journal of Research, 5*(4), 264–280.

Norman, M. D., Karavas, Y. G., & Reed, H. (2018, June 4). *The emergence of trust and value in public blockchain networks* (Working Paper). http://s3.amazonaws.com/arenaattachments/2332393/536b3b1208a6debfa6eaf5b9c9c9187a.pdf?1529445044.

Nourani, M., Malim, M., & Mia, M. A. (2020). Revisiting efficiency of microfinance institutions (MFIs): An application of network data envelopment analysis. *Economic Research—Ekonomska Istraživanja, 34*, 1146–1169.

Paul, E., et al. (2018). Performance-based financing in low-income and middle-income countries: Isn't it time for a rethink? *BMJ Global Health, 3*(1).

Pedrini, M., Bramanti, V., Minciullo, M., & Ferri, M. L. (2016). Rethinking microfinance for developed countries. *Journal of International Development, 28*(2), 281–302.

Postelnicu, L., Hermes, N., & Szafarz, A. (2014). Defining social collateral in microfinance group lending. In R. Mersland & R. Ø. Strøm (Eds.), *Microfinance institutions*. Palgrave Studies in Impact Finance. Palgrave Macmillan.

Pythowska, J., & Korynski, P. (2017). *Digitalizing microfinance in Europe*. Available at https://www.european-microfinance.org/sites/default/files/document/file/Digitalization-research-paper.pdf.

Reinhardt, R., Hietschold, N., & Gurtner, S. (2019). Overcoming consumer resistance to innovations—An analysis of adoption triggers. *R&D Management, 49*(2), 139–154.

Riggins, F., & Weber, D. M. (2016). Exploring the impact of information and communication technology (ICT) on intermediation market structure in the microfinance industry. *The African Journal of Information Systems*, *8*(3).

Russel, J. & Norvig, P. (2015). *Artificial intelligence. A modern approach*. Pearson.

Saberi, S., Kouhizadeh, M., Sarkis, J., & Shen, L. (2018). Blockchain technology and its relationships to sustainable supply chain management. *International Journal of production researching*, 2117–2135.

Sarkar, S., & Alvari, H. (2018). Mitigating bias in online microfinance platforms: A case study on Kiva.org. In I. Koprinska et al. (Eds.), *ECML PKDD 2020 workshops*. Communications in Computer and Information Science (Vol. 1323). Springer Verlag.

Shah, S., Rahman, M., & Khan, J. A. (2019). The mediating role of group lending between poverty and microfinance. *NICE Research Journal of Social Science*, *12*(2).

Sharma, S. K., & Al-Muharrami, S. (2018). Mobile banking adoption: Key challenges and opportunities and implications for a developing country. In Y. Dwivedi et al. (Eds.), *Emerging markets from a multidisciplinary perspective. Advances in theory and practice of emerging markets*. Springer Verlag.

Sharma, S., Singh, P., Singh, K., & Chauhan, B. (2017). Group lending model—A panacea to reduce transaction cost? *Zagreb International Review of Economics and Business, 20*(2), 46–63.

Srinivas, V., & Mahal, R. (2017, September). Digital transformation: The next big leap in microfinance, *PARIDNYA. The MIBM Research Journal, 5*(1).

Sun, S. L., & Liang, H. (2021). Globalization and affordability of microfinance. *Journal of Business Venturing, 36*(1), 1–18.

Sundaresan, S. (2009). *Microfinance emerging trends and challenges*. Edward Elgar.

Tomic, V., & Stojanovic, D. (2018). *Trends and innovations in mobile banking*. Available at https://www.researchgate.net/publication/330468035.

Usman, G., Tahseen, B. M., & Naseeb, A. (2018). The impact of technology on the sustainable development of microfinance. *Global Sci-Tech, 10*(1), 22–29.

Vandeputte, P., & De Toffol, B. (2017). *The rmicrofinance institutions in Western Europe: A qualitative study*. Louvain School of Managemole of FinTechs in the business model of ent, Université Catholique de Louvain. Available at http://hdl.handle.net/2078.1/thesis:11338.

World Bank. (2017). *The Global Findex Database. Measuring financial inclusion and the FinTech revolution*. Available at http://documents.worldbank.org/curated/en/332881525873182837/The-Global-Findex-Database-2017-Measuring-Financial-Inclusion-and-the-Fintech-Revolution.

World Bank. (2020). *Smart contract technology and financial inclusion*. Available at https://openknowledge.worldbank.org/bitstream/handle/10986/

33723/Smart-Contract-Technology-and-Financial-Inclusion.pdf?sequence=1&isAllowed=y.

Yunus, M., & Jolis, A. (1999). *Banker to the poor: Micro-lending and the battle against world poverty*. PublicAffairs.

Zamore, S., Beisland, L. A., & Mersland, R. (2021). Excessive focus on risk? Non-performing loans and efficiency of microfinance institutions. *International Journal of Finance and Economics*, 1–18. Available at https://onlinelibrary.wiley.com/doi/full/10.1002/ijfe.2477.

CHAPTER 5

Fintechs

The supply chain/business model canvas anticipated in the introduction is recalled in Fig. 5.1.

5.1 Fintech Applications

While FinTechs are disrupting the formal financial sector in developed countries, their ability to provide ubiquitous and low-cost access to financial services is seen as a key enabler for financial inclusion in developing countries. Technology is the way to go. Despite the obstacles along the way of digitalization, microfinance institutions will be able to reap the benefits from the adoption of FinTechs (Dang, 2020; Vandeputte & De Toffol, 2017).

FinTech covers digital innovations and technology-enabled business model innovations in the financial sector. Such innovations[1] can disrupt existing industry structures and blur industry boundaries, facilitate strategic disintermediation, revolutionize how existing firms create and deliver products and services, provide new gateways for entrepreneurship, democratize access to financial services, but also create significant privacy, regulatory, and law enforcement challenges. Examples of innovations that are central to FinTech today include cryptocurrencies and

[1] See Anikina et al., (2016).

R. Moro-Visconti, *MicroFinTech*, Palgrave Studies in Financial Services Technology, https://doi.org/10.1007/978-3-030-80394-0_5

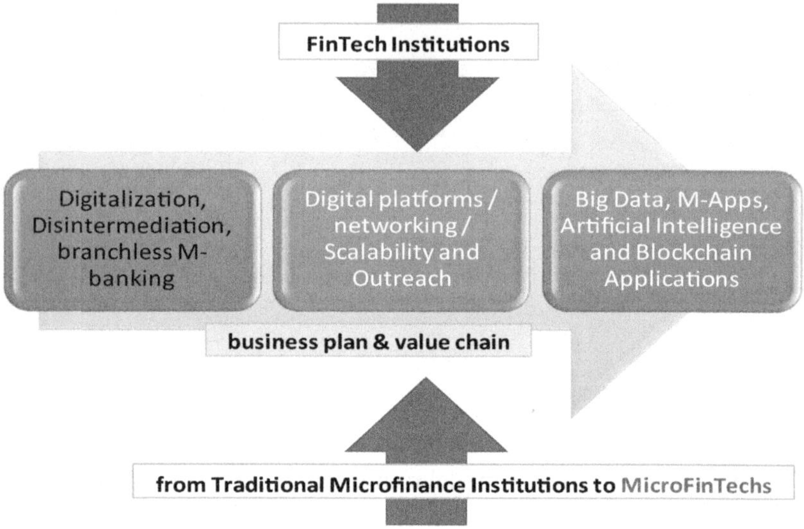

Fig. 5.1 The Impact of Technology on Microfinance

the blockchain, new digital advisory and trading systems, artificial intelligence and machine learning, peer-to-peer lending, equity crowdfunding, and mobile payment systems.[2]

Financial technology (FinTech) is an industry composed of diversified companies that use technology to make financial services more efficient.

FinTech is recognized as one of the most critical innovations in the financial industry and is evolving at a rapid speed, driven in part by the sharing economy, favorable regulation, and information technology. FinTech promises to disrupt and reshape the financial industry by cutting costs, improving the quality of financial services, and creating a more diverse and stable financial landscape.

With the advances in e-finance and mobile technologies for financial firms, FinTech innovation emerged after the worldwide financial crisis in 2008 by combining e-finance, internet technologies, social networking services, social media[3], artificial intelligence, and big data analytics.

[2] See Philippon, 2019a, b.

[3] See Daowd et al., (2020).

Technological startups include companies operating in the Financial Technology segment (FinTech), providing services and financial products with ICT technologies. FinTechs reformulate business models, making use of innovative software and algorithms, value chains based on interactive computer platforms, artificial intelligence, and big data. Software as a Service (SaaS) can be useful for MFIs that rely on flexible external devices[4].

Financial services, which focus on the transmission of information on digital platforms, rely on innovative activities concerning the processing of data and their interpretation in real-time with automated descriptive, prescriptive, and predictive technologies.

FinTech has become a hot term due to many forces, which include technical development, business innovation expectations (market), cost-saving requirements, and customer demands (Gai et al., 2018). Other factors concern the regulatory framework and the macroeconomic scenario characterized by low-interest rates, leading to a reduction of the institutions' profitability, and promoting investments aimed to increase the organizations' efficiency (Piobbici et al., 2019).

FinTech refers to a vast and diverse industry that disrupts the industry, solving friction points for consumers and businesses. It can also impact the circular economy (Pizzi et al., 2021).

The banking industry is facing radical transformation and restructuring, as well as a move toward a customer-centric platform-based model. The competition will increase as new players enter the industry, but the long-term impact is more open. The regulation will decisively influence to what extent BigTech will enter the industry and who the dominant players will be. The challenge for regulators will be to keep a level playing field that strikes the right balance between fostering innovation and preserving financial stability. Consumer protection concerns rise to the forefront (Vives, 2019).

The main areas of activity are (Haddad & Hornuf, 2019; Gai et al., 2018):

- Financial technologies applied to blockchains and distributed ledger technology based on data archives, whose records are public on a computer network and without the need for a central register;

[4] See Ashta & Patel (2010).

- Crypto and digital money;
- Peer-to-peer loans (P2P)[5];
- Smart contracts (using the blockchain) that automatically execute contracts between buyers and sellers;
- Open banking supported by the blockchain applications that create a service through a connected network of financial institutions and third-party providers.
- IT security, through or decentralized storage of data, and anti-fraud systems;
- Applications in the insurance field (InsurTech) or regulation (RegTech);
- Asset management (robo-advice, social trading, wealth management, personal financial management apps, or software).
- The FinTech revolution captures the simultaneous attack of technologies like mobile telephones and blockchain, outreaching niche markets. Banks may freeze, fight, form alliances with challengers, or be forced into flight by the BigTech (Ashta, Biot-Paquerot, 2018). FinTech applications may concern alternative finance (through online marketplaces that host crowdfunding, P2P lending, invoice trading, payment platforms, etc.), blockchain technology, InsurTech, and apps for financial inclusion, smart payments, and transfers, etc.
- FinTech or financial services technology is broadly defined as any technological innovation in financial services leading to using digital technologies that transform business models to generate new revenues and value-adding opportunities. These digital tools often disrupt established business models by creating new and efficient means of providing services. Financial technology leads to the digitalization of internal processes, customer interactions with financial institutions, and digital financial products like digital credit or deposits. New organizations have the advantage of being "digital natives" and be able to create an environment for a digital business whereby digital information is at the core, while the older ones need to digitize the content and re-organize the old processes by using digital solutions. In the context of financial inclusion, FinTech brings many opportunities (Arner et al., 2018; Bernards,

[5] Riggins & Weber (2017).

2019; Makina, 2019; Ravikumar, 2019; Thomas and Hedrick-Wong, 2019). Adopting financial technology has large potential to financially include people whom the traditional methods failed to reach. More and more traditional banks, MFIs, and developmental organizations make use of financial technology to deliver their services. FinTech opens channels to include a considerable number of excluded individuals and smaller companies, offering solutions that can be applied at scale. In microfinance, often referred to like people- and paper-intensive industry, digital solutions could allow for speedy credit decisions and loan disbursal, releasing loan officers' time to serve more clients in more places than ever before. Equipping MFIs with technology allows the institutions to work more efficiently and cost-effectively, be more agile, and responsive to the client's needs[6].

- MicroFinTech is a neologism that describes financial technology (FinTech) applications to microfinance (Dang, 2020).
- FinTech refers to the use of software and digital platforms to deliver financial services to consumers. These digital tools often disrupt established business models by creating new and efficient means of providing services. FinTech applications are so fully consistent with the research question of this study. FinTech can re-engineer business models, revolutionizing (and often bypassing) back office, middle office, and front office operations of MFI, with consequent economic savings and increased resilience of the supply chain.
- Business models are going to be disrupted, re-engineered, and rebuilt from scratch by technology, following a Schumpeterian pattern. This is the case especially in the banking industry, from which microfinance derives most of its business modeling ideas. Catalytic innovations are involved in satisfying the consumers' unmet needs through low-cost, simpler models.
- Access to financial products is becoming more attainable, with consequent improvements in credit inclusion, especially for unbanked households located in remote rural areas. FinTech makes financial products cheaper and more accessible, lowering operating costs for MFI. To the extent that part of these savings (after guaranteeing

[6] Pytkowska & Korynski (2017).

better sustainability for the MFI) can be passed on to consumers, outreach directly improves, to the benefit of unbanked customers.

- Digital payments like the ones with M-banking are a fundamental component of FinTech applications.
- The digital revolution is probably the greatest boon to financial inclusion, and the rise of FinTech along with blockchain, regulatory sandboxes, and other innovations that support FinTech speaks to this dominance in financial ecosystems[7].
- Global Findex data reveal many opportunities to increase account ownership among the 1.7 billion adults who remain unbanked. New products and technologies can boost the use of accounts among those who already have one (World Bank, 2017; chapter 6).
- Blockchain and distributed ledger technology have the potential to universally reshape the way business transacts across nearly every industry. The key benefit of blockchain technology is the distributed infrastructure's ability to share secure information and provide for the unalterable transfer of data—ensuring data integrity. This makes the technology an important tool in building trust among businesses and consumers. Both can provide and access accurate data about transactions across nearly every financial service industry from retail banking to insurance to investment banking. Even microfinance can use blockchain technology to secure digital payments, minimizing the need for middlemen. Lack of trust and knowledge in MFIs is a major cause for the non-adoption of its services. Blockchain technology can secure payments, solving part of these problems since it relies on shared trust, rather than on a centralized institution that is unknown and potentially mistrusted by the potential customer.
- Another important technological application that is typically used within FinTech devices is represented by Mobile Apps (M-Apps). A Mobile App or mobile application is a computer program designed to run on a mobile device such as a phone/tablet or watch.
- Mobile applications often stand in contrast to desktop applications which run on desktop computers, and web applications that run in mobile web browsers rather than directly on the mobile device.

[7] https://www.developmentbookshelf.com/doi/full/10.3362/1755-1986.2018.29-2.ED.

- M-Apps normally run on smartphones, but they can be used also with less sophisticated mobile phones, more diffused in backward environments. M-Apps can guarantee last-mile connectivity, easing contacts with remote users. They are a fundamental component of M-banking strategies.
- Intuitive and ready-to-use apps, tailor-made for the needs of basic clients, represent an important bridge toward the application of technology, in a microfinance relationship where the MFI needs to have direct and simple contact with the customer.

Figure 5.2 contains a complementary taxonomy of the main FinTech

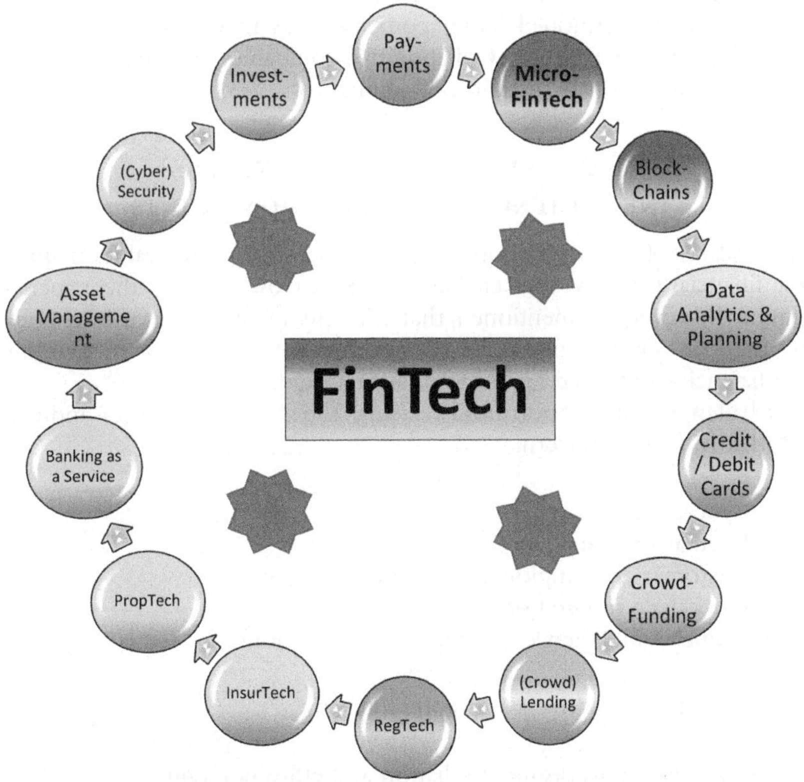

Fig. 5.2 Main FinTech Activities

areas.

While cryptocurrencies raise several questions, including the lack of market transparency, controls, and money laundering, other blockchain applications are based on more solid perspectives.

The valuation issues of FinTech companies must be adapted to often young companies, given the novelty of the sector, which have all the prerogatives of startups (in terms of expected growth, survival rate, volatility, etc. ...). The valuation methodologies must consider first the underlying business model.

According to Accenture (2016), there are two types of FinTech companies: competitive and collaborative. Competitive companies are mature firms, not necessarily specializing in FinTech, looking to squeeze out new competitors applying lower prices. In this case, it would be any of the previously mentioned larger companies, as they make up the bulk of investments in FinTech. Collaborative companies are those that offer services to enhance the position of competitors.

5.2 Financial Bottlenecks: Inefficiencies and Friction Points

An analysis of the main bottlenecks of the supply and value chain of the financial industry goes far beyond the narrow scope of this paper. It might, however, be mentioned that frictions increase the costs charged to the consumers, burdening the intermediation process with undue inefficiencies and longer passages that fuel rigidity.

Challenges and opportunities facing the financial services industry (Burlakov, 2019) concern:

- Cybercrime threats;
- Regulatory compliance;
- Customer and employee retention;
- Blockchain integration;
- Artificial intelligence and big data applications.

Two main value drivers are represented by:

a) Savings due to disintermediation and efficiency gains;
b) Improved availability and fungibility of access to the services.

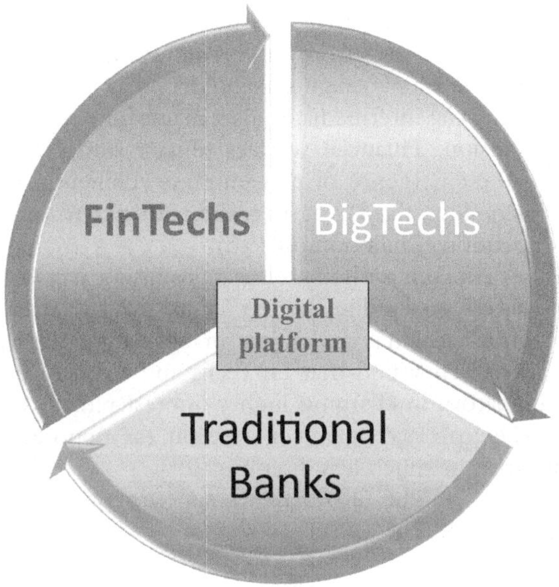

Fig. 5.3 Interaction of FinTech with BigTechs and Traditional Banks

Cheaper and always available financial services substantially increase the perceived value for money for the consumers and the other stakeholders that form the financial ecosystem, fostering its long-term sustainability[8]. The joint impact of savings and improved fungibility is likely to have a scalable impact in terms of client outreach. Higher volumes (due to more frequent negotiations and a wider set of products) may partially offset lower margins for traditional banking intermediaries (Fig. 5.3).

Bottlenecks determine the throughput of a supply chain. Recognizing this fact and making improvements will increase the cash flow. A bottleneck (or constraint) in a supply chain means the resource that requires the longest time in operations of the supply chain for certain demands.

Financial bottlenecks are intrinsic in the supply chain design, where intermediation is a long labor-intensive process. Each additional chain increases the marginal costs eventually charged to the final user and makes the whole supply chain more rigid. Digital applications contribute to

[8] See Al Hammadi & Nobanee (2019).

shortening the supply chain that also becomes more resilient. Positive economic marginality derives from this reengineering process and should be shared among the supply chain stakeholders that include consumers.

The cost of financial intermediation is a major bottleneck and a source of financial exclusion. Financial services remain surprisingly expensive, which explains the emergence of new entrants (Philippon, 2019a). This cost has declined since the Great Recession, thanks to technology and increased competition (Philippon, 2019b).

The advent of FinTech is often seen as a promising avenue for reducing inequality in access to credit. Bartlett et al. (2018) study this issue, analyzing the role of FinTech lenders in alleviating discrimination in mortgage markets. They find that FinTechs and face-to-face lenders are equally discriminatory in charging higher interest rates from minorities. However, in the loan accept/reject decision (as opposed to pricing), FinTechs appear to be much less discriminatory.

FinTech lenders might also have a superior ability for screening borrowers (Berg et al., 2019).

5.3 FinTech Business Models

A business model describes the rationale for how an organization creates, delivers, and captures value.

FinTech is an elastic business that can concentrate on market niches and specific customer segments, leveraging an innovative use of (big) data.

There are several common business model elements: value proposition, target customer, distribution channel, relationship, value configuration, core competency, partner network, cost structure, and revenue model. Value propositions provide information on what products and services a company is offering. Target customer describes to whom the company intends to offer its products and services, i.e., the value; distribution channels are the means and ways of how a company reaches out to its customers; and relationship refers to the links a company creates between its target customers and itself. These three elements (target customer, distribution channel, relationship) can also be subsumed under the customer interface. Value configuration is how resources are arranged about a company's activities; core competencies highlight the competencies that are needed to carry out the (desired) business model. Partner networks are the company's cooperation with other actors that are needed to co-create value. Value configuration, core competency, and partner network can be categorized further as infrastructure management. Finally, the last two elements of a business model highlight financial aspects. The cost structure describes the "monetary consequences" for a business model to operate, and the revenue model is the way the company receives money from its revenue streams.

FinTechs can complementarily be a:

a) A catalyzer/upgrader (digital enabler) of traditional business models, bringing to efficiency gains and pollinating the activity of ordinary banks or other financial intermediaries;
b) A pioneer of innovative products and services, normally through a B2B channel.

Table 5.1 synthesizes the FinTechs main typologies and business models (see also Tanda & Schena, 2019; Das, 2019).

Although the adoption of IT has significantly decreased the operational expenses of financial companies in the past, it seems that the adoption of innovative technologies reduces them even more. Technologies have considerably impacted the costs of running a physical infrastructure or a "branch," the costs of storing sensitive data, and finally on the IT investment, development, and maintenance costs (Vandeputte & De Toffol, 2017).

The era of mobile devices is slowly undermining the advantages of the physical distribution of financial services (Dietz et al., 2016).

The shifting customer preferences toward ubiquitous banking services is reducing high touchpoints between clients and branch employees. Moreover, a high number of customer-facing transactions are being replaced by immediate, automated digital functions (du Toit & Burns, 2016). By cutting out a part of their intermediaries, financial institutions avoid substantial costs such as property rentals and payroll. Consequently, significant cost savings are made and are passed on to the customers in the form of lower interest rates (Dietz et al., 2016).

Besides lowering operational costs, FinTechs boost the performance of the remaining branches by reassigning branch employees to the core and higher-value activities (Broeders & Khanna, 2015; du Toit & Burns, 2016).

FinTechs are central to streamline operational capabilities within a financial service firm. On the one hand, the partial or full automation

Table 5.1 FinTech typologies and business models

Typology	*Business Model*
Financing solutions	Pure equity crowdfunding (retail); club deals; funding from institutional investors
Blockchain	The blockchain is a decentralized and distributed digital ledger that corresponds to an open database with a pattern of sharable and unmodifiable data that are sequenced in chronological order. The main applications are cryptocurrencies; banking and payments; cyber-security; supply chain management; forecasting; networking & IoT; insurance; private transport & ride-sharing; cloud storage; charity; voting; healthcare; and crowdfunding
Payment systems and processing (PayTech)	Credit cards; mobile payments through apps; virtual POS; online wallet; and money transfers. Payment innovations throughout the year have been largely all about mobile e-wallets and contactless payments. PayTech firms also focused on ensuring the security of transactions leveraging artificial intelligence (AI) and machine learning (ML) technologies Global consumers have grown less reliant on cash, enhancing the growth profile of mobile payments firms
P2P loans	Peer-to-peer (P2P) lending is the practice of lending money to individuals or businesses through online services that match lenders with borrowers. Peer-to-peer lending companies often offer their services online and attempt to operate with lower overhead and provide their services more cheaply than traditional financial institutions
Open Banking	In October 2015, the European Parliament adopted a revised Payment Services Directive, known as PSD2. The new rules included aims to promote the development of neobanks or challenger banks' use of innovative online and mobile payments through open banking

(continued)

of decision-making processes reduces the overall lead time of services. On the other hand, standardized technologies enable a faster reaction to new market demands (Vandeputte & De Toffol, 2017).

Table 5.1 (continued)

Typology	*Business Model*
Big Data & Analytics	Big data analytics is the often complex process of examining large and varied data sets, or big data, to uncover information—such as hidden patterns, unknown correlations, market trends, and customer preferences—that can help organizations make informed business decisions. Big data based on payment transaction data provide insight into customer retention, identification of criminal activities, or future customer behavior
InsurTech	InsurTech refers to the use of technology innovations designed to squeeze out savings and efficiency from the current insurance industry model
RegTech	Regulatory technology, in short, RegTech, is a new technology that uses information technology to enhance regulatory processes. With its main application in the financial sector, it is expanding into any regulated business with an appeal for the Consumer Goods Industry. Regtech, post-financial crisis—with MiFiD II, Basel III, and GDPR—may have been the initial external driver to ensure full compliance, and this has ensured a dramatic rise in technological solutions, and crucial in increasing efficiency, for example, by reducing gap-analysis time
MicroFinTech	FinTech applications to microfinance activities (microcredit; microdeposits; microinsurance; micro-consulting). M-banking boosts volumes and fosters marginality gains
Artificial Intelligence	AI will transform nearly every aspect of the financial service industry. Automated wealth management, customer verification, and open banking all provide opportunities for AI solution providers
PropTech	Property technology, in short called PropTech, sometimes also called real estate technology, is a term that encompasses the application of information technology and platform economics to real estate markets
Banking as a Service (BaaS)	End-to-end process ensuring the overall execution of a financial service provided over the web

5.4 Banks Versus FinTechs: Cross-Pollination and Scalability

The business model of a bank is vastly different from that of a typical FinTech, and this difference reflects in the balance sheet and the income statement.

The balance sheet of a bank is characterized by a binding structure, due to the presence of the supervisory capital and bank deposits (in the liabilities) and loans to customers (within the assets). The assets and liabilities structure of a typical FinTech is much "lighter," being represented by net working capital and some capitalized assets (tangible and intangible), against equity and financial debt in the liabilities.

The income statement reflects these differences:

- the bank has economic margins represented by the interest rate differential and the net contribution of commissions;
- the FinTech has a more standard EBITDA and EBIT, sourced by the difference between operating revenues (from services) and monetary OPEX (to get to the EBITDA) or comprehensive OPEX, including depreciation and amortization, to determine the EBIT.

The different income statements, driven by the respective business model of either the bank or the FinTech, reflect a completely different attitude toward (digital) scalability.

FinTechs have a revenue model that is much more scalable than that of a typical bank. Whereas a bank is limited in its growth potential by constraints such as the supervisory capital (a percentage of its loans, weighted for risk), huge fixed costs for personnel, and difficult upside in a mature market, FinTechs incorporate a digital potential in an intrinsically scalable business model.

Even if FinTechs have a higher marginality potential, they still need the volumes (client base, etc.) and the market caption that is bound to traditional banks.

5.5 FinTech Valuation

The appraisal methodology may conveniently start from a strategic interpretation of the business model (that derives from accounting data) to extract the key evaluation parameters to insert in the model, as shown in Fig. 5.4.

An analysis of the business model may conveniently consider (Fig. 5.5):

1. The revenue model;
2. The strategic goals;
3. The growth drivers;
4. The expected investments;
5. The market trends.

FinTechs cooperate with banks (Bömer & Maxin, 2018). Cooperation is primarily geared to the integration or use of a FinTech application (product-related cooperation).

5.5.1 *Insights from Listed FinTechs*

FinTechs have a hybrid business model, as they operate in the financial (banking) sector deploying their technological attitudes. Evaluators may so wonder if FinTechs follow the typical evaluation patterns of bank/financial intermediaries or those of technological firms. Preliminary empirical evidence—reported below—shows that the latter interpretation is the one consistent with the stock market mood.

This indication is important for the assessment of the best evaluation criteria.

The following graph (with data sourced from Bloomberg) contains the comparative stock market price (from August 1, 2015, to June 30, 2020) of (Fig. 5.6):

a) IFINXNT—Indxx Global FinTech Thematic Index;
b) MXW00BK—MSCI World Banks Weighted Equity Index;
c) MXW00IT—MSCI World (ex-Australia) Information Technology Index.

Despite the young age of FinTechs, many of these firms are experiencing significantly faster growth than their traditional financial services peers. This reflects in the performance of FinTech companies tracked by the Indxx Global FinTech Thematic Index, the underlying index for

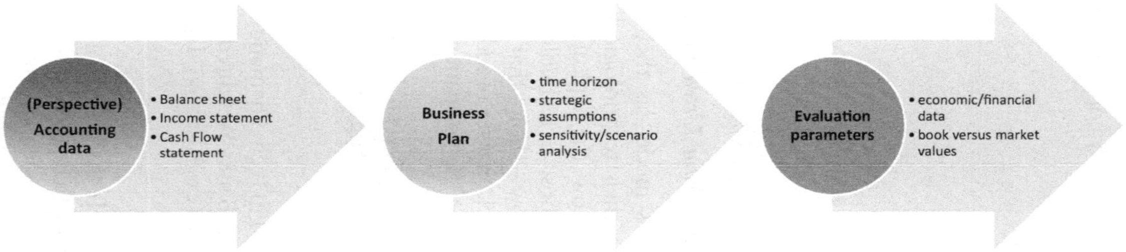

Fig. 5.4 Evaluation Methodology

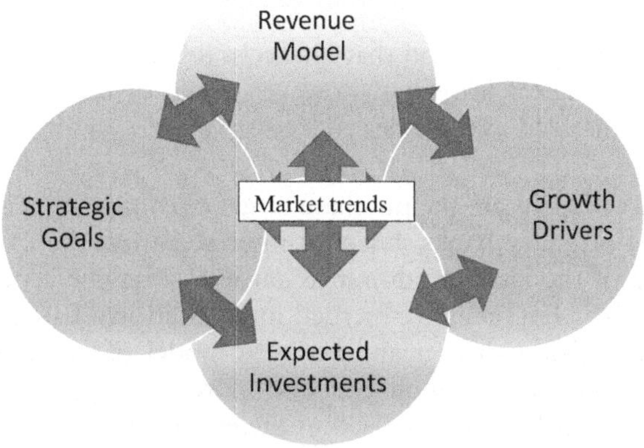

Fig. 5.5 Business model and Value Drivers

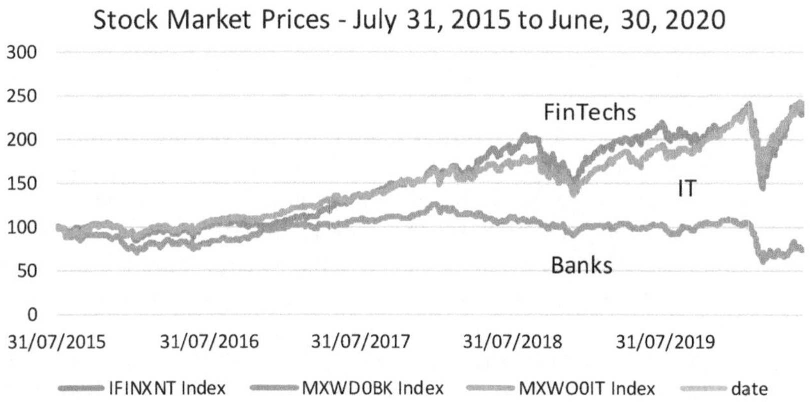

Fig. 5.6 FinTech versus Technological and Banking Stock Market Index

the Global X FinTech ETF (FINX), relative to the Financial Select Sector Index.

FinTechs seem far from the banks even because they have a different model, as they do not collect deposits and lend money, intermediating financial resources; FinTechs are not hyper-regulated deposit-taking institutions, and they just provide financial service and do not intermediate "money" as a product, and they do not need a supervisory capital like banks.

The preliminary conclusion that FinTechs follow the evaluation parameters of technological firms has, however, some caveats that may tentatively be summarized as follows:

a) If FinTech firms are the purchase target of (much bigger and consolidated) ordinary banks/financial intermediaries, then the valuation criteria of the latter predominate, at least after the acquisition (and especially if FinTechs are merged into traditional banks);
b) The underlying market and business model of maturing FinTechs may become less technological and more "client-based";
c) Some established criteria used in the evaluation of traditional banks are, however, hardly applicable even in perspective (e.g., consideration of "physical" banking branches as a positive element).

5.5.2 *The Accounting Background for Valuation*

The valuation of FinTech companies concerns promising startups and some seasoned firms.

FinTechs have a hybrid business model, as they operate in the financial (banking) sector deploying their technological attitudes. Evaluators may so wonder if FinTechs follow the typical evaluation patterns of bank/financial intermediaries or those of technological firms. Preliminary empirical evidence shows that the latter interpretation is the one consistent with the stock market mood and the business model of FinTechs.

The appraisal methodology may conveniently start from a strategic interpretation of the business model to extract the key evaluation parameters to insert in the model. Evaluation patterns typically follow Discounted Cash Flows (DCF) or other metrics based on market comparables.

The evaluation is sensitive to forward-looking data that can be used to build up a sound business plan with a time horizon coherent with the average life cycle of the products and services of FinTech.

A business plan is a formal accounting statement that numerically describes a set of business goals, the reasons why they are believed attainable, and the strategic plan and managerial steps for reaching those goals. Hypotheses and visionary ideas of game-changers must be transformed into numbers and need to be backed by reasonable and verifiable assumptions about future events and milestones (Moro Visconti, 2021).

The accounting background is composed of pro forma balance sheets (of some 3–5 years) and perspective income statements. The matching of these two documents produces expected cash flow statements. Economic and financial margins are the key accounting parameters for valuation that are represented by the EBITDA, the EBIT, the operating and net cash flows, and the Net Financial Position, as it will be shown in the formulation of the appraisal approaches.

5.6 Valuation Methods

The evaluation criteria typically follow the (actual and prospective) business model of the target company.

The technological value driver seems, at least in this historical phase, prevalent over the banking/financial activity, as shown in Fig. 5.7. A

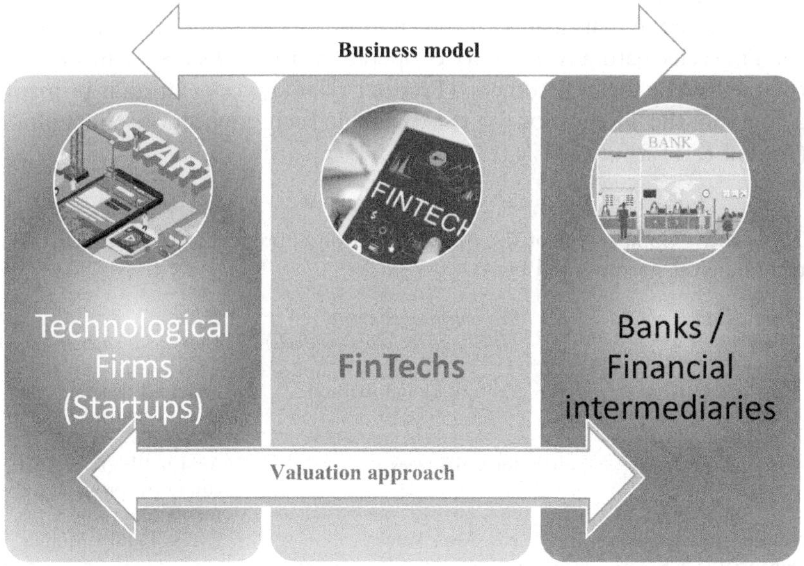

Fig. 5.7 Business Model and Valuation Approach of FinTechs

preliminary consideration may, however, indicate that the business model is slightly more "bank-centric" than the evaluation criteria. The reasons for this business model divergence are manifold: Banks are capital- and labor-intensive institutions and are strictly supervised (not only since they are financial institutions but also because they collect deposits and are so regulated by Central Bank authorities). FinTechs are quite different, although they share with banks a common underlying framework.

A comparison of the primary evaluation criteria in traditional (non-financial) firms, high-tech firms (startups), and banks/financial intermediaries is reported in Table 5.2.

Banking and financial activities (Madrid Damodaran, 2009) follow peculiar valuation patterns that often concentrate on parameters like adjusted equity or dividends. These parameters are, however, not particularly meaningful with FinTechs since they are not capital-intensive firms, and their capacity to pay out dividends is absent in the startup phase.

If the FinTech activity is developed within a banking group by a captive company, its strategic meaning may be that of a catalyzer of (traditional) banking activity. In this case, what mostly matters is not the value of FinTech as a stand-alone reality, but rather its contribution to the incremental marginality of the (traditional) banking group it belongs to. FinTechs naturally tend to cooperate with banks, as in most cases they represent their customers. (Product-related) cooperation is primarily geared to the integration or use of a FinTech application cooperation (Brandl & Hornuf, 2017).

Table 5.2 Comparison of the main evaluation approaches of traditional firms, technological startups, and banks

Traditional Firm	*Technological Startup (IPEV, 2018; other methods)*	*Bank (Financial intermediary)*
Balance-sheet based (Fernandez, 2001)	Venture capital method	Expected dividends per share/Dividend Discount Models
Income	Binomial trees	Adjusted book value of equity (to proxy Market value)
Mixed capital-income	Net Asset Value	Excess Return Models
Financial (DCF)		
Market multiples (comparable firms)		

In this case, the value may be inferred even with differential income methodologies, traditionally used in the evaluation of intangible assets (within the income approaches).

According to the International Valuation Standard IVS 210, § 80:

> *80. Premium Profit Method or With-And-Without Method*
> *80.1 The premium profit method, sometimes referred to as the with-and-without method, indicates the value of an intangible asset by comparing two scenarios: one in which the business uses the subject intangible asset and one in which the business does not use the subject intangible asset (but all other factors are kept constant). (…).*
> *80.2 The Comparison of the Two Scenarios Can Be Done in Two Ways:*
> *a) calculating the value of the business under each scenario with the difference in the business values being the value of the subject intangible asset, and*
> *b) calculating for each future period the difference between the profits in the two scenarios. The present value of those amounts is then used to reach the value of the subject intangible asset.*

In this case, what matters for the evaluation is the with-an-without availability of the FinTech business that can be considered as the "intangible" asset indicated in IVS 210.

Demyanova (2018) considers several methodologies that, in most cases, are hardly applicable to FinTechs. For example, the liquidation value or book value method is not consistent with the innovative nature of startups that become valueless if wound up and derive most of their potential value from intangible assets. The Berkus method appears too undetermined, and real options may be embedded in the estimate of future cash flows with multiple scenarios.

Among the main evaluation methodologies of FinTech companies, the following are the most relevant:

1. Financial approach (Discounted Cash Flows—DCF);
2. Market comparables.

5.6.1 *The Financial approach*

The financial approach is based on the principle that the market value of the company is equal to the discounted value of the cash flows that the company can generate ("cash is king"). The determination of the cash flows is of primary importance in the application of the approach, as is the consistency of the discount rates adopted.

The doctrine (especially the Anglo-Saxon one) believes that the financial approach is the "ideal" solution for estimating the market value for limited periods. It is not possible to make reliable estimates of cash flows for longer periods. "The conceptually correct methods are those based on cash flow discounting. I briefly comment on other methods since - even though they are conceptually incorrect - they continue to be used frequently" (Fernandez, 2001).

This approach is of practical importance if the individual investor or company with high cash flows (leasing companies, retail trade, public and motorway services, financial trading, project financing SPVs, etc.) are valued.

Financial evaluation can be particularly appropriate when the company's ability to generate cash flow for investors is significantly different from its ability to generate income, and forecasts can be formulated with a sufficient degree of credibility and are demonstrable.

There are two complementary criteria for determining the cash flows:

a.1 The cash flow available to the company (Free cash flow to the firm)

This configuration of expected flows is the one most used in the practice of company valuations, given its greater simplicity of application compared to the methodology based on flows to partners. It is a measure of cash flows independent of the financial structure of the company (unlevered cash flows) that is particularly suitable to evaluate companies with high levels of indebtedness, or that do not have a debt plan. In these cases, the calculation of the cash flow available to shareholders is more difficult because of the volatility resulting from the forecast of how to repay debts.

This methodology is based on the operating flows generated by the typical management of the company, based on the operating income available for the remuneration of own and third-party means net of the relative tax effect. Unlevered cash flows are determined by using operating income before taxes and finance charges.

Net operating income

− taxes on operating income

+ amortization/depreciation and provisions (non-monetary operating costs)

+ technical divestments (−investments)

+ divestments (-investments) in other assets

+ decrease (−increase) in operating net working capital

= **Cash flow available to shareholders and lenders (operating cash flow)**

The cash flow available to the company is, therefore, determined as the cash flow available to shareholders, plus financial charges after tax, plus loan repayments and equity repayments, minus new borrowings and flows arising from equity increases.

The difference between the two approaches is, therefore, given by the different meanings of cash flows associated with debt and equity repayments.

Cash flows from operating activities are discounted to present value at the weighted average cost of capital.

This configuration of flows offers an evaluation of the whole company, independently from its financial structure. The value of the debt must be subtracted from the value of the company to rejoin the value of the market value, obtained through the cash flows for the shareholders.

The relationship between the two concepts of cash flow is as follows:

$$\begin{aligned}\text{cash flowavailable to the company} &= \text{cash flow available to shareholders}\\ &+ \text{financial charges (net of taxes)}\\ &+ \text{loan repayments} - \text{new loans}\end{aligned} \tag{5.1}$$

a.2. The (residual) cash flow available to shareholders

This configuration considers the only expected flow available for members' remuneration. It is a measure of cash flow that considers the financial structure of the company (levered cash flow). It is the cash flow that remains after the payment of interest and the repayment of equity shares and after the coverage of equity expenditures necessary to maintain existing assets and to create the conditions for business growth.

In M&A operations, the Free Cash Flow to the Firm (operating cash flow) is normally calculated to estimate the Enterprise Value (comprehensive of debt). The residual Equity Value is then derived by subtracting the Net Financial Position.

The cash flow for the shareholders is determined, starting from the net profit:

Net profit (loss)

\+ amortization/depreciation and provisions
\+ divestments (−investments) in technical equipment
\+ divestments (−investments) in other assets
\+ decrease (−increase) in net operating working capital
\+ increases (−decreases) in loans
\+ equity increases (−decreases)
= **Cash flows available to shareholders (Free cash flow to equity)**

The discounting of the free cash flow for the shareholders takes place at a rate equal to the cost of the shareholders' equity. This flow identifies the theoretical measure of the company's ability to distribute dividends, even if it does not coincide with the dividend paid.

Cash flow estimates can be applied to any type of asset. The differential element is represented by their duration. Many assets have a defined time horizon, while others assume a perpetual time horizon, such as shares.

Cash flows (CF) can, therefore, be estimated using a normalized projection of cash flows that it uses, alternatively:

- unlimited capitalization:

$$W1 = CF / i \tag{5.2}$$

- limited capitalization:

$$W2 = CF\ a\ n\neg i \tag{5.3}$$

where W_1 and W_2 represent the present value of future cash flows.

The discount rate to be applied to expected cash flows is determined as the sum of the cost of equity and the cost of debt, appropriately weighted according to the leverage of the company (the ratio between financial debt and equity). This produces the Weighted Average Cost of Capital (WACC):

$$WACC = k_i(1 - t)\frac{D}{D + E} + k_e\frac{E}{D + E} \tag{5.4}$$

where:
k_i = cost of debt;
t = corporate tax rate;
D = market value of debt;
E = market value of equity;
$D + E$ = raised capital;
k_e = cost of equity (to be estimated with the Capital Asset Pricing Model—CAPM or the Dividend Discount Model).

The cost of debt capital is easy to determine, as it can be inferred from the financial statements of the company. The cost of equity or share capital, which represents the minimum rate of return required by investors for equity investments, is instead more complex and may use the CAPM or the Dividend Discount Model (a method of valuing a company's stock price considering the sum of all its future dividend payments, discounted back to their present value. It is used to value stocks based on the net present value of future dividends).

The formula of the CAPM is the following:

$$E(r)_{FinTech} = r_{free} + \beta_{FinTech}[(E(r)_{market} - r_{free}] \tag{5.5}$$

where:

$$E(r)_{FinTech} = expectedreturnoftheFinTechlistedstock;$$

$r_{free} = risk - freerateofreturn(e.g., ofalongtermGovernmentbond);$

$\beta_{FinTech} = sensitivityoftheFinTech'sstocktothemarketprice;$

$(E(r)_{market} = expectedreturnofthe(benchmark)Stockmarket.$

A central element is represented by the beta (β) of the FinTech to be evaluated that consists of the ratio between the covariance of the FinTech security with its stock market, divided by the variance of the market. Market betas, subdivided by industry, may be detected from the data set of A. Damodaran (see for instance http://pages.stern.nyu.edu/~adamodar/New_Home_Page/datafile/Betas.html).

Once the present value of the cash flows has been determined, the calculation of the market value W of the company may correspond to:

(a) the unlevered cash flow approach:

$$W = \sum \frac{CF_0}{WACC} + VR - D \tag{5.6}$$

(b) the levered cash flow approach:

$$W = \sum \frac{CF_n}{K_e} + VR \tag{5.7}$$

where:
$\sum CF_0/WACC =$ present value of operating cash flows;
$\sum CF_n/K_e =$ present value of net cash flows;
$VR =$ terminal (residual) value;
$D =$ initial net financial position (financial debt – liquidity).

The residual value is the result of discounting the value at the time n (before which the cash flows are estimated analytically). It is often the greatest component of the global value W (above all in intangible-intensive companies) and tends to zero if the time horizon of the capitalization is infinite (VR / ∞ = 0).

The two variants (levered versus unlevered) give the same result if the value of the firm, determined through the cash flows available to the lenders, is deducted from the value of the net financial debts.

Operating cash flows (unlevered) and net cash flows for shareholders (levered) are determined by comparing the last two balance sheets (to dispose of changes in operating net working capital, fixed assets, financial liabilities, and shareholders' equity) with the income statement of the last year.

The accounting derivation of the cash flow and its link to the cost of capital (to get DCF—Discounted Cash Flows) is illustrated in Table 5.3.

The net cash flow for the shareholders coincides with the free cash flow to equity and, therefore, with the dividends that can be paid out, once it has been verified that enough internal liquidity resources remain in the company. This feature, associated with the ability to raise equity from third parties and shareholders, is such as to allow the company to find adequate financial coverage for the investments deemed necessary to

Table 5.3 Cash flow statement and link with the cost of capital

Cash flow statement	
EBIT + Depreciation and amortization	
= EBITDA (A)	
± Δ Operating Net Working Capital ± Δ fixed assets (CAPEX)	
= Operating cash flow (unlevered cash flow to the firm) (B)	To be discounted at the **Weighted average cost of capital** (WACC)
- Financial charges ± Δ net financial liabilities ± Extraordinary income and charges - Taxes ± Δ Equity	
= Net (free) cash flow to the shareholders (levered cash flow) (C)	To be discounted at the **cost of equity** (Ke)
Reconciliation statement:	
Closing cash and cash equivalents - Opening cash and cash equivalents	
= Change in net cash flow = liquidity (D) = (C)	

maintain the company's continuity and remain on the market in economic conditions (minimum objectives). They should allow for the creation of incremental value in favor of shareholders, who are the residual claimants (being, as subscribers of risky capital, the only beneficiaries of the variable net returns, which, as such, are residual and subordinate to the fixed remuneration of the other stakeholders).

The estimate of cash flows can be applied to any activity.

The differential element is service life. Many activities have a defined time horizon, while others assume a perpetual time horizon, such as company shares.

The discounted cash flow (DCF) approach can be complemented with real options that incorporate intangible-driven flexibility in the forecasts.

DCF is ubiquitous in financial valuation and constitutes the cornerstone of contemporary valuation theory (Singh, 2013). The robustness of the model, as well as its compatibility with the conventional two-dimensional risk-return structure of investment appraisal, makes it suited to a multitude of valuations. Accounting standards across the globe recognize the efficacy of this model and advocate its use wherever practicable. FAS 141 and 142 of the United States and IAS 39 that relate to the accounting of intangible assets recommend the use of DCF methodology for attributing a value to such assets.

Some caveats should be considered. According to OECD (2017):

- "*Valuation techniques that estimate the discounted value of projected future cash flows derived from the exploitation of the transferred intangible or intangibles can be particularly useful when properly applied. There are many variations of these valuation techniques. In general terms, such techniques measure the value of an intangible by the estimated value of future cash flows it may generate over its expected remaining lifetime. The value can be calculated by discounting the expected future cash flows to present value. Under this approach valuation requires, among other things, defining realistic and reliable financial projections, growth rates, discount rates, the useful life of intangibles, and the tax effects of the transaction. Moreover, it entails consideration of terminal values when appropriate*" (Sect. 6.157).
- "*When applying valuation techniques, including valuation techniques based on projected cash flows, it is important to recognize that the estimates of value based on such techniques can be volatile. Small*

changes in one or another of the assumptions underlying the valuation approach or in one or more of the valuation parameters can lead to large differences in the intangible value the approach produces. A small percentage change in the discount rate, a small percentage change in the growth rates assumed in producing financial projections, or a small change in the assumptions regarding the useful life of the intangible can each have a profound effect on the ultimate valuation. Moreover, this volatility is often compounded when changes are made simultaneously to two or more valuation assumptions or parameters" (Sect. 6.158).

- "*The reliability of a valuation of a transferred intangible using discounted cash flow valuation techniques is dependent on the accuracy of the projections of future cash flows or income on which the valuation is based*" (Sect. 6.163).
- "*The discount rate or rates used in converting a stream of projected cash flows into a present value is a critical element of a valuation approach. The discount rate considers the time value of money and the risk or uncertainty of the anticipated cash flows. As small variations in selected discount rates can generate large variations in the calculated value of intangibles using these techniques*" (Sect. 6.170).
- "*It should be recognized in determining and evaluating discount rates that in some instances, particularly those associated with the valuation of intangibles still in development, intangibles may be among the riskiest components*" (Sect. 6.172).

5.6.2 Empirical approaches (Market multipliers)

The market value identifies:

(a) The value attributable to a share of the equity expressed at stock exchange prices;
(b) The price of the controlling interest or the entire share equity;
(c) The traded value for the controlling equity of comparable undertakings;
(d) The value derived from the stock exchange quotations of comparable undertakings.

Sometimes comparable trades of companies belonging to the same product sector with similar characteristics (in terms of cash flows, sales, costs, etc.) are used.

In practice, an examination of the prices used in negotiations with companies in the same sector leads to quantifying average parameters:

- *Price/EBIT;*
- *Price/cash-flow;*
- *Price/book-value;*
- *Price/earnings;*
- *Price/dividend.*

These ratios seek to estimate the average rate to be applied to the company being assessed. However, there may be distorting effects of prices based on special interest rates, in a historical context, on difficulties of comparison, etc.

In financial market practice, the multiples methodology is frequently applied. Based on multiples, the company's value is derived from the market price profit referring to comparable listed companies, such as net profit, before tax or operating profit, cash flow, equity, or turnover.

The attractiveness of the multiples approach stems from its ease of use: Multiples can be used to obtain quick but dirty estimates of the company's value and are useful when there are many comparable companies listed on the financial markets and the market sets correct prices for them on average.

Because of the simplicity of the calculation, these indicators are easily manipulated and susceptible to misuse, especially if they refer to companies that are not entirely similar. Since there are no identical companies in terms of entrepreneurial risk and growth rate, the assumption of multiples for the processing of the valuation can be misleading, bringing to "fake multipliers."

The use of multiples can be implemented through:

A. Use of fundamentals;
B. Use of comparable data:

    B.1. Comparable companies;
    B.2. Comparable transactions.

The first approach links multiples to the fundamentals of the company being assessed: profit growth and cash flow, dividend distribution ratio, and risk. It is equivalent to the use of cash flow discounting approaches.

Discount factors incorporate risk. According to OECD (2017):

- *"When identifying risks in relation to an investment with specificity, it is important to distinguish between the financial risks that are linked to the funding provided for the investments and the operational risks that are linked to the operational activities for which the funding is used, such as for example the development risk when the funding is used for developing a new intangible" (Sect. 6.61).*
- *"Particular types of risk that may have importance in a functional analysis relating to transactions involving intangibles include:*
    (i) *risks related to development of intangibles, including the risk that costly research and development or marketing activities will prove to be unsuccessful, and considering the timing of the investment (for example, whether the investment is made at an early stage, mid-way through the development process, or at a late stage will impact the level of the underlying investment risk);*
    (ii) *the Risk of Product Obsolescence, Including the Possibility that Technological Advances of Competitors Will Adversely Affect the Value of the Intangibles;*
    (iii) *infringement risk, including the risk that defense of intangible rights or defense against other persons' claims of infringement may prove to be time-consuming, costly and/or unavailing;*
    (iv) *product liability and similar risks related to products and services based on the intangibles;*
    (v) *exploitation risks, uncertainties in relation to the returns to be generated by the intangible"* (sect. 6.65).

For the second approach, it is necessary to distinguish whether it is a valuation of comparable companies or comparable transactions.

The comparability concerns different firms but is also related to their contents.

In the case of comparable companies, the approach estimates multiples by observing similar companies. The problem is to determine what is meant by similar companies. In theory, the analyst should check all the variables that influence the multiple.

In practice, companies should estimate the most likely price for a non-listed company, taking as a reference some listed companies, operating in the same sector, and considered homogeneous. Two companies can be defined as homogeneous when they present, for the same risk, similar characteristics, and expectations.

The calculation is:

- A company whose price is known (P_1);
- A variable closely related to its value (X_1);

the ratio $(P_1)/(X_1)$ is assumed to apply to the company to be valued, for which the size of the reference variable (X_2) is known.

Therefore:

$$(P_1)/(X_1) = (P_2)/(X_2) \tag{5.8}$$

so that the desired value P_2 will be:

$$P_2 = X_2[(P_1)/(X_1)] \tag{5.9}$$

According to widespread estimates, the main factors in establishing whether a company is comparable are:

- Size;
- Belonging to the same sector[9];
- Financial risks (leverage);
- Historical trends and prospects for the development of results and markets;
- Geographical diversification;
- Degree of reputation and credibility;
- Management skills;
- Ability to pay dividends.

[9] See, for instance, the Statistical Classification of Economic Activities in the European Community, commonly referred to as NACE.

Founded on comparable transactions, the basis of valuation is information about actual negotiations (or mergers) of similar—i.e., comparable—companies.

The use of profitability parameters is usually considered to be the most representative of company dynamics.

Comparables may be looked for consulting databases like Orbis (https://www.forbes.com/sites/ronshevlin/2019/07/29/why-fintech-startups-fail/#30c33e6a6440).

Among the empirical criteria, the approach of the multiplier of the EBITDA (Earnings Before Interest, Taxes, Depreciation, and Amortization) is widely diffused. The Net Financial Position must be added algebraically to the EBITDA, to pass from the estimate of the enterprise value (total value of the company) to that of the equity value (value of the net assets). The formulation is as follows:

$$\begin{aligned} W &= \text{average perspective EBITDA} \\ &\quad * \text{ Enterprise Value / sector EBITDA} \\ &= \text{Enterprise Value of the company} \end{aligned} \tag{5.10}$$

And then:

$$\text{Equity Value} = \text{Enterprise Value} \pm \text{Net Financial Position} \tag{5.11}$$

The DCF approach can be linked to the market approach since they both share as a starting parameter the EBITDA.

5.7 Challenges and Failures: Why Fintechs Burn Out

Startup failures are so common that they cannot refrain from influencing valuation, for instance, increasing the risk embedded in the discount rate of expected cash flows.

Failures have common features among the different startups but are industry-specific. And the financial sector has its own rules.

Among the reasons that may cause the default of FinTech startups, the following are worth mentioning[10]:

[10] See https://www.forbes.com/sites/ronshevlin/2019/07/29/why-fintech-startups-fail/#30c33e6a6440.

- **Underfunding;**
- **Choosing an inexperienced venture capital;**
- **Overlooking compliance.** Regulatory complexity is often underestimated;
- **Thinking a FinTech startup is the same as any other tech startup;** psychological behaviors around money, credit, savings, and payments are different from those concerning IT, biotechnologies, etc.;
- **Competing solely on cost;** banks have massive (traditional) scale advantages.
- **Going digital,** FinTechs may re-engineer traditional business models but the task is uneasy and risky.
- **Overconfidence;** creating a new market is no easy task. Many FinTechs think that their business model is so innovative that they have no competitors. Whenever there is competition, geographical segmentation may represent a weak barrier, due to increasing financial globalization. Innovation may become increasingly challenging in a crowded and over-competitive market.
- **Underestimation of the length of the sales cycle;** financial institutions are notoriously slow purchasers of anything new.
- **Missing sales strategy**; FinTech startups are often the brainchild of software experts that have limited sales and marketing skills.
- **Lack of understanding of the financial market;** FinTech startups pursuing a B2C business model often overestimate the extent to which consumers will: 1) change their behavior and 2) pay for a new product or service in addition to all the things they already pay for. While a B2B model may be a better path for some FinTech startups, some fail by not understanding that they are a vendor—not a partner—which may require a completely different set of skills and capabilities from those they already have.

According to a survey (Endeavor Insight, Mapping Milan FinTech, 2019):

- Decision-makers in the private sector and the public sector alike should focus on helping companies reaching scale;
- FinTech entrepreneurs identified access to capital, access to talent, and compliance with the regulation as their top challenges in scaling their companies today;

- Network Analysis points to challenges and opportunities:
  - There is an absence of productive mentorship and angel investment connections between FinTech entrepreneurs;
  - The FinTech community has strong ties with the banking sector because of former employment;
  - Entrepreneurial networks are the most influential actors in the entrepreneurship community and they can become a vehicle to transmit resources;
- Decision-makers in the public sector and the private sector who wish to support FinTech entrepreneurship need to focus on:
  - Channel resources to companies with scale-up potential;
  - Foster relationships with international investors;
  - Address the shortage of tech talent and non-financial managerial talent in the sector;
  - Leverage entrepreneurship networks to foster angel investment and mentorship among entrepreneurs in the sector.

References

Al Hammadi, M., & Nobanee, H. (2019). *FinTech and sustainability: A mini-review*. https://ssrn.com/abstract=3500873.

Anikina, I. D., Gukova, V. A., Golodova, A. A., & Chekalkina, A. A. (2016). Methodological Fintech as Financial Innovation – The possibilities and problems of implementation 972 aspects of prioritization of financial tools for stimulation of innovative activities. *European Research Studies Journal, 19*(2), 100–112.

Arner, D. W., Buckley, R. P., & Zetzsche, D. A. (2018). *FinTech for financial inclusion: A framework for digital financial transformation*. https://ssrn.com/abstract=3245287.

Ashta, A., & Patel, J. (2010). *Is SaaS the appropriate technology for microfinance?* https://ssrn.com/abstract=1604741.

Ashta, A., & Biot-Paquerot, G. (2018). FinTech evolution: Strategic value management issues in a fast changing industry. *Strategic Change, 27*(4), 301–311.

Bartlett, R., Morse, A., Stanton, R., & Wallace, N. (2018). *Consumer–lending discrimination in the era of Fintech*. https://law.utexas.edu/wp-content/uploads/sites/25/BMSW_20181115.pdf.

Berg, T., Burg, V., Gombović, A., & Puri, M. (2019). On the rise of Fintechs – Credit scoring using digital footprints. *The Review of Financial Studies, 33*(7), 2845–2897.

Bernards, N. (2019). Fintech and financial inclusion. In T. Shaw, L. Mahrenbach, R. Modi, & X. Yi-Chong (Eds.), The Palgrave Handbook of Contemporary International Political Economy. Palgrave Macmillan.

Bömer, M., & Maxin, H. (2018). Why Fintechs cooperate with banks - evidence from Germany. *ZVersWiss, 107*, 359–386.

Brandl, B., & Hornuf, L. (2017). *Where did FinTechs come from, and where do they go? The transformation of the financial industry in Germany after digitalization* (SSRN Working Paper). Available at https://ssrn.com/abstract=3036555.

Broeders, H., & Khanna, S. (2015). *Strategic choices for banks in the digital age*. Mckinsey & Company – Financial Services. Available at http://Www.Mckinsey.Com/Industries/Financial-Services/Our-Insights/Strategicchoices-For-Banks-In-The-Digital-Age.

Burlakov, G. (2019). *10 challenges for the financial services industry in 2019*. Available at https://technorely.com/blog/financialindustry-challenges/.

Dang, T. T. (2020). Fintech in microfinance: A new direction for microfinance institutions in Vietnam. *The Journal of Business Economics and Environmental Studies, 10*(3), 13–22.

Daowd, A., Kamal, M. M., & Dey, B. L. (2020). The impact of social media on the performance of microfinance institutions in developing countries: A quantitative approach. *Information Technology and People, 34*(1), 25–49.

Das, S. R. (2019). The future of fintech. *Financial Management, 48*, 981–1007.

Demyanova, E. A., (2018). The topical issues of valuation of companies under the conditions of fintech. *Strategic Decisions and Risk Management, 1*, 88–103.

Dietz, M., Khanna, S., Olanrewaju, T., & Rajgopal, K. (2016). *Cutting through the noise around financial technology*. http://www.mckinsey.com/industries/financial-services/our-insights/cuttingthrough-the-noise-around-financial-technology.

du Toit, G., & Burns, M. (2016). *Customer loyalty in retail banking*. http://www.bain.com/publications/articles/customer-loyalty-in-retail-banking-2016.aspx.

Fernandez, P. (2001). Valuation using multiples. How do analysts reach their conclusions? *IESE Business School*.

Gai, K., Qiu, M., & Sun, X. (2018). A survey on Fintech. *Journal of Network and Computer Applications, 103*(1), 262–273.

Haddad, C., & Hornuf, L. (2019, June). The emergence of the global fintech market: Economic and technological determinants. *Small Business Economics, 53*(1), 81–105.

IPEV, (2018). *Valuation guidelines*. Available at http://www.privateequityvaluation.com/Valuation-Guidelines.

Madrid Damodaran, A. (2009). *Valuing financial service firms*. Available at http://people.stern.nyu.edu/adamodar/pdfiles/papers/finfirm09.pdf.

Makina, D. (2019). The potential of FinTech in enabling financial inclusion. In Extending Financial Inclusion in Africa (pp. 299–318). Academic Press.

Moro-Visconti, R. (2021). *Startup valuation: From strategic business planning to digital networking*. Palgrave Macmillan, Chapter 2.

OECD. (2017, July). *Transfer pricing guidelines for multinational enterprises and tax administrations*. Available at https://www.oecd.org/tax/oecdtransfer-pricing-guidelines-for-multinational-enterprises-and-tax-administrations-20769717.htm.

Philippon, T. (2019a). *The FinTech opportunity*. National Bureau of Economic Research.

Philippon, T. (2019b). *On FinTech and financial inclusion*. Stern School of Business. (Working Paper). Available at https://www.bis.org/events/conf190628/philippon.pdf.

Piobbici, F., Rajola, F., & Frigerio, C. (2019). Open innovation effectiveness in the financial services sector. In N. Mehandjiev, & B. Saadouni (Eds.), *Enterprise applications, markets and services in the finance industry* (Vol. 345). Springer Verlag.

Pizzi, S., Corbo, L., Caputo, A. (2021). Fintech and SMEs sustainable business models: Reflections and considerations for a circular economy. *Journal of Cleaner Production*, 281, 125217

Pythowska, J., & Korynski, P. (2017). *Digitalizing Microfinance in Europe*. https://www.european-microfinance.org/sites/default/files/document/file/Digitalization-research-paper.pdf.

Ravikumar, T. (2019). Digital financial inclusion: A payoff of financial technology and digital finance uprising in India. *International Journal of Scientific & Technology Research, 8*(11), 3434–3438.

Riggins, F., & Weber, D. M. (2017). Information asymmetries and identification bias in P2P social microlending. *Information Technology for Development, 23*(1), 107–126.

Tanda, A., & Schena, C. (2019). *FinTech, bigTech and banks: Digitalisation and its impact on banking business models*. Palgrave Macmillan.

Singh, J. P. (2013). On the Intricacies of cash flow corporate valuation. *Advances in Management, 6*(3), 15–22.

Thomas, H., & Hedrick-Wong, Y. (2019). *How digital finance and FinTech can improve financial inclusion* (pp. 27–41). Emerald Publishing Limited.

Vandeputte, P., & De Toffol, B. (2017). *The role of FinTechs in the business model of microfinance institutions in Western Europe: a qualitative study*. Louvain School of Management, Université Catholique de Louvain. http://hdl.handle.net/2078.1/thesis:11338.

Vives, X. (2019). Digital disruption in banking. *Annual Review of Finance, 11*, 243–272.

World Bank. (2017). *The Global Findex Database. Measuring Financial Inclusion and the Fintech Revolution*. http://documents.worldbank.org/curated/en/332881525873182837/The-Global-Findex-Database-2017-Measuring-Financial-Inclusion-and-the-Fintech-Revolution.

CHAPTER 6

Microfintech Applications

The supply chain/business model canvas anticipated in the introduction is recalled in Fig. 6.1.

6.1 From Fintech to Microfintech: Upgrading and Adapting the Business Model

FinTech product and service developers in advanced economies often understand how difficult many customers find their relationship with banks. They are aided in easing this link by their similarities to their customers in terms of background, education, and technological literacy. However, these similarities do not exist when products and services are being designed for customers in developing countries. In these markets, product designers need to rely on an evidence-based assessment of customer needs and wants, which will usually have to be specially commissioned, coupled, ideally, with visiting local villages and speaking to the local people who will be the potential customers for the products and services. The failure to appreciate the nuances of local customer journeys underlies many of the FinTech failures in the developing world (Buckley & Webster, 2016).

MicroFinTech derives from the convergence of microfinance patterns with FinTech applications, as shown in Fig. 6.2.

R. Moro-Visconti, *MicroFinTech*, Palgrave Studies in Financial Services Technology, https://doi.org/10.1007/978-3-030-80394-0_6

MicroFinTech Applications
From FinTech to MicroFinTech
Impact of Technology on Scalability and Outreach
Sponsoring Technology with Results-Based Financing

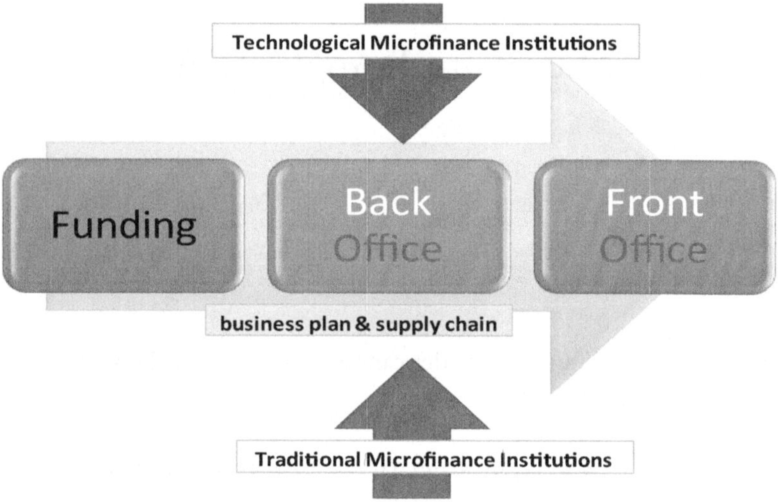

Fig. 6.1 Impact of MicroFinTech applications on the supply chain/business model

The microfinance background, illustrated in Chapter 2, shows the core characteristics of microcredit, introducing some governance criticalities. The main trends of microfinance[1] are analyzed in Chapter 3 that evidences the trade-off between sustainability and outreach. This issue is examined in Chapter 4, with a description of the impact of technology on microfinance. Whereas FinTech applications (examined in Chapter 5) describe the impact of technology on (standard) banking practices, upgrading old-fashioned business model, this chapter is eventually dedicated to the core topic of the book—MicroFinTech. The outline of the book can be synthetized in Fig. 6.2.

The same concepts can be complementarily represented by Fig. 6.3 which shows the "gearing" interaction of microfinance and FinTech to sort out MicroFinTech.

[1] See ASHTA (2018).

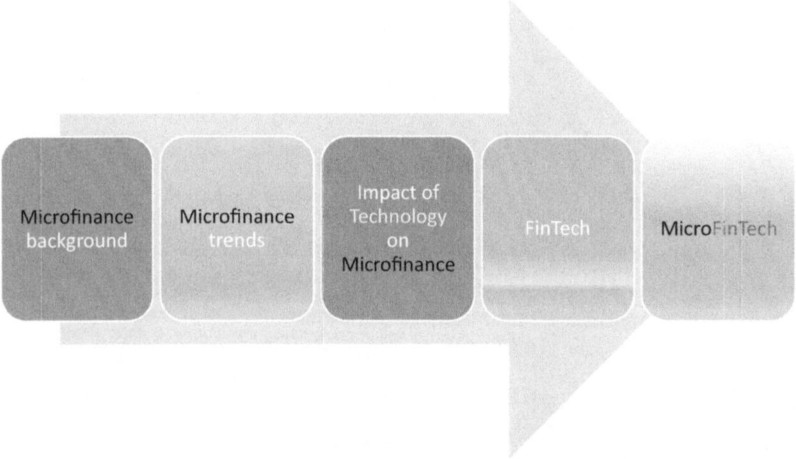

Fig. 6.2 From microfinance to MicroFinTech

The main thesis is that MicroFinTech brings efficiency gains and savings that eventually foster sustainability, so enabling a wider outreach. Cheaper intermediation costs should be reflected on improved outreach that increases volumes, supported by enhanced economic and financial margins. The FinTech-driven delivery model changes, and it is going to impact microfinance.

The emergence of FinTech, the new breed between financial innovation[2] and financial technology, which has been challenging the prevailing position of incumbent financial institutions, is providing a promising vehicle of tackling financial exclusion by closing the gap between unbanked, underbanked, and developed societies, opening the door to the global digital economy, bringing a long-term societal transformational change for the financially excluded/underserved, while leading to inclusive economic growth helping move toward a more just and equitable society (Salampasis & Mention, 2018).

The best practices in the use of digital technologies[3] by innovative FinTech firms could be of use to MFIs in diverse sectors such as

[2] Saksonova and Kuzmina-Merlino (2017) and Sinha et al. (2018).

[3] See Benami and Carter (2021).

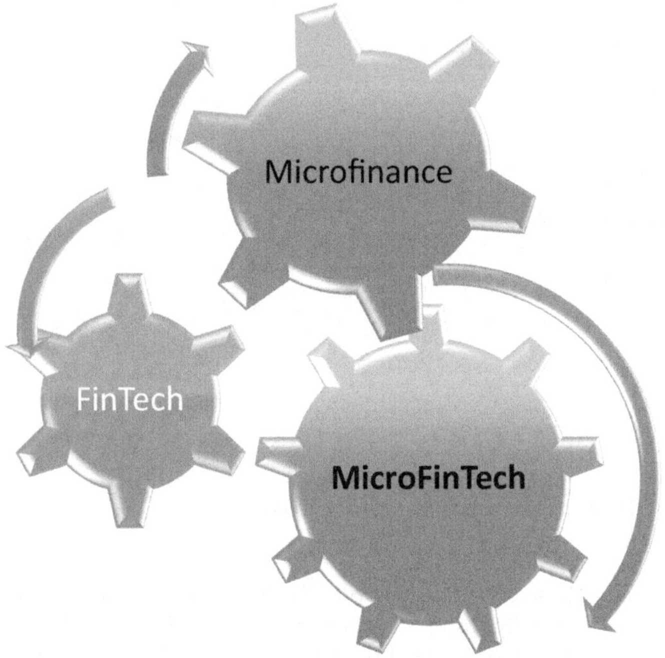

Fig. 6.3 MicroFinTech as a synthesis of microfinance and FinTech

mobile payments, credit scoring, card readers, ATMs, and management information systems.

According to CGAP (2019):

- FinTechs are bringing innovation to every part of the financial services sector;
- five innovation areas display the potential for FinTechs to impact financial inclusion:
  - Interactive customer engagement;
  - Smartphone-based payments;
  - Connections-based finance;
  - Location-based finance;

- De-risked nonproductive finance (FinTechs are helping low-income people pay sizable or unexpected expenses while using unique features to reduce the risk for the financier).

Not all FinTech activities apply to the MicroFinTech business. For instance, the asset management or the investment segment is inapplicable and other sections like WealthTech are hardly conceivable for the microfinance business. RegTech may be useful in limited cases (especially for deposit-taking MFIs). Credit/debit card applications may also be applicable in limited cases.

Crowdfunding or crowdlending may be related to group lending, a key feature of microfinance (Allison et al., 2015; Anglin et al., 2019; Attuel-Mendes, 2016; Berns et al., 2020, 2021; Blakstad & Allen, 2018; Cai et al., 2019; Dorfleitner et al., 2020; Jenik et al., 2017; Kim & De Moor, 2017; Marakkath & Attuel-Mendes, 2015; Martínez-Climent et al., 2019; Royal & Windsor, 2014; Sancha-Navarro et al., 2018; Sherwani et al., 2018).

Figure 5.1 may so be adapted to Fig. 6.4.

Whereas many activities are less sophisticated in the microfinance context, others (as the payment segment, applied to M-banking) are more developed. Another issue is represented by scale: microfinance numbers are big and potentially unlimited (should we consider the unbanked population). And so, even if economic margins may be smaller—to make products affordable—overall profit may benefit from volumes and scale potential.

Further consideration should focus on the interaction between FinTech and MicroFinTech. Whereas it may seem obvious that it is FinTech that inspires MicroFinTech, pollination may also follow the other way. Evidence shows that in some relevant cases (as M-payments), developing areas where microfinance is popular lead the innovative trend, and are more advanced than other sophisticated environments. A further characteristic of less developed playgrounds is represented by scale: the underbanked/unbanked are represented by billions of potential customers. Even if margins may be tiny, potential volumes are massive.

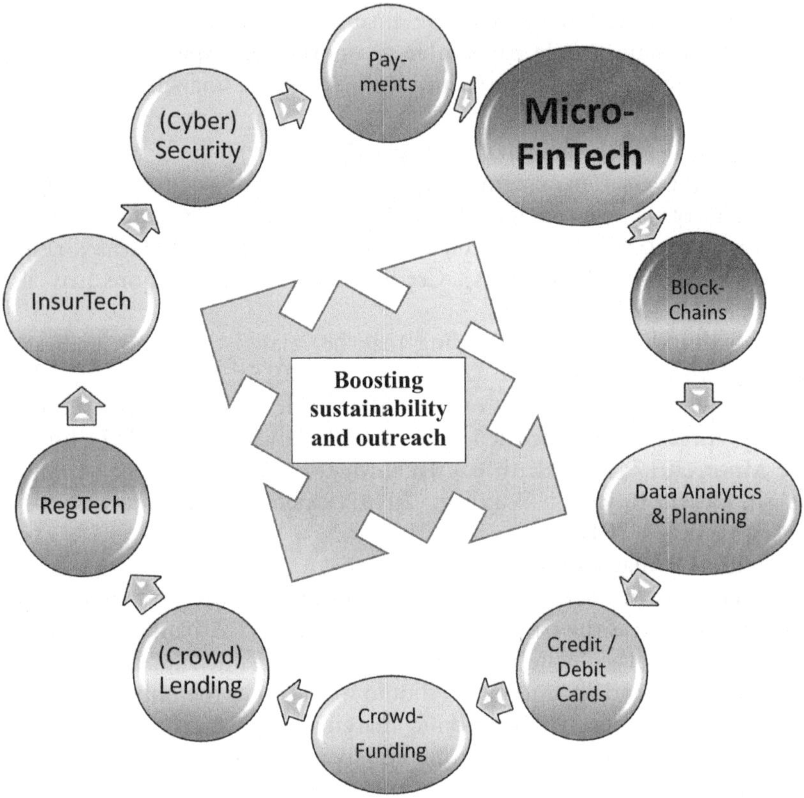

Fig. 6.4 Main MicroFinTech activities

6.2 The Uneasy Adoption of FinTech Strategies for Financial Inclusion

Section 6.1 (and Chapter 5, concerning Sects. 5.1 and 5.3) has shown that FinTechs can adopt different business models, driven by financial innovation, digital technologies, and the desire to reshape the financial intermediation supply and value chain with new solutions (more comfortable, customer-centric, cheaper, etc.).

Low-income consumers in developing economies have limited access and low sustained usage of financial services. FinTech provides an opportunity to promote the financial inclusion of low-income households in developing countries, starting from M-banking applications.[4] Greater financial inclusion can be a catalyst for eradicating poverty, and for developing the small business sector. FinTech must include both access and usage of financial services focusing on affordability, appropriateness, financial literacy, regulations, and fair competition (Chetty et al., 2019).

Financial inclusion statistics at present tend to exclude the key factor of usage, referring instead predominantly to consumers' access to financial products. In countries such as Kenya or South Africa, the rates of access to financial facilities are among the highest in emerging economies, but this betrays the severe challenges experienced by the customers in these countries, leading to low rates of usage and dependence on cash (Villasenor et al., 2016).

As Chetty et al. (2019) indicate, the drivers of financial inclusion differ depending on the local context. The most significant challenges identified by FinTech stakeholders in Southern and East Africa are:

1. Mobile-wallet transaction costs for low-value transfers are unsustainably high for the low-income segment, in both East and Southern African countries. Given the irregular receipt of income within the informal sectors of these countries and the high costs of mobile devices and Internet access, the true costs of mobile transactions are unaffordable for the poor, leading to decreased usage of products.
2. Products are not designed appropriately for the needs of the low-income segment. Various respondents argued that products are designed for the top of the pyramid instead of recognizing the unique needs of the poor. Low-income consumers have been unable to transition from mobile-wallet payments to savings, credit, insurance, or wealth management.
3. Financial literacy remains a challenge among the low-income segment and is compounded by limited capabilities in literacy, numeracy, digital literacy, and general awareness of financial products. Importantly, many respondents agree that policymakers should not mistake the effects of poor product designs, and not catering to the needs of the low-income segment, for low financial literacy. Recognizing this caveat, greater support is needed to develop

[4] Hussain (2017).

general and financial general education programs in low-income areas.

4. The regulatory environment has been identified as a challenge within Southern and East Africa. While the regulator works to protect the financial services ecosystem, improving safety and standardizing the industry, restrictive regulations will have an exclusionary effect on innovations. Often the regulation landscape is unclear, and innovators are unaware how to develop new technologies aligned to the regulatory needs of the country. Further, this uncertainty inhibits partnerships with foreign large-scale FinTech operators, as they are unclear of the medium- to long-term prospects of their products in a new market.

A further strategy can be represented by demonetization.[5]

6.2.1 Matching the Demand with the Supply of Financial Products

The demand and the supply of financial products depend on a series of factors that might be intermediated by MicroFinTech institutions.

Each demand-side driver corresponds to a characteristic, requisite, state of need, etc., of actual and potential consumers (micro-borrowers) concerning financial access.

On the other side, the supply side is concerned with the characteristics of MicroFinTechs and their ecosystem. Technological companies can operate only in a friendly environment where basic technology works, is compliant with the regulation, and is sufficiently known and accepted by potential customers.

The better the environment, the higher the probability to foster financial inclusion[6] and sustainable outreach, overcoming microfinance banana skins.

Figure 6.5 recalls the key demand and supply drivers, bridged by the business purposes and potential of MicroFintech institutions.

[5] See Palanivelu and Narmada (2020).

[6] See Macchiavello (2017).

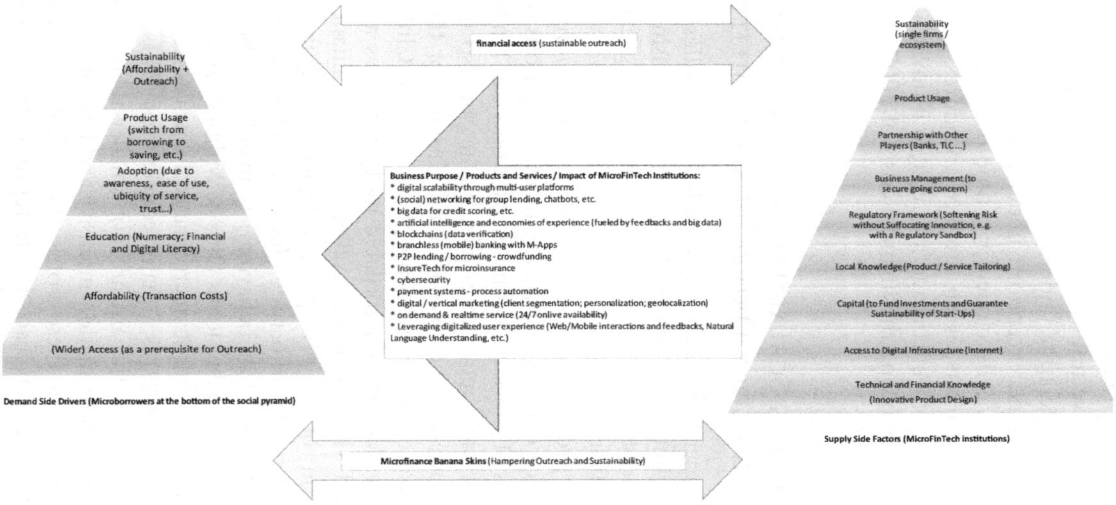

Fig. 6.5 Demand and supply drivers of Technology-driven Financial Inclusion

6.2.2 *Regulatory Sandboxes*

A regulatory sandbox is a framework set up by a financial sector regulator to allow small-scale, live testing of innovations by private firms in a controlled environment (operating under a special exemption, allowance, or other limited, time-bound exception) under the regulator's supervision. The concept, which was developed in a time of rapid technological innovation in financial markets, is an attempt to address the frictions between regulators' desire to encourage and enable innovation and the emphasis on regulation following the financial crisis of 2007–2008 (Jenik & Lauer, 2017).

6.3 Boosting Scalability and Outreach with Technology-Driven Sustainability

In the context of financial inclusion, FinTech holds boundless potential. As new tools and technologies are developed, and old business models are challenged, financial services can be provided with greater speed, accountability, and efficiency.

Access to financial products and services is becoming more attainable than ever, especially for consumers that live in rural locations or regions without the structures of a modern economy. Not only can FinTech make these products and services more accessible, but it can also make them more affordable by lowering the cost of doing business for the financial institution, savings that can be passed onto the consumer. Club this with the near abundant availability of affordable mobile phones and cellular networks, and a world where no one is excluded from the financial system may not be that far out of reach (https://www.accion.org/fintech).

In the literature, the trade-off between financial and social performance (that may produce mission drift behaviors) is mainly attributed to the higher costs of giving out smaller loans (Bos & Millone, 2015).

The small unitary scale of most microfinance loans (especially for the formerly unbanked new clients) is a major concern for MFIs (as already mentioned, the problems of the ant are not smaller than those of the elephant). Microloans are information-intensive and bear high monitoring costs. Technology can soften these bottle-chains first by reducing the unitary cost of processing each loan, and fostering outreach that implies volume increases, and further potential economies of scale.

Innovation improves scalability whenever operating leverage is positively affected by a change in sales (or, in the case of an MFI, total income generated by positive interests).

Technology enhances productivity and it may greatly help in fostering outreach, even if it should never be forgotten that proper management and "human software" stay always behind—and above—it.

Outreach is strongly threatened by unsustainability. When the business model[7] is not self-sustainable, the MFI is condemned to death, sooner or later reaching a cash burnout situation out of which it is uneasy to recover.

Technology is not a panacea and alone it cannot solve all problems, but it can help to do it, especially if it is synergistically backed by a favorable environment. Operating costs can be reduced using technological devices, such as:

- mobile banking;
- access to Internet cafés;
- biometric technology (to obtain loan approval and credit history), for example, applied to Automated Telling Machines and barcode-reading point-of-sale (POS) terminals;
- satellite navigators, to map clients' residences.

Internet dramatically reduces the necessary time to match borrowers and lenders; it virtually eliminates geographical distances, allowing remote banking applications without needing physical branches and enabling customers to access the service at any time, even beyond job hours.

Technology can help to lower the break-even point and extending the MFI's survival threshold and consequently its outreach, making the business more scalable—this being one of the weakest points of microfinance, whose labor-intensive business model absorbs most of the available cash and resources, leaving little or even any margin for the rest.

To the extent that technology can reduce intermediation and transaction costs—or even eliminate them—substantial margins are being saved to the benefit of both the MFIs and its clients. Lower costs have a strong beneficial impact on both sustainability and outreach. IT can lower intermediation costs, especially in businesses with a virtual component, where

[7] See Chauvin Alarcon (2011).

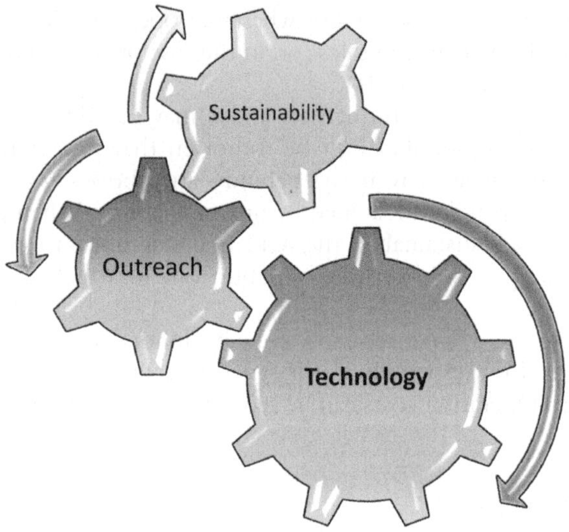

Fig. 6.6 Technology fosters microfinance sustainability and outreach

a physical (hardware) production and distribution are not necessary. This can be the case with virtual branches, transfer of dematerialized money, and so on—young and innovative business models are at hand (Fig. 6.6).

A rough but impressive idea of the outreach potential of the technology can be given by comparing the number of people who have a mobile phone but not a bank account: "Banks and cell phone companies are taking advantage of new handset technology and the expansion of cell phone use in developing economies to extend financial services to roughly 2 billion people who use cell phones but lack bank accounts."[8]

M-payments are expanding everywhere, and they have enormous scaling potential.

IT also has a profound impact on the MFI's organizational model. And computerized e-government of resources—beyond an old-fashioned "brick and mortar" pattern—changes the equilibriums between different stakeholders, easing the management process. To conveniently leverage

[8] Source: Global Envision, Microfinance Goes Mobile, http://www.globalenvision.org/library/4/1708/.

up the full power of new IT devices, e-governance must be service-oriented, addressing its efforts to clients and the market needs (with new e-governance-driven marketplaces), so as to ease their direct participation in a shared adventure, creating a working virtual community.

According to Sachs (2008), p. 307, contributions of ICT to sustainable development are represented by:

- connectivity, bypassing geographical obstacles;
- division of labor, among connected communities within the production chain;
- economies of scale, minimizing variable costs, due also to almost costless replication;
- accountability, due to the easiness of monitoring electronic transactions;
- matching buyers and sellers with B2B or B2C web intermediation;
- building social networks;
- easing education with distance learning.

The relationship between economic and financial flows is synthetized in Sect. 6.3.1.

6.3.1 Sustainability Metrics

Is microfinance business sustainable and affordable? If it is so, outreach may be pushed, provided that economic and financial positive marginality is not diluted up to the point of turning the business into an unprofitable adventure.

Considering a deposit-taking MFI, the basic model can be described in Table 6.1.

The starting point to answer this key question is accounting metrics of economic and financial flows, together with their assets and liability structure.[9] The answer should possibly be not static, following an evolutionary pattern where different scenarios may be envisaged and tested.

MFIs can reach their economic equilibrium only if revenues exceed costs and they can reach financial equilibrium only if cash inflows are

[9] See http://www.cgap.org/gm/document-1.9.8956/accounting%20course%20summary%2008%20final.pdf.

Table 6.1 MFI balance sheet

Assets and liabilities statement (balance sheet)	
Assets	*Equity and liabilities*
Cash & Bank (liquidity)	
Loans to clients (accounts receivable)	Paid in Capital
– Current	Reserves (cumulated profits and capital contributions)
– Past-Due	Net Profit/(Loss) current year (L)
– Restructured	**Total Equity (D)**
Net Outstanding Loans	
Intra-bank loans	Deposits
Other Current Assets	Short-term Borrowings*
Total Current Assets (A)	**Total Current Liabilities (E)**
Participations and Long-term Investments	Long-term Debt*
Fixed assets	**Total Long-Term Liabilities (F)**
Net Property and Equipment	
Total Long-Term Assets (B)	
Total Assets (C) = (A) + (B) = (G)	**Total Liabilities (G) = (D) + (E) + (F) = (C)**

*In domestic or foreign (hard) currency, creating in the latter case a forex mismatch with mainly domestic assets

higher than cash outflows. A positive cash flow balance is essential to maintain the capacity to cover the expenses in the medium to long term.

The main costs of an MFI are concerned with staff and infrastructural amounts and with the payment of negative interests to depositors, should the institution be enabled to collect funds from savers. We already know that the business model of an MFI is hardly scalable, especially if its dimensions are small and the clients are poor, with limited *pro capite* loans that are time and human resources consuming.

In the understanding of the MFI metrics, it is necessary to make a comprehensive, integrated analysis of the assets & liabilities statement, the income statement, and the cash flow statement, to link the structural dimension of the MFI's assets and liabilities (with its equity emerging as a differential) with its economic marginality and the cash flow balance. To the extent that the MFI is profitable, its net result increases the equity, and it is likely to produce a positive net cash flow, whereas a negative result erodes the equity and absorbs cash, typically demanding capital contributions or liquidity injections. This metrics quantitatively

Table 6.2 MFI's income statement and cash flow statement

INCOME STATEMENT	CASH FLOW STATEMENT
Positive Interest and fees on loans	Intermediation margin (J)
Positive Interest from investments	Depreciation and amortization (non-monetary costs)
Total income (H)	
	Δ accounts receivable
Negative Interest on debt	Paid advances
Negative Interest on deposits	Interests receivable
Provision for loan losses	Short-term liabilities
Administrative expenses	Tax liabilities
Staff costs	**Net Cash Flow from operating activities (N)**
Depreciation, Amortization and other Sundry operating charges	
Total operating expenses (I)	Δ tangible and intangible fixed assets
	Net Cash Flow from investment activities (O)
INTERMEDIATION MARGIN (J) = (H) – (I)	
	Δ Intra-bank and other short-term loans
Non-operating income	Δ Long-term loans
Grants and donations	**Net Cash Flow from financial activities (P) = = (N) + (O)**
Profit/(loss) before taxation (K)	**NET CASH FLOW (Q) = (S) – (R)**
Profit tax (L)	Cash Balance at the beginning of the year (R)
	Cash Balance at the end of the year (S)
NET RESULT (M) = (K) – (L)	

defines sustainability and—with it—the possibility of extending the MFI's outreach.

The assets & liabilities statement (balance sheet), with its variation from one year to the other, is to be linked to the income statement, to automatically generate the cash flow statement.[10]

Cashed-in incomes and cashed-out expenses are recorded in the income statement and then reported in the cash flow statement.

Survival liquidity is a key indicator both for the MFIs and its clients; when cash burnouts occur, rapid intervention is needed; the problem is particularly challenging if it concerns a deposit-taking MFI, with a potential systematic impact on the market that Central Banks accurately must monitor and, eventually, solve as a lender of last resort.

Sources of cash for the MFI are also to be considered, together with their different origin: domestic sources, not linked to foreign fundraising, are more stable during international crises and do not bear any currency risk, whereas they are more exposed to local shocks (Table 6.2).

[10] See, for instance, IAS 7 for an International accounting standard.

Table 6.3 Income statement of the MFI and its clients'

(Microfinance) client income statement		MFI income statement
Revenues from economic activities		
– (running) costs		
– (negative) interest rates on loans	⟷	Positive interest rates on lent funds
+ positive interests in deposits	⟷	– (negative) interest rates on deposits
		– staff and other operating costs
= net income		
– living costs (consumption)		= net income (if positive, making the MFI sustainable and allowing for outreaching new investments)
= net savings		
– borrowed funds		
+ deposits		
Free cash flow (available for savings and investments)		

The income statement of the MFI must go along with that of the poor clients, with positive margins acting as a safety net for both. In any other state of the world, subsidies are needed to make ends meet (Table 6.3).

Economic sustainability can be detected considering the income statement of a typical MFI and the impact of technology that can disrupt (Rothman & Grunstein, 2020) and re-engineer existing business models, as shown in Table 6.4.

The dynamic interpretation of Table 6.4 represents the canvas for the answer to the research question.

MFIs traditionally face high staff costs (6.a) and related operating expenses (6.c) for their core credit scoring and lending activities. Delinquency from untrustworthy borrowers represents another significant cost that contributes to the economic and financial absorption of resources.

To the extent that technology contributes to decreasing costs, economic marginality automatically improves. This surplus can be allocated, at least partially, to decreasing unitary interest rate margins, converging toward fair loan rates (Jarrow & Protter, 2019). MFIs may be tempted to cash in these extra margins, with a consequent mission drift from their original vocation; competition and the will of philanthropic shareholders may, however, minimize this risk, pushing toward a decrease in the level of interest rates. This reduction improves outreach, and so higher volumes of loans may partially compensate for lower marginality, preventing sustainability concerns.

Table 6.4 MFI income statement and impact of technology

Traditional MFI income statement		*Impact of technology*
1. Interest income		Savings in staff costs and loan delinquency (obtained combining product and process innovation) reduce unitary interest rate margins increasing volumes through expanded outreach
2. Interest expenses		
3. **Net interest margin**		
4. Net operating (non-interest) inco	4.a. Fees and commissions receivable	
	4.b. Fees and commissions payable	
	4.c. Net profit or loss on financial operations	
	4.d. Other operating income	Big data revenues …
5. Contribution margin		
6. Operating expenses	6.a. Staff costs	Automatization decreases staff costs; blockchains validate transactions
	6.b. Property costs	Clouding and dematerialization reduce branch costs
	6.c. Other operating expenses	
7. Net income before provisions		
8. Net provisions	8.a. Provisions on loans	Digitalized credit scoring reduces delinquency
	8.b. Other net provisions	
9. Income before tax		
10. Income tax		
11. Net income after tax		
Template adapted from	https://stats.oecd.org/index.aspx?DataSetCode=BPF1	

Technology can improve the supply and value chain on different layers, reducing the costs but also improving the revenues, not only with outreach-driven higher volumes but even with extra gains from innovative business models. For instance, the digitalization of information from profiling customers produces big data that represent a worthy asset, whose revenues can be shared with the clients, following a value co-creation pattern.

Business model extensions can also derive from the interaction with complementary activities and stakeholders. For instance, digital group lending through social networks eases the convergence with peer-to-peer lending, as shown later.

A core component of sustainability[11] is represented by the business' scalability that represents the capability to handle growing revenues, dramatically improving economic marginality, so contributing to making the business profitable.

6.3.2 *Operating Leverage and Scalability*

Operating leverage is a measure of how revenue growth translates into growth in operating income. It is a measure of leverage, and of how risky, or volatile, a company's operating income is.

Operating leverage is the degree to which a firm or project can increase operating income by increasing its revenues (positive interests for the MFI). A business that generates sales with a high gross margin and low variable costs has high operating leverage. The higher the degree of operating leverage, the greater the potential danger from forecasting risk, where a relatively small error in forecasting sales can be magnified into large errors in cash flow projections.

When a company reaches its break-even point (where operating revenues equal costs), then it can translate most of its incremental revenues on the EBIT if variable costs are negligible and fixed costs relevant. The opposite occurs when revenues shrink: in this case, the presence of fixed costs is a burden that increases the operating losses. There is so a boomerang effect and companies with higher fixed costs are more volatile and riskier.

[11] See Garcia-Perez et al. (2020).

The formula is the following:

$$\textbf{operating leverage} = \frac{\Delta\textbf{EBIT}/\textbf{EBIT}}{\Delta\textbf{revenues}/\textbf{revenues}} \tag{6.1}$$

Operating leverage so expresses the ratio between the percentage variation in the operating income (Earnings Before Interests and Taxes, EBIT) and the percentage variation of revenues.

The elements that influence the operating leverage are:

- Sale prices
- Volumes of sale
- Variable costs
- Fixed costs

We can consider an income statement where fixed and variable costs are represented separately.

Revenues
(variable costs)
= Contribution margin (1-2)
(fixed costs)
= Operating Profit = EBIT (3-4)

The contribution margin is the selling price per unit minus the variable cost per unit. It represents the portion of revenue that is not consumed by variable costs and so contributes to the coverage of fixed costs. This concept is one of the key building blocks of break-even analysis.

The contribution margin analysis is a measure of operating leverage; it expresses how growth in sales translates to growth in operating profits (EBIT).

The contribution margin is computed by using a management accounting version of the income statement that has been reformatted to group a business's fixed and variable costs.

The overall contribution margin is given by the product of the unitary contribution margin and the sold quantities (or the services given). The unitary contribution margin is mainly determined by the relationship between "prices and revenues" of the sold products and the "prices and costs" of the variable input factors of production.

Companies with a greater structure of fixed costs (that do not follow the variation of sold quantities, remaining unchanged—fixed) experiment a higher operating leverage. If a company has only variable costs, then the operating leverage has a unitary level and its contribution margin will coincide with the EBIT; to double the EBIT, sales will have to double, as they grow at the same pace of the variable costs and the contribution margin.

A classic dilemma is represented by the difference between a company with only fixed costs and another one with just variable costs: which one is better?

Both corner solutions have pros and cons: the former companies find it more difficult to reach a break-even point but when it does, the marginal growth of revenues is fully translated into higher EBIT, with a scalable impact on marginality. Companies with higher variable costs are on the contrary safer but less profitable when the outlook is positive, compensating lower risk with smaller returns.

The contribution margin can be increased:

a .With a higher profit margin, expressed by the difference "price/revenue" vs. "price/cost";
b .Improving the efficiency of variable factors of production;
c .Increasing the volumes of sales.

Fixed costs are the second determinant of EBIT. Costs are "fixed" if they do not vary when production changes. The cost structure and the mix of fixed vs. variable costs is a strategic option of any company but it also depends on the industry. For example, retail companies can choose from shops that are fully owned or in franchising; staff can be represented by employees or freelance workers, etc. Some sectors however have strategic constraints that limit the possibility of the company to select its cost structure. For instance, in the automotive sector, fixed costs and investments are typically high and they are difficult to reduce below certain thresholds.

Fixed costs are typically significant in the banking sector, where staff costs and IT investments matter.

Labor cost is just partially fixed, and it has extraordinary components that are linked to performance (stock options, etc.).

The degree of operating leverage (DOL) is a synthetic indicator of the operating risk, estimated comparing the contribution margin (total revenues – total variable costs) to the EBIT (EBIT = total revenues – total variable costs – fixed costs):

$$DOL = (TR-VC)/(TR - VC - FC) = CM/EBIT \quad (6.2)$$

Where:

DOL = degree of operating leverage

TR = total revenues

VC = variable costs

FC = fixed costs

CM = contribution margin.

The break-even point (BEP) in economics, business—and specifically cost accounting—is the point at which total cost and total revenue are equal, i.e., "even." There is no net loss or gain, and one has "broken even," though opportunity costs have been paid and capital has received the risk-adjusted, expected return. In short, all costs that must be paid are paid, and there is neither profit nor loss.

The break-even point (BEP) or break-even level represents the sales amount—in either unit (quantity) or revenue (sales) terms—that is required to cover total costs, consisting of both fixed and variable costs to the company. Total profit at the break-even point is zero. It is only possible for a firm to pass the break-even point if the dollar value of sales is higher than the variable cost per unit. This means that the selling price of the good must be higher than what the company paid for the good or its components for them to cover the initial price they paid (variable costs). Once they surpass the break-even price, the company can start making a profit.

The break-even point is one of the most used concepts of financial analysis and is not only limited to economic use but can also be used by entrepreneurs, accountants, financial planners, managers, and even marketers. Break-even points can be useful to all avenues of a business, as it allows employees to identify required outputs and work toward meeting these.

The break-even value is not generic and will vary dependent on the individual business. Some businesses may have a higher or lower break-even point, however, each business must develop a break-even point calculation, as this will enable them to see the number of units they need to sell to cover their variable costs. Each sale will contribute to the payment of fixed costs. The break-even point (BEP) or break-even level represents the sales amount—in either unit (quantity) or revenue (sales) terms—that is required to cover total costs, consisting of both fixed and variable costs to the company. Total profit at the break-even point is zero. It is only possible for a firm to pass the break-even point if the dollar value of sales is higher than the variable cost per unit. This means that the selling price of the good must be higher than what the company paid for the good or its components for them to cover the initial price they paid (variable costs). Once they surpass the break-even price, the company can start making a profit.

The main purpose of break-even analysis is to determine the minimum output that must be exceeded for a business to profit. It also is a rough indicator of the earnings impact of marketing activity. A firm can analyze ideal output levels to be knowledgeable on the number of sales and revenues that would meet and surpass the break-even point. If a business doesn't meet this level, it often becomes difficult to continue operation.

The break-even point is one of the simplest, yet least-used analytical tools. Identifying a break-even point helps provide a dynamic view of the relationships between sales, costs, and profits. For example, expressing break-even sales as a percentage of actual sales can help managers understand when to expect to break even (by linking the percent to when in the week or month this percent of sales might occur).

The break-even point is a special case of target income sales, where target income is 0 (breaking even). This is very important for financial analysis. Any sales made past the break-even point can be considered profit (after all initial costs have been paid).

Break-even analysis can also provide data that can be useful to the marketing department of a business as well, as it provides financial goals that the business can pass on to marketers, so they can try to increase sales.

Break-even analysis can also help businesses see where they could restructure or cut costs for optimum results. This may help the business become more effective and achieve higher returns. In many cases, if an entrepreneurial venture is seeking to get off the ground and enter into a market it is advised that they formulate a break-even analysis to suggest to potential financial backers that the business has the potential to be viable and at what points.

The break-even point (BEP) is the point at which cost, or expenses and revenue are equal: there is no net loss or gain (Fig. 6.7).

A company's scalability implies that the underlying business model offers the potential for economic growth within the company. In broader terms, scalability is the capability of a system, network, or process to handle a growing amount of work, or its potential to be enlarged to accommodate that growth (Fig. 6.8).

These general considerations may be applied to the MicroFinTech industry. According to Philippon (2019), changes in fixed versus variable costs are likely to improve access to financial services and reduce inequality.

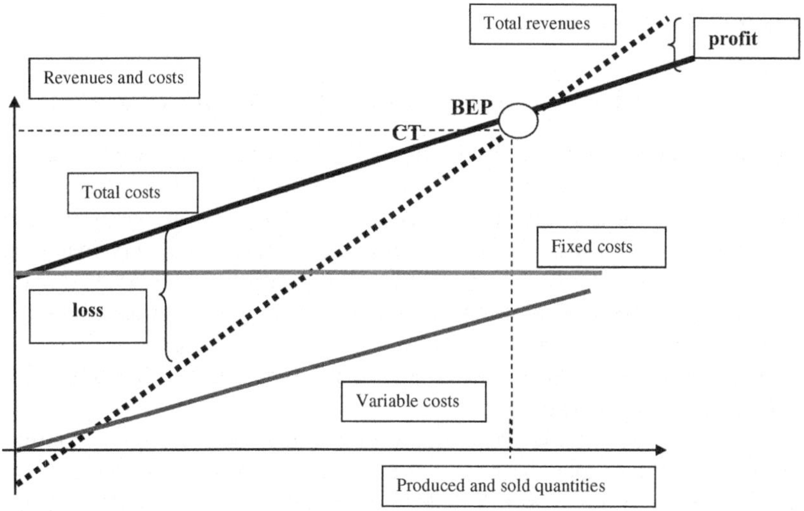

Fig. 6.7 Break-even analysis

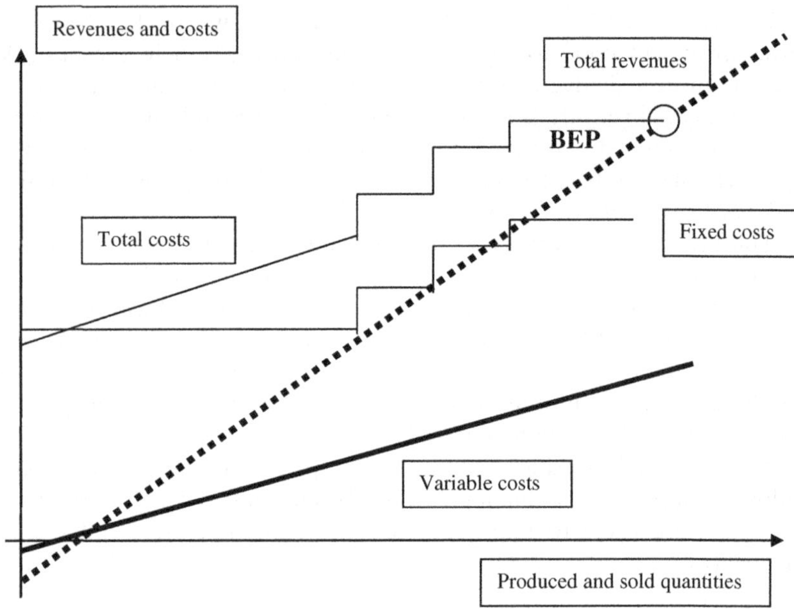

Fig. 6.8 Break-even point

6.3.3 Metcalfe's Law and Network Scalability

Metcalfe's law states the effect of a TLC network is proportional to the square of the number of connected users of the system (n^2). Metcalfe's law was originally presented c. 1980, not in terms of users but rather of "compatible communicating devices" (e.g., fax machines, telephones, etc.). Only later with the globalization of the Web did this law carry over to users and networks as its original intent was to describe Ethernet purchases and connections. The law is also very much related to economics and business management, especially with competitive companies looking to merge.

Metcalfe's law characterizes many of the network effects of communication technologies and networks such as the Internet, social networking, and the World Wide Web. Metcalfe's law is related to the fact that the number of unique possible connections in a network of n nodes can be expressed mathematically. If a network is composed of n people and each of them assigns to the network a value that is proportional to the number of other participants, then the value that all the n people assign to the network is the following:

$$n * (n - 1) = n^2 - n \tag{6.3}$$

The law has often been illustrated using the example of fax machines: a single fax machine is useless, but the value of every fax machine increases with the total number of fax machines in the network because of the total number of people with whom each user may send and receive documents increases. Likewise, in social networks, the greater number of users with the service, the more valuable the service becomes to the community (Fig. 6.9).

Two telephones can make only one connection, five can make 10 connections, and twelve can make 66 connections.

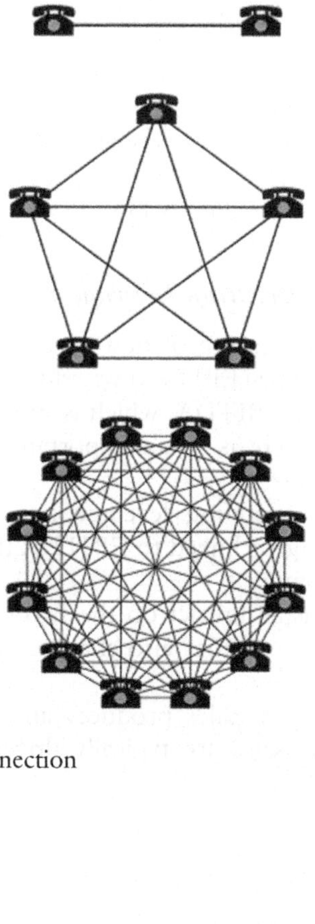

Fig. 6.9 Telephone connection

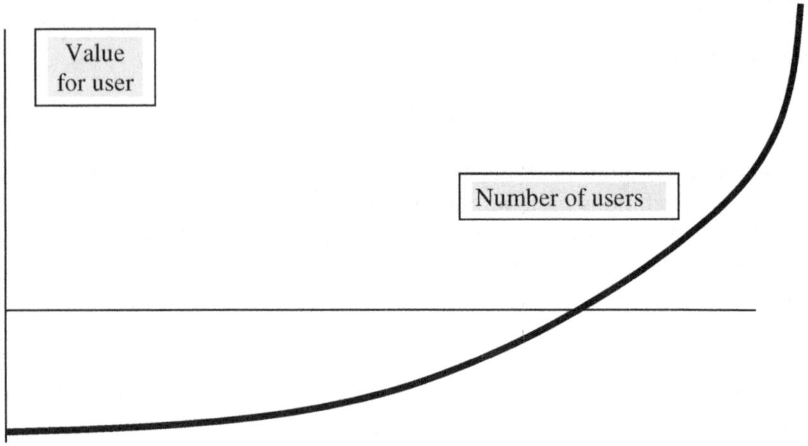

Fig. 6.10 Value for the user according to Metcalfe's law

Metcalfe's law is fully consistent with a network scenario (Barabási, 2016) where group lending and P2P members interact through digital platforms. Network scalability is so compatible with microfinance potentialities (Fig. 6.10).

The BEP is the following (Fig. 6.11).

6.3.4 *Operating Leverage and Liquidity*

Operating leverage is a measure of how revenue growth translates into growth in operating income (EBIT). If we add up depreciation and amortization to EBIT, we get EBITDA, which is simultaneously an economic and liquidity margin. There is so an important link between operating leverage and liquidity.

Any change in the operating leverage has an impact on liquidity because operating leverage is linked to EBITDA that is the first parameter of the cash flow statement.

Any sales increase has an impact on the EBITDA and the EBIT. The mix of fixed vs. variable costs may also change, influencing the operating net working capital.

Normally, an increase in sales produces an increase in both receivables and stock; higher sales are typically driven by higher purchases,

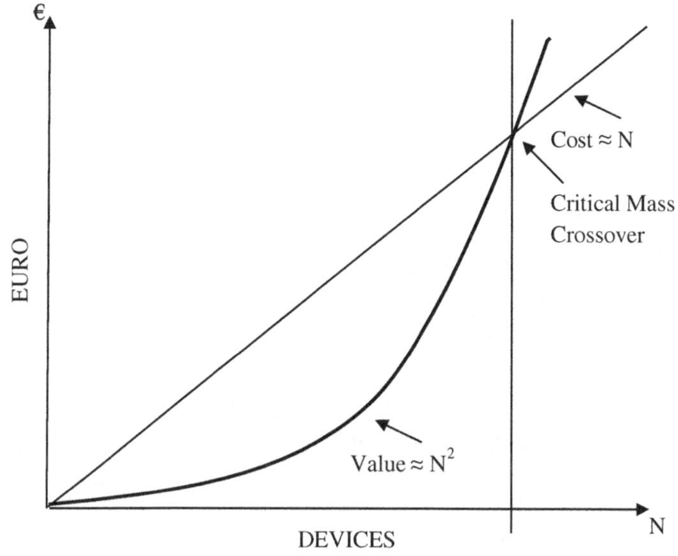

Fig. 6.11 Break-Even Point with Metcalfe's law

with a consequent increase also in payables. If the economic marginality of the sales increase remains positive, then the net working capital is likely to grow since the increase in receivables and stock exceeds the growth of payables. A higher net working capital absorbs cash, and so part of the liquidity that is generated by a higher EBIT/EBITDA is used for financing this growth. Higher sales are often fuelled also by an increase in investments/Capital Expenditure (CAPEX) that also absorbs cash (Fig. 6.12).

6.4 Sponsoring Technology with Impact Investment and Results-Based Financing

The adoption of technology is an expensive and risky process that may cause a digital divide (Ozili, 2020) not only among the MFI's clients but also considering the institution. Some MFIs may be unable to adopt technology for lack of funds, missing expertise, managerial drawbacks, technical shortcomings, etc.

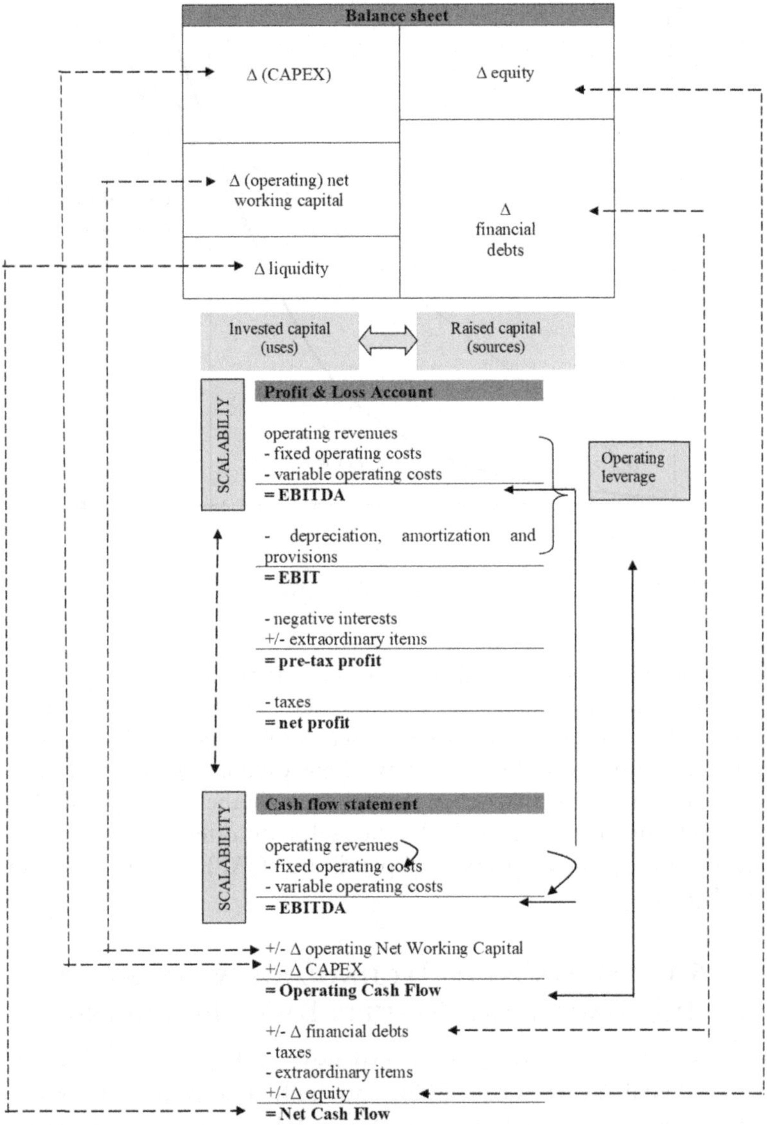

Fig. 6.12 Operating leverage and cash flows

Small-scale MFIs may also be deprived of the necessary critical mass to efficiently use technological assets, scaling up the investments to find a break-even point.

Donors and social investors may also be cautious about the unpredictable returns of technology adoption.

All these bottlenecks may hamper optimal technology adoption.

There are however incentives that contrast these pitfalls and soften criticalities.

Impact investing refers to investments "made into companies, organizations, and funds to generate a measurable, beneficial social or environmental impact alongside a financial return." [12] Impact investing is a rapidly growing industry powered by investors who are determined to generate social and environmental impact as well as financial returns. This is taking place all over the world, and across all asset classes. Impact investing is unlocking significant sums of private investment capital to complement public resources and philanthropy in addressing global challenges.

According to Ashta (2012), the question to be addressed is how venture capital will help this MFI scale its business and profits? Can developed country investors, facing a lack of profitable investment opportunities in the wake of the financial crisis, marry their business acumen with social responsibility toward the poor?

If impact investors may provide the institutional framework for the incubation of technological investments, results-based financing (or similar instruments as performance-based financing or payment by result) could represent a complementary tool to make ventures conditional upon results, so minimizing the overall investment risk.

The rationale behind results-based financing (RBF) approach is that the financier only disburses when the agreed results have been achieved. The approach, therefore, differs from more traditional approaches where aid is given in advance to finance input for activities that are expected to produce results, with the risk that these do not materialize if the cooperation partner does not use the funds well, or if the program logic has been misjudged. An RBF approach makes it possible to move the focus from

[12] https://web.archive.org/web/20170708185027/https://thegiin.org/assets/GIIN_AnnualImpactInvestorSurvey_2017_Web_Final.pdf.

activities and plans to the monitoring of results and learning about what works.[13]

Technology providers are stimulated by RBF to reach verifiable performance goals that can be scaled up in similar industries (e.g., MFI located in different continents but with similar targets), being international donors often keen to invest in diversified environments.

6.5 Leveraging MFIs With P2P Lending and Crowdfunding

Crowdfunding represents the latest incarnation of social lending, which has existed for centuries (Everett, 2019), and is so consistent with microfinance, representing a trendy pattern of technological upgrading.

Peer-to-peer lending platforms (P2P) and microfinance (Assadi et al., 2018; Yum et al., 2012) are both innovative instruments, having the potential of promoting financial inclusion and respond to the lack of trust in traditional financial institutions experienced with the financial crisis. They both have recently experienced great development and, at the same time, challenged legal systems' traditional legal categories and regulations (Macchiavello, 2013).

Internet-based P2P lending features have already been anticipated in Sect. 4.11.3.

Crowdfunding, similarly to microfinance, emerged from philanthropy, each taking a different and unique approach. Microfinance's focus on providing financial services to those excluded from formal financial services, most of which are poor, has greatly supported its spread throughout the developing world, where it is most needed. Crowdfunding builds upon the power of the masses both as a source of funds and as a source of their collective capabilities, which combined are greater than any individual. To date, crowdfunding has taken several forms, some acting on a pure philanthropic and donation basis, with others exploring various forms of for-profit and entrepreneurial support, all of which provide improved access to funding by removing intermediaries,

[13] https://www.sida.se/contentassets/1b13c3b7a75947a2a4487e2b0f61267c/18235.pdf.

such as venture capital funds, business angels, and banks. This approach can be found mostly in the developed world, where social networks have grown dramatically, and communication has been made easier with the spread of the Internet (Marom, 2013).

Peer-to-peer lending has sprung up in recent years, defined by its flexibility to meet the needs of loan applicants from a range of financial backgrounds. Institutional investors' reluctance to fund small business owners has facilitated the widespread acceptance of peer-to-peer lending, which represents a convenient investment medium for prospective borrowers, individual investors, and P2P companies. The inclusive model inherent in P2P lending concerns for investors who expect to maximize returns while minimizing default risks (Jones, 2016).

Information asymmetry is one of the fundamental problems that online peer-to-peer (P2P) lending platforms face. This problem becomes more acute when platforms are used for microfinance, where the targeted customers are mostly economically underprivileged people (Yum et al., 2012).

6.6 The Networked Digital Ecosystem

Digital-based financial inclusion is a form of organizing development interventions through networks of state institutions, international development organizations, philanthropic investment, and FinTech companies. The FinTech–philanthropy–development complex generates digital ecosystems that map, expand, and monetize digital footprints (Gabor & Brooks, 2017).

MicroFinTech applications are likely to reshape the whole microfinance ecosystem. The impact of technology concerns the digital networks that collect and exchange (big) data in real-time.

An analysis of the ecosystem will be conducted considering (Fig. 6.13, which reproduces Fig. 2.2):

a. The main properties of a microfinance network;
b. Digital nodes as a bridging vertex that re-engineers the ecosystem, catalyzing innovation;
c. A reinterpretation of the (traditional) microfinance system described in Sect. 2.2.

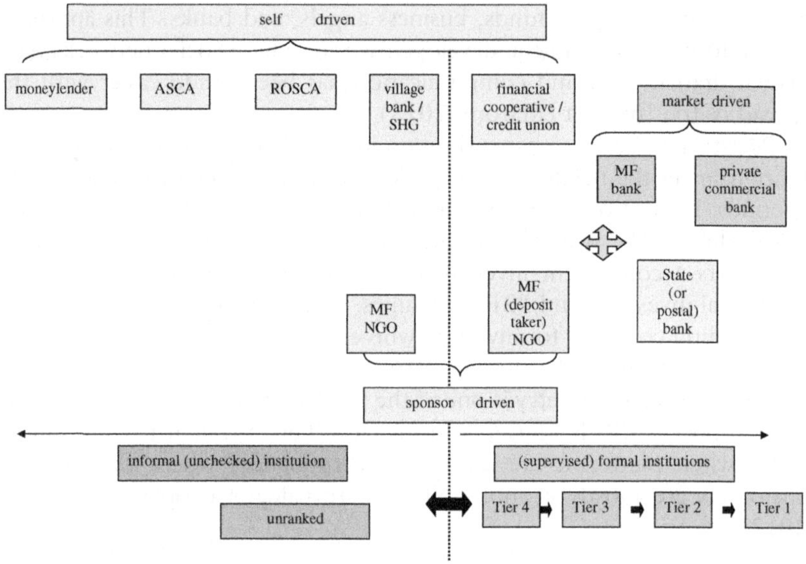

Fig. 6.13 Technology-driven microfinance evolution

6.7 Digitalization of Self-Help Groups

A self-help group (SHG) is a financial intermediary committee usually composed of 10–20 local women or men between 18 and 40 years. Most self-help groups are located in India, though SHGs can be found in other countries, especially in South Asia and Southeast Asia. SHG is nothing but a group of people who are on daily wages, they form a group and from that group, one person collects the money and gives the money to the person who is in need.

Members also make small regular savings contributions over a few months until there is enough money in the group to begin lending. Funds may then be lent back to the members or others in the village for any purpose. In India, many SHGs are "linked" to banks for the delivery of microcredit.

According to Badruddin (2017), these are the benefits and challenges of SHGs (Table 6.5).

Table 6.5 Benefits and challenges of Self-Help Groups (SHGs)

Benefits of digitalization of SHGs	*Challenges in digitalization of SHGs*
The advantages of implementing technology for the digitization of SHGs to increase the outreach are: • Main-streaming of SHG members with financial inclusion agenda enabling access to a wider range of financial services; • Digitization of SHG accounts will increase bankers' comfort in credit appraisal and linkage of SHGs; • Automatic and accurate rating of SHGs will be available online for banks; • Mapping of persons not covered under Aadhaar platform and bringing them under Aadhaar fold; • Ease of transfer of social benefits and Direct Benefit Transfer (DBT) through Aadhaar linked accounts and convergence with other government benefits; • A comprehensive information base and robust MIS can be developed about poor community covered, which may facilitate suitable interventions and convergence of other program for social and financial empowerment; • It will help in identifying suitable interventions and support for proper nurturing and strengthening of SHGs	• Convincing rural community, stakeholders including banks for full participation; • Sourcing of information from poor database and records; • Large-scale training and capacity building of SHGs, SHPIs, and others involved in implementation of the program; • Capture of field level information from SHGs in a limited time and periodic upload of savings and credit details of SHGs

6.8 The Dark Side of MicroFinTech

Like many technology-driven applications, MicroFinTech improves the capacity of microfinance services, so exacerbating its pitfalls. It should not be forgotten that being poor and indebted is worse than being just poor.

Technology reduces the segmentation of the stakeholders, making contagion (of instability, etc.) more likely and pervasive.

FinTech providers can promote economic growth during good economic times by increasing the volume of financial transactions in the financial system, although it is still unknown whether FinTech providers and their activities can exacerbate economic crises during bad economic times (Ozili, 2018).

Cybercrimes are also made possible by technological apps.

Digitalization goes beyond the empathic face-to-face confrontation and may exacerbate some psychological issues.

6.9 Microfinance Digitizers: From Kiva to M-pesa and Lendwithcare

MFIs are increasingly digitizing their business models, and examples from larger institutions are growing, representing a template for smaller operators.

Digitalization is embedded in operational activities since its inception in newly formed startups. In other cases, established MFIs are reinventing their businesses by introducing IT features, from m-banking to other applications. Cross-pollination with microfinance-oriented FinTechs represents a useful chance both for established players and newcomers.

Kiva is a non-profit organization headquartered in San Francisco, California that allows people to lend money via the Internet to low-income entrepreneurs and students in 77 countries. Kiva's mission is "to expand financial access to help underserved communities thrive" (https://www.kiva.org/about).

Kiva relies on a network of field partners to administer the loans on the ground. These field partners can be MFIs, social impact businesses, schools, or non-profit organizations. Borrowers pay interest on most loans to the field partners, and the field partners are charged small fees by Kiva. Kiva is supported by grants, loans, and donations from its users, corporations, and national institutions.

Kiva is a lending platform that follows this working scheme:

1. Choose a borrower
   Browse by category and find an entrepreneur to support
2. Make a loan
   Help fund a loan with as little as $25.
3. Get repaid
   Kiva borrowers have a 96% repayment rate historically.
4. Repeat
   Relend your money or withdraw your funds.

Acting as an intermediator, Kiva does not retain any commission.

M-Pesa (M stands for mobile, pesa is Swahili for money) is a mobile phone-based money transfer service, payments, and micro-financing service, launched in 2007 by Vodafone Group plc and Safaricom, the largest mobile network operator in Kenya. M-Pesa allows users to deposit, withdraw, transfer money, pay for goods and services, access credit and savings, all with a mobile device. Mobile financial services such as M-Pesa in Kenya are said to promote inclusion (Van Hove & Dubus, 2019).

Telecom microfinance banking is a further trendy issue. Bigger TLC operators, dealing with mobile information of their clients, gather and use big data that are increasingly valuable. Their financial resources also allow them to enter the banking industry, representing a threat to incumbent traditional banks.[14]

Another example is represented by Lendwithcare, an institution that works with several MFIs in the countries in which it operates. If the MFI is happy with an entrepreneur's idea or business plan, they approve the proposal and provide the initial loan requested. They also help the entrepreneur construct their profile for lendwithcare.org.

[14] Younas and Kalimuthu (2021).

Lenders can browse the list of entrepreneurs on the Web site, read about their businesses, see the value of the loan they have requested, the percentage of the loan already provided by other lenders, and then choose an entrepreneur to lend to. Once the entrepreneur's loan is fully funded, the money is transferred to the MFI to replace the initial loan already paid out to the entrepreneur. During this process lenders receive progress updates regarding the entrepreneur's progress. The entrepreneur gradually pays back their loan according to a repayment schedule. The MFI transfers these repayments to CARE International who then credits the payment into lenders' lendwithcare.org accounts. Lenders can then either withdraw their money using a PayPal account or can use the credit to provide a loan to another entrepreneur.

Lendwithcare is among the first crowdfunding platforms specifically dedicated to supporting individual and group entrepreneurs in developing countries through partner microfinance institutions. A key objective of Lendwithcare is to identify the attributes (i.e., the characteristics of crowdfunding projects in their online descriptions) that affect investors/potential investors when taking their investment decision (Chakhar et al., 2020).

6.10 Reinterpreting the Key Microfinance Principles

The key microfinance principles examined in Chapters 2 and 3 are synthetically reconsidered here, analyzing the impact of technology (Table 6.6).

Table 6.6 The impact of technology on the Key Principles in Microfinance

Key principle	*Impact of technology*
1. Poor people need a variety of financial services, not just loans In addition to credit, they want savings, insurance, and money transfer services	FinTech-driven technology provides a wider set of instruments
2. Microfinance is a powerful tool to fight poverty Poor households use financial services to raise income, build their assets, and cushion themselves against external shocks	Technology can cut operating costs and improve outreach
3. Microfinance means building financial systems that serve the poor Microfinance will reach its full potential only if it is integrated into a country's mainstream financial system	Technology-driven scale-up strengthens the financial ecosystem
4. Microfinance can pay for itself and must do so if it is to reach very large numbers of poor people Unless microfinance providers charge enough to cover their costs, they will always be limited by the scarce and uncertain supply of subsidies from donors and governments	Technology reduces unitary lending costs, easing the reach of operational and financial self-sufficiency
5. Microfinance is about building permanent local financial institutions That can attract domestic deposits, recycle them into loans, and provide other financial services	Technology dematerializes physical locations
6. Microcredit is not always the answer Other kinds of support may work better for people who are so destitute that they are without income or means of repayment	Technology broadens the microfinance scope
7. Interest rate ceilings hurt poor people by making it harder for them to get credit	Technology-driven operational savings can be partially converted to an interest rate reduction

(continued)

Table 6.6 (continued)

Key principle	*Impact of technology*
Making many small loans costs more than making a few large ones. Interest rate ceilings prevent microfinance institutions from covering their costs, and thereby choke off the supply of credit for poor people	
8. The job of the government is to enable financial services, not to provide them directly	Technology is not government-driven
Governments can rarely do a good job of lending, but they can set a supporting policy environment	
9. Donor funds should complement private capital, not compete with it	Technology-driven crowdfunding platforms can collect private capital in many complementary forms, from donations to reward-based schemes or equity injections
Donors should use the appropriate grant, loan, and equity instruments temporarily to build the institutional capacity of financial providers, develop support infrastructure, and support experimental services and products	
10. The key bottleneck is the shortage of strong institutions and managers	Technology, improving self-sufficiency, reinforces MFIs
Donors should focus their support on building capacity	
11. Microfinance works best when it measures—and discloses—its performance	Technology can improve performance management and make it timelier
Reporting not only helps stakeholders judge costs and benefits but also improves performance. MFIs need to produce accurate and comparable reporting on financial performance (e.g., loan repayment and cost recovery) as well as social performance (e.g., number and poverty level of clients)	

Source (of the first column): CGAP (2006), *Good Practice Guidelines for Funders of Microfinance*, www.cgap.org

References

Allison, T. H., Davis, B. C., Short, J. C., & Webb, J. W. (2015). Crowdfunding in a prosocial microlending environment: Examining the role of intrinsic versus extrinsic Cues. *Entrepreneurship Theory and Practice, 39*(1), 53–73.

Anglin, A. H., Short, J. C., Ketchen, D. J., Allison, T. H., & McKenny, A. F. (2019). Third–party signals in crowdfunded microfinance: The role of microfinance institutions. *Entrepreneurship Theory and Practice, 44*(4), 623–644.

Ashta, A. (2012). Co–creation for impact investment in microfinance. *Strategic Change, 21*, 71–81.

Ashta, A. (2018a). News and trends in fintech and digital microfinance: Why are European MFIs invisible? *FIIB Business Review, 7*(4).

Assadi, D., Ashta, A., & Jung, A. (2018). A tale of three musketeers of alternative finance: Stagnating microcredit, growing P2P online lending and striving for slow money. *Journal of Innovation Economics, 26*(2), 13–36.

Attuel-Mendes, L. (2016). Crowdfunding and crowdmicrofinance, an evolution of models for entrepreneurship of the poor. *Open Access Library Journal, 3*, 1–7.

Badruddin, A. (2017). Conceptualization of the effectiveness of fintech in financial inclusion. *International Journal of Engineering Technology Science and Research, 4*(7), 959–965.

Barabási, A. (2016). *Network science*. Cambridge University Press.

Benami, E., & Carter, M. R. (2021). Can digital technologies reshape rural microfinance? Implications for savings, credit & insurance. *Applied Economic Perspectives and Policy* (in press).

Berns, J. P., Figueroa-Armijos, M., da Motta Veiga, S. P., & Dunne, T. C. (2020). Dynamics of lending–based prosocial crowdfunding: Using a social responsibility lens. *Journal of Business Ethics, 161*(1), 169–185.

Berns, J. P., Shahriar, A. Z. M., & Unda, L. A. (2021). Delegated monitoring in crowdfunded microfinance: Evidence from Kiva. *Journal of Corporate Finance, 66*, 101864.

Blakstad, S., & Allen, R. (2018). SME microfinance, fractional ownership and crowdfunding. In *FinTech revolution*. Palgrave Macmillan.

Bos, J. W. P., & Millone, M. (2015). Practice what you preach: Microfinance business models and operational efficiency. *World Development, 70*, 28–42.

Buckley, R. P., & Webster, S. (2016). Fintech in developing countries: Charting new customer journeys. *Journal of Financial Transformation, 44*, 151–159.

Cai, W., Polzin, F., & Stam, E. (2019). *Crowdfunding and social capital: A systematic literature review*. Available at https://ssrn.com/abstract=3361748.

CGAP. (2019). *Fintechs and financial inclusion. Looking past the hype and exploring their potential*. Available at https://www.cgap.org/sites/default/

files/publications/2019_05_Focus_Note_Fintech_and_Financial_Inclusion_1_0.pdf.

Chakhar, S., Ishizaka, A., Thorpe, A., Cox, J., Nguyen, T., & Ford, L. (2020). Calculating the relative importance of condition attributes based on the characteristics of decision rules and attribute reducts: Application to crowdfunding. *European Journal of Operational Research, 286*(2), 689–712.

Chauvin Alarcon, M. F. (2011). *The business model of microfinance institutions: Value creation and sustainability*. Akademiker Verlag.

Chetty, K., Josie, J. et al. (2019). *Review of fintech strategies for financial inclusion in Sub–Saharan Africa*. Available at https://www.g20-insights.org/wp-content/uploads/2019/05/t20-japan-tf2-10-fintech-strategies-financial-inclusion-sub-saharan-africa-1.pdf.

Dorfleitner, G., Oswald, E.-M., & Röhe, M. (2020). The access of microfinance institutions to financing via the worldwide crowd. *The Quarterly Review of Economics and Finance, 75*, 133–146.

Everett, C. R. (2019). *Origins and development of credit–based crowdfunding*. Available at https://ssrn.com/abstract=2442897.

Gabor, D., & Brooks, S. (2017). The digital revolution in financial inclusion: International development in the fintech era. *New Political Economy, 22*(4), 423–436.

Hussain, A. H. M. (2017). Financial inclusion through mobile micro banking: Building a prototype for transaction cost efficiency in microfinance practice. *Global Disclosure of Economics and Business, 6*(1), 19–28.

Jarrow, R., & Protter, P. (2019, December). Fair microfinance loan rates. *International Review of Finance, 19*(4), 909–918.

Jenik, I., & Lauer, K. (2017). *Regulatory sandboxes and financial inclusion*. Available at https://www.cgap.org/sites/default/files/Working-Paper-Regulatory-Sandboxes-Oct-2017.pdf.

Jenik, I., Lyman, T., & Nava, A. (2017). *Crowdfunding and financial inclusion*. Available at https://www.cgap.org/sites/default/files/Working-Paper-Crowdfunding-and-Financial-Inclusion-Mar-2017.pdf.

Jones, J. (2016). How microfinance can close asymmetrical information on peer–to–peer platforms. *Bsu Honors Program Theses and Projects*, item 152. Available at https://Vc.Bridgew.Edu/Honors_Proj/152.

Kim, H., & De Moor, L. (2017). The case of crowdfunding in financial inclusion: A survey. *Strategic Change-Briefings in Entrepreneurial Finance, 26*(2), 193–212.

Macchiavello, E. (2013). A new frontier of socially responsible financial sector: Microfinance and peer–to–peer lending. *Banca Impresa Società, 2*, 277–336.

Macchiavello, E. (2017). *Microfinance and financial inclusion: The challenge of regulating alternative forms of finance*. Routledge.

Marakkath, N., & Attuel-Mendes, L. (2015). Can microfinance crowdfunding reduce financial exclusion? Regulatory issues. *International Journal of Bank Marketing, 33*(5), 624–636.

Marom, D. (2013). Crowd-empowered microfinance. In J. P. Gueyie, R. Manos, & J. Yaron (Eds.),*Microfinance in developing countries*. Palgrave Macmillan.

Martínez-Climent, C., Costa-Climent, R., & Oghazi, P. (2019). Sustainable Financing through Crowdfunding. *Sustainability, 11*, 934.

Ozili, P. K. (2018). Impact of digital finance on financial inclusion and stability. *Borsa Istanbul Review, 18*(4), 329–340.

Ozili, P. K. (2020). Contesting digital finance for the poor. *Digital Policy, Regulation and Governance, 22*(2), 135–151.

Palanivelu, V. R., & Narmada, S. (2020). Impact of demonetisation on the micro finance sector. *International Journal of Advanced Science and Technology, 29*(4), 705–712.

Philippon, T. (2019). *On FinTech and financial inclusion*. Stern School of Business. Available at https://www.bis.org/events/conf190628/philippon.pdf.

Rothman, T., & Grunstein, D. (2020). *Valuation of early-stage companies and disruptive technologies*. Palgrave Macmillan.

Royal, C., & Windsor, S. (2014). Microfinance, crowdfunding, and sustainability: A case study of telecenters in a South Asian developing country. *Strategic Change, 23*(7–8), 425–438.

Saksonova, S., & Kuzmina-Merlino, I. (2017). Fintech as financial innovation—The possibilities and problems of implementation. *European Research Studies Journal, XX*(3A), 961–973.

Salampasis D., & Mention A. (2018). FinTech: Harnessing innovation for financial inclusion. In *Handbook of blockchain, digital finance, and inclusion* (Vol. 2, pp. 451–461). Academic Press.

Sancha-Navarro, J. M., Sanchís-Pedregosa, C., & Oliver-Alfonso, M. D. (2018). Relationship between crowdfunding and microfinance: A theoretical approach. *Finance, Markets and Valuation, 4*(2), 63–72.

Sherwani, N. U. K., Junaid, I., & Zeba, M. (2018). Microfinance and crowdfunding: Alternative approaches for entrepreneurship development. *International Journal of Management, IT and Engineering, 8*(2), 233–243.

Sinha, S., Pandey, K., & Madan, N. (2018). Fintech and the demand side challenge in financial inclusion. *Enterprise Development and Microfinance, 29*(1), 94–98.

Van Hove, L., & Dubus, A. (2019, January 22). M-PESA and financial inclusion in Kenya: Of paying comes saving? *Sustainability, 11*(3), 568.

Villasenor, J. D., West, D. M., & Lewis, R. J. (2016). *The 2016 Brookings Financial and Digital Inclusion Project Report: Advancing equitable financial ecosystems*. Available at https://www.brookings.edu/wp-content/uploads/2016/08/fdip_20160816_project_report.pdf.

Younas, W., & Kalimuthu, K. R. (2021). Telecom microfinance banking versus commercial banking: a battle in the financial services sector. *Journal of Financial Services Marketing* (in press).

Yum, H., Lee, B., & Chae, M. (2012). From the wisdom of crowds to my own judgment In microfinance through online peer–to–peer lending platforms. *Electronic Commerce Research and Applications, 11*(5), 469–483.

Conclusion

After the pioneer experiment of Grameen Bank some 30 years ago, microfinance has entered the adult age, and thousands of mostly small MFIs are competing in a market where demand for financial services from the poorest is potentially unlimited, while supply is not.

While the success of microfinance has gone beyond any expectation, enormous problems are still on the ground and the road toward what is now considered microfinance's optimal goal—maximization of outreach to the poorest, combined with financial self-sustainability of MFIs—is still full of obstacles.

Academic research, both on theoretical and empirical grounds, is broad and it is proving useful in a field where flexibility and financial innovation, to overcome problems that make the poorest unbankable according to commercial banking standards, are greatly needed.

Local experiences are, however, showing a challenging universal application and what works in Bangladesh is not always successful in Bolivia or in sub-Saharan Africa, even if international cross-pollination plays a substantial role. Empirical evidence from millions of micro-cases is represented in models that often have just a local application: precisely the contrary of the fundamental rules of a scientific approach, from Galileo onwards… A disappointing but healthy lesson for those who believe that science alone is a solution to every problem, while the poorest need and deserve much more. And learning comes more from confusion and trial and error than from certainty.

R. Moro-Visconti, *MicroFinTech*, Palgrave Studies in Financial Services Technology, https://doi.org/10.1007/978-3-030-80394-0

Even in microfinance, the last mile to the client seems the most challenging, requiring a flexible cultural and technical adaptation to local habits and needs.

From empirical evidence and academic research, we might, however, draw precious indications for policy issues such as for instance the determination of the optimal level of interest rates; while significant rate charges, to cover great operating costs that derive from small unitary loans and weekly on-field money collection, are an evident obstacle to borrowing, rate ceilings or endless subsidies are—perhaps surprisingly—an even worse remedy.

The life cycle growth of MFIs that are surviving a Darwinian selection allows them to reach commercial banking status, being enabled to collect deposits and—in the best cases—to have links with international funders, mainly through Microfinance Investment Vehicles. For the few MFIs that until now have been able to jump on the train of global financial markets, smart opportunities of lower funding costs and more sophisticated financial services are on hand.

Further research and on-field application are strongly needed to make substantial progress in meeting the core needs of the destitute and underserved. Since the poorest are naturally humble, even scientists and practitioners addressing their problems should accordingly be.

The supply chain/business plan representation of a traditional versus technological MFI can be represented here in a more comprehensive way.

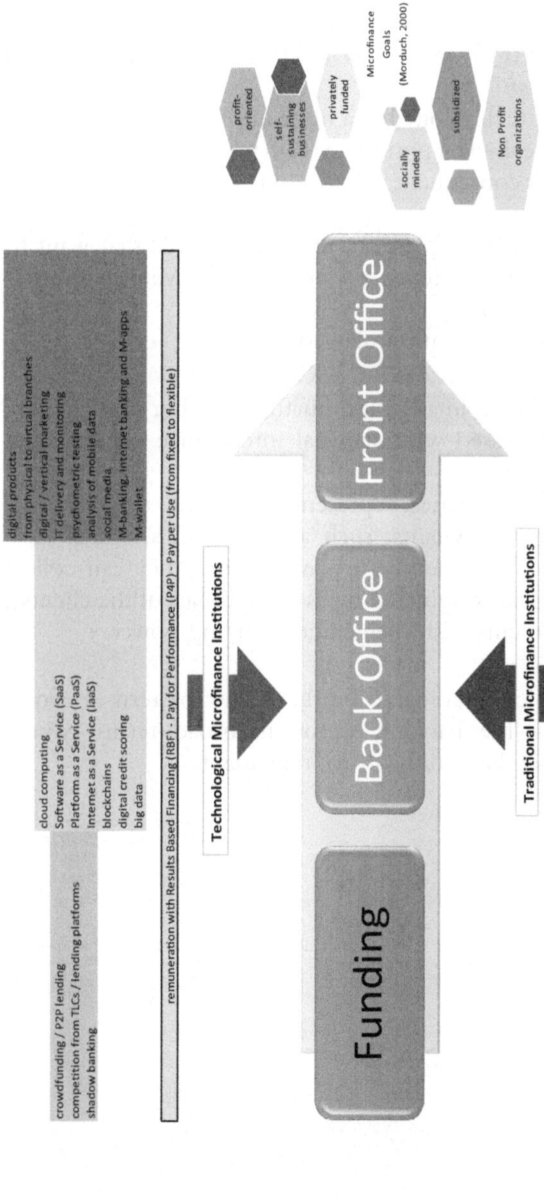

MicroFintech comprehensive outlook

The research question that has inspired this book is the following: *given the economic and organizational bottlenecks that prevent traditional microfinance in underdeveloped countries from outreach most of its potential clients, which is the impact on microfinance sustainability of technology-driven innovation?*

It has been shown that technology has a huge impact on sustainability, lowering the economic break-even point of MFIs (whose business is operationally intensive), with a consequent positive impact on outreach to the unbanked.

FinTechs represent a good template for upgrading MFIs that want to exploit technological advances. Hence the neologism "MicroFinTech," recalled in the title of the book.

Two trendy streams of investigation may concern:

1. The interaction of digital intangibles, nurtured by big data that are stored in cloud, processed with artificial intelligence patterns and verified by blockchains;
2. The role of new intermediaries, represented not only by MicroFinTechs, but also by Tech Giants, such as big TelCos, which have a competitive edge over incumbent players, since they can collect and process digital data (originated by the cellphones of the clients), levering tech investments with their huge spending power.

Only time will tell which is going to be the trendy pattern of evolution within an industry—the banking sector, in broad terms—where innovation has traditionally been difficult to implement.

References

Abrar, A., & Javaid, A. Y. (2016). The impact of capital structure on the profitability of microfinance institutions. *South Asian Journal of Management Sciences, 10*(1), 21–37.

Achleiter, A. K. (2008). *Social entrepreneurship and venture philanthropy in Germany*. TUM Business School, Technische Universität München.

Adeyeye, P., & Oyetayo, O. (2016). Balance sheet management and outreach success for microfinance banks in Nigeria. *International Journal of Economic Development Research and Investment, 7*(1), 473–499.

AFI. (2018). Digital transformation of microfinance and digitization of microfinance services to deepen financial inclusion in Africa. Available at https://www.afi-global.org/publications/2830/Digital-Transformation-of-Microfinance-Digitization-of-Microfinance-Services-to-Deepen-Financial-Inclusion-in-Africa.

Aggarwal, R., Goodell, J. W., & Selleck, L. J. (2015). Lending to women in microfinance: Role of social trust. *International Business Review, 24*(1), 55–65.

Agrawal, P., & Sen, S. (2017). Digital economy and microfinance. *The MIBM Research Journal, 5*(1), 27–35.

Agyemang-Badu, A. (2018). Financial inclusion, poverty and income inequality: Evidence from Africa. *Spiritan International Journal of Poverty Studies, 2*(2).

Akerlof, G. A. (1970, August). The market for "lemons": Quality uncertainty and the market mechanism. *Quarterly Journal of Economics, 84*, 488.

Al Hammadi, M., & Nobanee, H. (2019). *FinTech and sustainability: A mini-review*. Available at https://ssrn.com/abstract=3500873.

R. Moro-Visconti, *MicroFinTech*, Palgrave Studies in Financial Services Technology, https://doi.org/10.1007/978-3-030-80394-0

Ali, A., Jamaludin, N., & Othman, Z. H. (2016). Modeling microfinance acceptance among social network women entrepreneurs. *International Journal of Economics and Financial Issues, 6*(S4), 72–77.

Allet, M., & Green, H. M. (2015). Microfinance: Characteristics of microfinance institutions involved in environmental management. *Journal of Business Ethics, 126*, 395–414.

Allet, M., & Hudon, M. (2015). Green microfinance: Characteristics of microfinance institutions involved in environmental management. *Journal of Business Ethics, 126*, 395–414.

Allison, T. H., Davis, B. C., Short, J. C., & Webb, J. W. (2015). Crowdfunding in a prosocial microlending environment: Examining the role of intrinsic versus extrinsic cues. *Entrepreneurship Theory and Practice, 39*(1), 53–73.

Almansour, A. Y., Alrawashdeh, N., & Almansour, B. Y. (2020). The impact of capital structure on the performance of microfinance institutions. *Management Science Letters, 10*(4), 881–888.

Altinok, A. (2018). *Group lending, sorting, and risk sharing*. Available at https://www.researchgate.net/publication/324953074_Group_Lending_Sorting_and_Risk_Sharing.

Anglin, A. H., Short, J. C., Ketchen, D. J., Allison, T. H., & McKenny, A. F. (2019). Third-party signals in crowdfunded microfinance: The role of microfinance institutions. *Entrepreneurship Theory and Practice, 44*(4), 623–644.

Anikina, I. D., Gukova, V. A., Golodova, A. A., & Chekalkina, A. A. (2016). Methodological FinTech as financial innovation—The possibilities and problems of implementation 972 aspects of prioritization of financial tools for stimulation of innovative activities. *European Research Studies Journal, 19*(2), 100–112.

Armendariz De Aghion, B. A., & Morduch, J. (2010). *The economics of microfinance*. MIT press.

Armendariz De Aghion, B. A., & Szafarz, A. (2009). *On mission drift in microfinance institutions* (Working Paper CEB 09.015.RS). Université libre de Bruxelles. Available at http://ideas.repec.org/p/sol/wpaper/09-015.html.

Arner, D. W., Buckley, R. P., & Zetzsche, D. A. (2018). *FinTech for financial inclusion: A framework for digital financial transformation*. Available at https://ssrn.com/abstract=3245287.

Ashta, A. (Eds.). (2011). *Advanced technologies for microfinance*. IGI Global.

Ashta, A. (2012). Co-creation for impact investment in microfinance. *Strategic Change, 21*, 71–81.

Ashta, A. (2018a). News and trends in FinTech and digital microfinance: Why are European MFIs invisible? *FIIB Business Review*, *7*(4), 232–243.

Ashta, A. (2018b). *Lessons from microfinance for social entrepreneurship theory: The life cycle of the social enterprise*. Available at SSRN: https://ssrn.com/abstract=3136710.

Ashta, A., & Biot-Paquerot, G. (2018). FinTech evolution: Strategic value management issues in a fast changing industry. *Strategic Change, 27*(4), 301–311.

Ashta, A., & Patel, J. (2010). *Is SaaS the appropriate technology for microfinance?* Available at https://ssrn.com/abstract=1604741.

Assadi, D., Ashta, A., & Jung, A. (2018). A tale of three musketeers of alternative finance: Stagnating microcredit, growing P2P online lending and striving for slow money. *Journal of Innovation Economics, 26*(2), 13–36.

Attuel-Mendes, L. (2016). Crowdfunding and crowdmicrofinance: An evolution of models for entrepreneurship of the poor. *Open Access Library Journal, 3*, 1–7.

Awaworyi Churchill, S. (2020). Microfinance financial sustainability and outreach: Is there a trade-off? *Empirical Economics, 59*(3), 1329–1350.

Badruddin, A. (2017). Conceptualization of the effectiveness of FinTech in financial inclusion. *International Journal of Engineering Technology Science and Research, 4*(7), 959–965.

Banerjee, A. V., Bénabour, R., & Mookherjee, D. (2006). *Understanding poverty*. Oxford University Press.

Banerjee, A., & Duflo, E. (2007, Winter). The economic lives of the poor. *The Journal of Economic Perspectives, 21*(1), 141–168.

Banerjee, A., Duflo, E., Glennerster, R., & Kinnan, C. (2015). The miracle of microfinance? Evidence from a randomized valuation. *American Economic Journal: Applied Economics, 7*(1), 22–53.

Barabási, A. (2016). *Network science*. Cambridge University Press.

Barnett, B. (2011, October). *Cloud computing & financial services for the poor*. Usaid. Available at https://Www.Microfinancegateway.Org/Sites/Default/Files/Mfg-En-Toolkit-Cloud-Computing-Financial-Services-For-The-Poor-Primer-Procurement-Guidance-Oct-2011.Pdf.

Bartlett, R., Morse, A., Stanton, R., & Wallace, N. (2018). *Consumer-lending discrimination in the era of FinTech*. Available at https://law.utexas.edu/wp-content/uploads/sites/25/BMSW_20181115.pdf.

Bateman, M., & Chang, H. (2012). Microfinance and the illusion of development: From hubris to nemesis in thirty years. *World Economic Review, 2012*(1), 1–13.

Bazarbash, M. (2019). *FinTech in financial inclusion: Machine learning applications in assessing credit risk* (IMF Working Papers, Wp/19/109). Available at https://www.imf.org/en/Publications/WP/Issues/2019/05/17/FinTech-in-Financial-Inclusion-Machine-Learning-Applications-in-Assessing-Credit-Risk-46883.

Beck, T. (2015). *Microfinance: A critical literature survey* (Independent Evaluation Group (IEG) Working Paper Series, no. 2015/4). World Bank Group.

Benami, E., & Carter, M. R. (2021). Can digital technologies reshape rural microfinance? Implications for savings, credit & insurance. *Applied Economic Perspectives and Policy* (in press).

Berg, T., Burg, V., Gombović, A., & Puri, M. (2019). On the rise of FinTechs—Credit scoring using digital footprints. *The Review of Financial Studies, 33*(7), 2845–2897.

Bernards, N. (2019). Fintech and financial inclusion. In: T. Shaw, L. Mahrenbach, R. Modi, & X. Yi-Chong (Eds.), *The Palgrave handbook of contemporary international political economy*. Palgrave Macmillan.

Berns, J. P., Figueroa-Armijos, M., da Motta Veiga, S. P., & Dunne, T. C. (2020). Dynamics of lending-based prosocial crowdfunding: Using a social responsibility lens. *Journal of Business Ethics, 161*(1), 169–185.

Berns, J. P., Shahriar, A. Z. M., & Unda, L. A. (2021). Delegated monitoring in crowdfunded microfinance: Evidence from Kiva. *Journal of Corporate Finance, 66*, 101864.

Bhanot, D., & Bapat, V. (2015). Sustainability index of micro finance institutions (MFIs) and contributory factors. *International Journal of Social Economics, 42*, 387–403.

Blakstad, S., & Allen, R. (2018). SME microfinance, fractional ownership and crowdfunding. In *FinTech revolution*. Palgrave Macmillan.

Bömer, M., & Maxin, H. (2018). Why FinTechs cooperate with banks—Evidence from Germany. *ZVersWiss, 107*, 359–386.

Bos, J. W. P., & Millone, M. (2015). Practice what you preach: Microfinance business models and operational efficiency. *World Development, 70*, 28–42.

Brandl, B., & Hornuf, L. (2017). *Where did FinTechs come from, and where do they go? The transformation of the financial industry in Germany after digitalization* (SSRN Working Paper). Available at https://ssrn.com/abstract=3036555.

Broeders, H., & Khanna, S. (2015). *Strategic choices for banks in the digital age*. Mckinsey & Company—Financial Services. Available at http://www.Mckinsey.Com/Industries/Financial-Services/Our-Insights/Strategicchoices-For-Banks-In-The-Digital-Age.

Bruton, G., Khavul, S., Siegel, D., & Wright, M. (2015). New financial alternatives in seeding entrepreneurship: Microfinance, crowdfunding, and peer-to-peer innovations. *Entrepreneurship: Theory and Practice, 29*(1), 9–26.

Buckley, R. P., & Webster, S. (2016). FinTech in developing countries: Charting new customer journeys. *Journal of Financial Transformation, 44*, 151–159.

Budampati, S. (2018). Impact of Information technology on microfinance industry. *Advanced Science and Technology Letters, 150*, 116–121.

Buera, F. J., Kaboski, J. P., & Shin, Y. (2021). The macroeconomics of microfinance. *The Review of Economic Studies, 88*(1), 126–161.

Burlakov, G. (2019). *10 challenges for the financial services industry in 2019.* Available at https://technorely.com/blog/financialindustry-challenges/.

Cai, W., Polzin, F., & Stam, E. (2019). *Crowdfunding and social capital: A systematic literature review.* Available at https://ssrn.com/abstract=3361748.

CGAP. (2019). *FinTechs and financial inclusion. Looking past the hype and exploring their potential.* Available at https://www.cgap.org/sites/default/files/publications/2019_05_Focus_Note_Fintech_and_Financial_Inclusion_1_0.pdf.

Chakhar, S., Ishizaka, A., Thorpe, A., Cox, J., Nguyen, T., & Ford, L. (2020). Calculating the relative importance of condition attributes based on the characteristics of decision rules and attribute reducts: Application to crowdfunding. *European Journal of Operational Research, 286*(2), 689–712.

Chauvin Alarcon, M. F. (2011). *The business model of microfinance institutions: Value creation and sustainability.* Akademiker Verlag.

Chetty, K., Josie, J., et al. (2019). *Review of FinTech strategies for financial inclusion in Sub-Saharan Africa.* Available at https://www.g20-insights.org/wp-content/uploads/2019/05/t20-japan-tf2-10-fintech-strategies-financial-inclusion-sub-saharan-africa-1.pdf.

Chiappini, H. (2017). *Social impact funds. Definition, assessment and performance.* Palgrave Macmillan.

Collier, P. (2007). *The bottom billion: Why the poorest countries are failing and what can be done about it.* Oxford University Press.

Collins, D., Murdoch, J., Rutherford, S., & Ruthven, O. (2009). *Portfolios of the poor: How the world's poor live on $2 a day.* Princeton University Press.

Cong, L. W., & He, Z. (2018, April). *Blockchain disruption and smart contracts* (NBER Working Paper no. 24399).

CSFI. (2011). *Microfinance banana skins 2011.* Available at www.cgap.org/p/site/c/template.rc/1.9.49643/.

Dang, T. T. (2020). FinTech in microfinance: A new direction for microfinance institutions in Vietnam. *The Journal of Business Economics and Environmental Studies, 10*(3), 13–22.

Daowd, A., Kamal, M. M., & Dey, B. L. (2020). The impact of social media on the performance of microfinance institutions in developing countries: A quantitative approach. *Information Technology and People, 34*(1), 25–49.

Das, S. R. (2019). The future of fintech. *Financial Management, 48*, 981–1007.

Davradakis, E., & Santos, R. (2019). *Blockchain, FinTechs and their relevance for international financial institutions* (EIB Working Papers no. 2019/01). European Investment Bank.

de Oliveira Leite, R., dos Santos Mendes, L., & Sacramento, L. C. (2019). To profit or not to profit? Assessing financial sustainability outcomes of microfinance institutions. *International Journal of Finance & Economics, 24*(3), 1287–1299.

Demirguc-Kunt, A., Klapper, L., Singer, D., Ansar, S., & Hess, J. (2018). *The Global Findex Database 2017: Measuring financial inclusion and the FinTech revolution.* Available at http://documents1.worldbank.org/curated/en/332881525873182837/pdf/126033-PUB-PUBLIC-pubdate-4-19-2018.pdf.

Demyanova, E. A., (2018). The topical issues of valuation of companies under the conditions of fintech. *Strategic Decisions and Risk Management, 1*, 88–103.

De Soto, H. (2003). The *mystery of capital. Why capitalism triumphs in the west and fails everywhere else.* Basic Books.

Deutsche Bank. (2007). *Microfinance. An emerging investment opportunity.* Available at https://www.db.com/usa/docs/Emerging_Investment_Opportunities.pdf.

Dietz, M., Khanna, S., Olanrewaju, T., & Rajgopal, K. (2016). *Cutting through the noise around financial technology.* Available at http://www.mckinsey.com/industries/financial-services/our-insights/cuttingthrough-the-noise-around-financial-technology.

Dorfleitner, G., Hornuf, L., Schmitt, M., & Weber, M. (2017). *FinTech in Germany.* Springer Verlag.

Dorfleitner, G., Nguyen, Q. A., & Röhe, M. (2019). Microfinance institutions and the provision of mobile financial services: First empirical evidence. *Finance Research Letters, 31*, 357–362.

Dorfleitner, G., Oswald, E.-M., & Röhe, M. (2020). The access of microfinance institutions to financing via the worldwide crowd. *The Quarterly Review of Economics and Finance, 75*, 133–146.

Dorfleitner, G., Oswald, E.-M., & Zhang, R. (2019). From credit risk to social impact: On the funding determinants in interest-free peer-to-peer lending. *Journal of Business Ethics, 170*, 375–400.

Dos Santos, P. L., & Kvangraven, I. H. (2017). Better than cash, but beware the costs: Electronic payments systems and financial inclusion. *Developing Economies, 48*(2), 205–227.

Dujak, D,. & Sajter, D. (2019). *Blockchain applications in supply chain.* Springer Verlag.

du Toit, G., & Burns, M. (2016). *Customer loyalty in retail banking.* Available at http://www.bain.com/publications/articles/customer-loyalty-in-retail-banking-2016.aspx.

Emengini, E. S. (2019). Subsidy/donation and performance of microfinance institutions. *Asian Journal of Economics, Business and Accounting, 13*(1), 1–12.

Engels, P. (2010). *Mission drift in microfinance*. Ibidem Verlag.

Ernst & Young. (2019). *FinTech ecosystem playbook*. Available at https://www.ey.com/Publication/vwLUAssets/EY-fintech-ecosystem-playbook/$FILE/EY-fintech-ecosystem-playbook.pdf.

European Commission. (2020). *Microfinance in the European Union: Market analysis and recommendations for delivery options in 2021–2027*. Available at https://ec.europa.eu/social/main.jsp?catId=738&langId=en&pubId=8347&furtherPubs=yes.

Everett, C. R. (2019). *Origins and development of credit-based crowdfunding*. Available at https://ssrn.com/abstract=2442897.

Fanconi, P., & Scheurle, P. (2017). *Small money—Big impact: Fighting poverty with microfinance*. Wiley.

Fernandez, P. (2001). Valuation using multiples. How do analysts reach their conclusions? *IESE Business School*.

Fosso Wamba, S., Kala Kamdjoug, J. R., Bawack, R., & Keogh, J. (2020), Bitcoin, blockchain, and FinTech: A systematic review and case studies in the supply chain. *Production Planning and Control, 31*(2–3), 115–142.

Gabor, D., & Brooks, S. (2017). The digital revolution in financial inclusion: International development in the FinTech era. *New Political Economy, 22*(4), 423–436.

Gai, K., Qiu, M., & Sun, X. (2018). A survey on FinTech. *Journal of Network and Computer Applications, 103*(1), 262–273.

Galvagno, M., & Dalli, D. (2014). Theory of value co-creation: A systematic literature review. *Managing Service Quality, 24*(6), 643–683.

Gander, J. (2015). *Designing digital business models*. Kingston University.

García-Pérez, I., Fernández-Izquierdo, M. Á., & Muñoz-Torres, M. J. (2020). Microfinance institutions fostering sustainable development by region. *Sustainability, 12*(7), 2682.

Garcia-Perez, I., Munoz-Torres, M. J., & Fernandez-Izquierdo, M. Á. (2017). Microfinance literature: A sustainability level perspective survey. *Journal of Cleaner Production, 142*, 3382–3395.

Godfroid, C. (2019). Relationship lending in microfinance: How does it impact client dropout? *Strategic Change, 28*(4), 289–300.

GSMA. (2019). *Mobile money: Key success factors of a National Financial Inclusion Strategy*. Available at https://www.gsma.com/mobilefordevelopment/wp-content/uploads/2019/03/GSMA_Key-Success-Factors-of-a-National-Financial-Inclusion-Strategy-1.pdf.

Gupta, A., Christie, R., & Manjula, R. (2017). Scalability in internet of things: Features, techniques and research challenges. *International Journal of Computational Intelligence Research, 13*(7), 1617–1627.

Gutiérrez-Nieto, B., & Serrano-Cinca, C. (2019). 20 years of research in microfinance: An information management approach. *International Journal of Information Management, 47*, 183–197.

Habib, M., & Jubb, C. (2015). Poverty alleviation with microfinance: Bangladesh evidence In A. Heshmati, E. Maasoumi, & G. Wan (Eds.), *Poverty reduction policies and practices in developing Asia*. Springer Verlag.

Haddad, C., & Hornuf, L. (2019, June). The emergence of the global fintech market: Economic and technological determinants. *Small Business Economics, 53*(1), 81–105.

Hudon, M., Labie, M., & Reichert, P. (2020). What is a fair level of profit for social enterprise? Insights from microfinance. *Journal of Business Ethics, 162*(3), 627–644.

Hussain, A. H. M. (2017). Financial inclusion through mobile micro banking: Building a prototype for transaction cost efficiency in microfinance practice. *Global Disclosure of Economics and Business, 6*(1), 19–28.

IPEV, (2018). *Valuation guidelines*. Available at http://www.privateequityvaluation.com/Valuation-Guidelines.

Jarrow, R., & Protter, P. (2019, December). Fair microfinance loan rates. *International Review of Finance, 19*(4), 909–918.

Jenik, I., & Lauer, K. (2017). *Regulatory sandboxes and financial inclusion*. Available at https://www.cgap.org/sites/default/files/Working-Paper-Regulatory-Sandboxes-Oct-2017.pdf.

Jenik, I., Lyman, T., & Nava, A. (2017). *Crowdfunding and financial inclusion*. Available at https://www.cgap.org/sites/default/files/Working-Paper-Crowdfunding-and-Financial-Inclusion-Mar-2017.pdf.

Jin, X., Wah, B. W., Cheng, X., & Wang, Y. (2015). Significance and challenges of big data research. *Big Data Research, 2*(2), 59–64.

Jones, J. (2016). *How microfinance can close asymmetrical information on peer-to-peer platforms* (item 152). Bsu Honors Program Theses and Projects. Available at https://vc.Bridgew.Edu/Honors_Proj/152.

Kaicer, M. (2020). Information technology performance management by artificial intelligence in microfinance institutions: An overview. *International Journal of Computational Intelligence Studies, 9*(3), 186–189.

Kapuscinski, R. (2003). *A reporter's self portrait*. SIW "Znak".

Kauffman, R. J., & Riggins, F. J. (2012). Information and communication technology and the sustainability of microfinance. *Electronic Commerce Research and Applications, 11*(5), 450–468.

Kim, H., & De Moor, L. (2017). The case of crowdfunding in financial inclusion: A survey. *Strategic Change-Briefings in Entrepreneurial Finance, 26*(2), 193–212.

Korpela, K., Hallikas, J., & Dahlber, T. (2017). *Digital supply chain transformation toward blockchain integration*. Paper presented at the 50*th* Hawaii International conference on system sciences (p. 4182).

Kshetri, N. (2017). Potential roles of blockchain in fighting poverty and reducing financial exclusion in the global South. *Journal of Global Information Technology Management, 20*(4), 201–204.

Kumar, K., McKay, C., & Rotman, S. (2010). *Microfinance and mobile banking: The story so far*. Available at https://www.cgap.org/sites/default/files/CGAP-Focus-Note-Microfinance-and-Mobile-Banking-The-Story-So-Far-Jul-2010.pdf.

Lui, P. T., (2016). *Medical record system using blockchain, big data and tokenization*. Paper presented at the Information and Communications security: 18th International Conference (pp. 254–261).

Macchiavello, E. (2013). A new frontier of socially responsible financial sector: Microfinance and peer-to-peer lending. *Banca Impresa Società, 2*, 277–336.

Macchiavello, E. (2017). *Microfinance and financial inclusion: The challenge of regulating alternative forms of finance*. Routledge.

Mader, P. (2017). Contesting financial inclusion. *Development and Change, 49*(2), 461–483.

Madrid Damodaran, A. (2009). *Valuing financial service firms*. Available at http://people.stern.nyu.edu/adamodar/pdfiles/papers/finfirm09.pdf.

Makina, D. (2019). The potential of FinTech in enabling financial inclusion. In *Extending financial inclusion in Africa* (pp. 299–318). Academic Press.

Mann, L. (2017). Left to other peoples' devices? A political economy perspective on the big data revolution in development. *Development and Change, 49*(1), 3–36.

Marakkath, N., & Attuel-Mendes, L. (2015). Can microfinance crowdfunding reduce financial exclusion? Regulatory issues. *International Journal of Bank Marketing, 33*(5), 624–636.

Marom, D. (2013). Crowd-empowered microfinance. In J. P. Gueyie, R. Manos, & J. Yaron (Eds.),*Microfinance in developing countries*. Palgrave Macmillan.

Martínez-Climent, C., Costa-Climent, R., & Oghazi, P. (2019). Sustainable financing through crowdfunding. *Sustainability, 11*, 934.

Mattila, J. (2017). *The blockchain phenomenon. The disruptive potential of distributed consensus architectures*. Available at https://brie.berkeley.edu/sites/default/files/juri-mattila-.pdf.

Meyer, J., & Krauss, A. (2021). The social performance of microfinance investment vehicles. *Journal of Sustainable Finance & Investment, 11*(2), 163–186.

Mia, M. A. (2020). Technological change and innovations in microfinance institutions: What matters? *Global Business Review, 17*(5), 1179–1195.

Mia, M. A., Dalla Pellegrina, L., Van Damme, P., & Wijesiri, M. (2019). Financial inclusion, deepening and efficiency in microfinance programs: Evidence from Bangladesh. *European Journal of Development Research, 31*(4), 809–835.

Mia, M. A., & Lee, H. (2017). Mission drift and ethical crisis in microfinance institutions: What matters? *Journal of Cleaner Production, 164*, 102–114.

Milana, C., & Ashta, A. (2012). Developing microfinance. A survey of the literature. *Strategic Change, 21*(7–8), 299–330.

Milana, C., & Ashta, A. (2020). Microfinance and financial inclusion: Challenges and opportunities. *Strategic Change, 29*(3), 257–266.

Morduch, J., Cull, R., & Demirgüç-Kunt, A. (2018). The microfinance business model: Enduring subsidy and modest profit. *The World Bank Economic Review, 32*(2), 221–244.

Moro Visconti, R. (2009). Are microfinance institutions in developing countries a safe harbor against the contagion of global recession? *International Finance Review, 10*, 389–438.

Moro Visconti, R. (2011). Global recession and microfinance risk governance in developing countries. *Risk Governance and Control Journal, 1*(3), 17–30.

Moro Visconti, R. (2012). Is African microfinance different? Evidence from banana skins. *African Journal of Microfinance and Enterprise Development, 2*(2), 25–45.

Moro Visconti, R. (2015). Leveraging development with technology and microfinance. *ACRN Oxford Journal of Finance and Risk Perspectives, 4*(3), 19–33.

Moro Visconti, R. (2020). *The valuation of digital intangibles. Technology, marketing and internet*. Palgrave Macmillan.

Moro-Visconti, R. (2021). *Startup valuation: From strategic business planning to digital networking*. Palgrave Macmillan, Chapter 2.

Moro Visconti, R., Larocca, A., & Marconi, M. (2017). Big data-driven value chains and digital platforms: From value co-creation to monetization. In A. K. Somani & G. Deka (Eds.), *Bigdata analytics: Tools, technology for effective planning*. CRC Press.

Moro Visconti, R., & Quirici, M. C. (2014). The impact of innovation and technology on microfinance sustainable governance. *Corporate Ownership & Control, 11*(3–2), 420–428.

Moss, T. W., Neubaum, D. O., & Meyskens, M. (2015). The effect of virtuous and entrepreneurial orientations on microfinance lending and repayment: A signaling theory perspective. *Entrepreneurship Theory and Practice, 39*(1), 27–52.

Mushtaq, R., & Bruneau, C. (2019). Microfinance, financial inclusion and ICT: Implications for poverty and inequality. *Technology in Society, 59*, 663–686.

Mwashiuya, H. T., & Mbamba, U. O. L. (2018). Relationship between information communication technology adoption in microfinance institutions and access to financial services. *International Journal of Research, 5*(4), 264–280.

Newman A., Schwarz S., Borgia D. J., & Wei, W. (2017). The influence of formal and informal institutions on microcredit: Financial inclusion for micro-entrepreneurs by lender type. In D. Cumming, Y. Dong, W. Hou, & B. Sen (Eds.), *Microfinance for entrepreneurial development*. Palgrave Macmillan.

Norman, M. D., Karavas, Y. G., & Reed, H. (2018, June 4). *The emergence of trust and value in public blockchain networks* (Working Paper). http://s3.amazonaws.com/arenaattachments/2332393/536b3b1208a6debfa6eaf5b9c9c9187a.pdf?1529445044.

Nourani, M., Malim, M., & Mia, M. A. (2020). Revisiting efficiency of microfinance institutions (MFIs): An application of network data envelopment analysis. *Economic Research—Ekonomska Istraživanja, 34*, 1146–1169.

OECD. (2017, July). *Transfer pricing guidelines for multinational enterprises and tax administrations*. Available at https://www.oecd.org/tax/oecdtransfer-pricing-guidelines-for-multinational-enterprises-and-tax-administrations-20769717.htm.

Özcan, G. (2020). Financial development and income inequality: An empirical analysis on the emerging market economies. *Theoretical and Applied Economics, 3*(624), 85–96.

Ozili, P. K. (2018). Impact of digital finance on financial inclusion and stability. *Borsa Istanbul Review, 18*(4), 329–340.

Ozili, P. K. (2020). Contesting digital finance for the poor. *Digital Policy, Regulation and Governance, 22*(2), 135–151.

Palanivelu, V. R., & Narmada, S. (2020). Impact of demonetisation on the micro finance sector. *International Journal of Advanced Science and Technology, 29*(4), 705–712.

Parvin, S. S., Hossain, B., Mohiuddin, M., & Cao, Q. (2020). Capital structure, financial performance, and sustainability of micro-finance institutions (MFIs) in Bangladesh. *Sustainability, 12*(15), 6222.

Patrick, F., & Squires, M. (2021). Linking mobile money networks to "e-ROSCAs": An experimental study. *Science Advances*, *7*(1).

Paul, E., et al. (2018). Performance-based financing in low-income and middle-income countries: Isn't it time for a rethink? *BMJ Global Health*, *3*(1).

Pedrini, M., Bramanti, V., Minciullo, M., & Ferri, M. L. (2016). Rethinking microfinance for developed countries. *Journal of International Development, 28*(2), 281–302.

Philippon, T. (2019a). *The FinTech opportunity*. National Bureau of Economic Research.

Philippon, T. (2019b). *On FinTech and financial inclusion*. Stern School of Business. (Working Paper). Available at https://www.bis.org/events/conf190628/philippon.pdf.

Piobbici, F., Rajola, F., & Frigerio, C. (2019). Open innovation effectiveness in the financial services sector. In N. Mehandjiev, & B. Saadouni (Eds.), *Enterprise applications, markets and services in the finance industry* (Vol. 345). Springer Verlag.

Pizzi, S., Corbo, L., & Caputo, A. (2021). FinTech and SMEs sustainable business models: Reflections and considerations for a circular economy. *Journal of Cleaner Production, 281,* 125217

Postelnicu, L., Hermes, N., & Szafarz, A. (2014). Defining social collateral in microfinance group lending. In R. Mersland & R. Ø. Strøm (Eds.), *Microfinance institutions*. Palgrave Studies in Impact Finance. Palgrave Macmillan.

Prahalad, C. K. (2006). *The fortune at the bottom of the pyramid*. Wharton School Publishing.

Pythowska, J., & Korynski, P. (2017). *Digitalizing microfinance in Europe*. Available at https://www.european-microfinance.org/sites/default/files/document/file/Digitalization-research-paper.pdf.

Rahman, M. M., Khanam, R., & Nghiem, S. (2017). The effects of microfinance on women's empowerment: New evidence from Bangladesh. *International Journal of Social Economics, 44*(12), 1745–1757.

Ravikumar, T. (2019). Digital financial inclusion: A payoff of financial technology and digital finance uprising in India. *International Journal of Scientific & Technology Research, 8*(11), 3434–3438.

Rawls, J. (1971). *A theory of justice*. Harvard University Press.

Reinhardt, R., Hietschold, N., & Gurtner, S. (2019). Overcoming consumer resistance to innovations—An analysis of adoption triggers. *R&D Management, 49*(2), 139–154.

Riggins, F., & Weber, D. M. (2016). Exploring the impact of information and communication technology (ICT) on intermediation market structure in the microfinance industry. *The African Journal of Information Systems*, *8*(3).

Riggins, F., & Weber, D. M. (2017). Information asymmetries and identification bias in P2P social microlending. *Information Technology for Development, 23*(1), 107–126.

Rothman, T., & Grunstein, D. (2020). *Valuation of early-stage companies and disruptive technologies*. Palgrave Macmillan.

Royal, C., & Windsor, S. (2014). Microfinance, crowdfunding, and sustainability: A case study of telecenters in a South Asian developing country. *Strategic Change, 23*(7–8), 425–438.

Russel, J. & Norvig, P. (2015). *Artificial intelligence. A modern approach*. Pearson.

Rutherford, S. (2000). *The poor and their money*. Oxford University Press.

Saberi, S., Kouhizadeh, M., Sarkis, J., & Shen, L. (2018). Blockchain technology and its relationships to sustainable supply chain management. *International Journal of production researching*, 2117–2135.

Saksonova, S., & Kuzmina-Merlino, I. (2017). FinTech as financial innovation—The possibilities and problems of implementation. *European Research Studies Journal*, *XX*(3A), 961–973.

Salampasis D., & Mention A. (2018). FinTech: Harnessing innovation for financial inclusion. In *Handbook of blockchain, digital finance, and inclusion* (Vol. 2, pp. 451–461). Academic Press.

Sancha-Navarro, J. M., Sanchís-Pedregosa, C., & Oliver-Alfonso, M. D. (2018). Relationship between crowdfunding and microfinance: A theoretical approach. *Finance, Markets and Valuation, 4*(2), 63–72.

Sangwan, S., & Nayak, N. C. (2020, July). Factors influencing the borrower loan size in microfinance group lending: A survey from Indian microfinance institutions. *Journal of Financial Economic Policy, 13*(2), 223–238.

Sarkar, S., & Alvari, H. (2018). Mitigating bias in online microfinance platforms: A case study on Kiva.org. In I. Koprinska et al. (Eds.), *ECML PKDD 2020 workshops*. Communications in Computer and Information Science (Vol. 1323). Springer Verlag.

Saxena, A., & Deb, A. T. (2014). Paradigm paranoia or mission drift? Lessons from microfinance crisis in India. *Journal of Business Thought, 4*, 38–49.

Shah, S., Rahman, M., & Khan, J. A. (2019). The mediating role of group lending between poverty and microfinance. *NICE Research Journal of Social Science, 12*(2).

Shaikh, A. A., & Karjaluoto, H. (2015). Mobile banking adoption: A literature review. *Telematics and Informatics, 32*(1), 129–142.

Sharma, S. K., & Al-Muharrami, S. (2018). Mobile banking adoption: Key challenges and opportunities and implications for a developing country. In Y. Dwivedi et al. (Eds.), *Emerging markets from a multidisciplinary perspective. Advances in theory and practice of emerging markets*. Springer Verlag.

Sharma, S., Singh, P., Singh, K., & Chauhan, B. (2017). Group lending model—A panacea to reduce transaction cost? *Zagreb International Review of Economics and Business, 20*(2), 46–63.

Sherwani, N. U. K., Junaid, I., & Zeba, M. (2018). Microfinance and crowdfunding: Alternative approaches for entrepreneurship development. *International Journal of Management, IT and Engineering, 8*(2), 233–243.

Sing, J., Dutt, P., & Adbi, A. (2021). Microfinance and entrepreneurship at the base of the pyramid. *Strategic Entrepreneurship Journal* (in press). Available at https://onlinelibrary.wiley.com/doi/10.1002/sej.1394.

Sinha, S., Pandey, K., & Madan, N. (2018). FinTech and the demand side challenge in financial inclusion. *Enterprise Development and Microfinance, 29*(1), 94–98.

Song, I., Lui, C., & Vong, J. (2014). Lowering the interest burden for microfinance. *International Journal of Process Management and Benchmarking, 4*(2), 213–229.

Soumaré, I., Tchakoute Tchuigou, H., & Hessou, H. T. (2020). Are microfinance institutions resilient to economic slowdown? Evidence from their capital ratio adjustment over the business cycle. *Economic Modelling, 92*, 1–22.

Sen, A. (1999). *Development as freedom*. Oxford University Press.

Singh, J. P. (2013). On the Intricacies of cash flow corporate valuation. *Advances in Management, 6*(3), 15–22.

Srinivas, V., & Mahal, R. (2017, September). Digital transformation: The next big leap in microfinance, *PARIDNYA. The MIBM Research Journal, 5*(1).

Stiglitz, J. (1990). Peer monitoring and credit markets. *World Bank Economic Review, 4*(3), 351–366.

Stiglitz, J. E., & Weiss, A. (1981, June). Credit rationing in markets with imperfect information. *American Economic Review, 71*(3), 393–410.

Sun, S. L., & Liang, H. (2021). Globalization and affordability of microfinance. *Journal of Business Venturing, 36*(1), 1–18.

Sundaresan, S. (2009). *Microfinance emerging trends and challenges*. Edward Elgar.

Tanda, A., & Schena, C. (2019). *FinTech, bigTech and banks: Digitalisation and its impact on banking business models*. Palgrave Macmillan.

Tanin, T. I. (2017). *Does environment, social and governance (ESG) drive the financial performance of microfinance institutions? A cross-country panel analysis* (Master dissertation). INCEIF, Kuala Lumpur. Available at https://ikr.inceif.org/handle/INCEIF/2637.

Tauhidul Islam, T. (2017). *Does environment, social and governance (ESG) drive the financial performance of microfinance institutions? A cross-country panel analysis*. INCEIF, Kuala Lumpur. Available at https://ikr.inceif.org/handle/INCEIF/2637.

Tchakoute Tchuigoua, H., Durrieu, F., & Kouao, G. S. (2017). Funding strategy and performance of microfinance institutions: An exploratory study. *Strategic Change, 26*(2), 133–143.

Tchakoute Tchuigoua, H., & Pignatel, I. (2020). Microfinance institutions and International Financial Reporting Standards: An exploratory analysis. *Research in International Business and Finance, 54*, 101309.

Tchakoute Tchuigoua, H., Soumaré, I., & Hessou, H. T. (2020). Lending and business cycle: Evidence from microfinance institutions. *Journal of Business Research, 119*, 1–12.

Thi-Hong, V. L., Vo, A. T., Nguyen, N. T., & Duc, D. H. (2021). Financial inclusion and economic growth: An international evidence. *Emerging Markets Finance and Trade, 57*(1), 239–263.

Thomas, H., & Hedrick-Wong, Y. (2019). *How digital finance and FinTech can improve financial inclusion* (pp. 27–41). Emerald Publishing Limited.

Tomic, V., & Stojanovic, D. (2018). *Trends and innovations in mobile banking*. Available at https://www.researchgate.net/publication/330468035.

Tutino, M. (2013). Matching outreach and financial sustainability. An assessed accounting framework in evaluating performance of microfinance project. *GSTF Journal on Business Review, 2*(3), 46–50.

Usman, G., Tahseen, B. M., & Naseeb, A. (2018). The impact of technology on the sustainable development of microfinance. *Global Sci-Tech, 10*(1), 22–29.

Vandeputte, P., & De Toffol, B. (2017). *The role of FinTechs in the business model of microfinance institutions in Western Europe: A qualitative study*. Louvain School of Management, Université Catholique de Louvain. Available at http://hdl.handle.net/2078.1/thesis:11338.

Van Hove, L., & Dubus, A. (2019). M-Pesa and financial inclusion in Kenya: Of paying comes saving? *Sustainability, 11*(3), 568.

Villasenor, J. D., West, D. M., & Lewis, R. J. (2016). *The 2016 brookings financial and digital inclusion project report: Advancing equitable financial ecosystems*. Available at https://www.brookings.edu/wp-content/uploads/2016/08/fdip_20160816_project_report.pdf.

Vives, X. (2019). Digital disruption in banking. *Annual Review of Finance, 11*, 243–272.

Vong, J., & Song, I. (2015). Mobility technology solutions can reduce interest rates of microfinance loans. *Emerging Technologies for Emerging Markets. Topics in Intelligent Engineering and Informatics, 11*, 11–24.

Wellalage, N. H., & Thrikawala, S. (2021). Bank credit, microfinance and female ownership: Are women more disadvantaged than men? *Finance Research Letters* (in press).

Williamson, O. E. (1979). Transaction-cost economics: The governance of contractual relations. *Journal of Law and Economics, 22*(2), 233–261.

World Bank. (2017). *The Global Findex Database. Measuring financial inclusion and the FinTech revolution*. Available at http://documents.worldbank.org/curated/en/332881525873182837/The-Global-Findex-Database-2017-Measuring-Financial-Inclusion-and-the-Fintech-Revolution.

World Bank. (2018). *Financial inclusion—Financial inclusion is a key enabler to reducing poverty and boosting prosperity*. Available at http://www.worldbank.org/en/topic/financialinclusion/overview.

World Bank. (2020). *Smart contract technology and financial inclusion*. Available at https://openknowledge.worldbank.org/bitstream/handle/10986/33723/Smart-Contract-Technology-and-Financial-Inclusion.pdf?sequence=1&isAllowed=y.

Younas, W., & Kalimuthu, K. R. (2021). Telecom microfinance banking versus commercial banking: A battle in the financial services sector. *Journal of Financial Services Marketing* (in press).

Yum, H., Lee, B., & Chae, M. (2012). From the wisdom of crowds to my own judgment in microfinance through online peer-to-peer lending platforms. *Electronic Commerce Research and Applications, 11*(5), 469–483.

Yunus, M., & Jolis, A. (1999). *Banker to the poor: Micro-lending and the battle against world poverty*. PublicAffairs.

Van Hove, L., & Dubus, A. (2019, January 22). M-PESA and financial inclusion in Kenya: Of paying comes saving? *Sustainability, 11*(3), 568.

Zamore, S., Beisland, L. A., & Mersland, R. (2021). Excessive focus on risk? Non-performing loans and efficiency of microfinance institutions. *International Journal of Finance and Economics*, 1–18.

Zetzsche, D. A., & Dewi, T. R. (2018, April 17). *The paradoxical case against interest rate caps for microfinance—And how FinTech and RegTech resolve the dilemma* (Working Paper no. 2018-003). University of Luxembourg Law. Available at https://ssrn.com/abstract=3159202.

Websites

ACCION www.accion.org.

Consultative Group to Assist the Poor (CGAP) www.cgap.org.

Development Gateway www.developmentgateway.com.

Economic Self-Reliance Review http://marriottschool.byu.edu/esrreview/.

EnterWeb www.enterweb.org.

Food and Agriculture Organization of the UN (FAO) www.fao.org.

Grameen Bank www.grameen-info.org.

GTZ—German Cooperation Agency www.gtz.de/.

Inter-American Development Bank www.iadb.org/Publications/.

MicroBanking Bulletin www.mixmbb.org/.

Microcapital www.microcapital.org.

Microfinance.com www.microfinance.com.

Microfinance Centre for EU & NIS www.mfc.org.pl.

Microfinance Information eXchange (MIX) www.themix.org.

Microfinance Network www.mfnetwork.org.

MicroSave www.microsave.org.

Microfinance Transparency http://mftransparency.org/.

PlaNet Finance www.planetfinance.org.

SEEP Network www.seepnetwork.org.

UN Capital Development Fund www.uncdf.org/english/microfinance/index.php.

USAID MicroLinks www.microlinks.org.

Virtual Library on Microcredit www.gdrc.org/icm/.
World Bank www.worldbank.org.

Index

R. Moro-Visconti, *MicroFinTech*, Palgrave Studies in Financial Services Technology, https://doi.org/10.1007/978-3-030-80394-0

The manufacturer's authorised representative in the EU is Springer
Nature Customer Service Centre GmbH, Europaplatz 3, 69115 Heidelberg,
Germany. If you have any concerns regarding our products, please
contact ProductSafety@springernature.com

Printed and bound by CPI Group (UK) Ltd, Croydon, CR0 4YY
30/09/2026
02225453-0006